LEADING
AT THE EDGE

Second Edition

LEADING
AT THE EDGE

Second Edition

Leadership Lessons *from the* Extraordinary Saga *of* Shackleton's Antarctic Expedition

Dennis N. T. Perkins
with Margaret P. Holtman and Jillian B. Murphy

AMACOM
American Management Association
New York • Atlanta • Brussels • Chicago • Mexico City • San Francisco
Shanghai • Tokyo • Toronto • Washington, D.C.

Bulk discounts available. For details visit:
www.amacombooks.org/go/specialsales
Or contact special sales:
Phone: 800-250-5308
Email: specialsls@amanet.org
View all the AMACOM titles at: www.amacombooks.org

Acknowledgments for permission to use previously published materials can be found on page 255.

Library of Congress Cataloging-in-Publication Data

Perkins, Dennis N. T., 1942–
    Leading at the edge : leadership lessons from the extraordinary saga of Shackleton's Antarctic expedition / Dennis N. T. Perkins ; with Margaret P. Holtman and Jillian B. Murphy. — 2nd ed.
        p. cm.
    Includes bibliographical references and index.
    ISBN 978-0-8144-3194-8 (pbk.) — ISBN 0-8144-3194-1 (pbk.) 1. Leadership. 2. Shackleton, Ernest Henry, Sir, 1874-1922. 3. Antarctica—Discovery and exploration—British. 4. Strategic planning. 5. Survival. 6. Explorers—Antarctica. I. Holtman, Margaret P. II. Murphy, Jillian B. III. Title.
    HD57.7.P46 2012
    658.4'092—dc23

                                                                            2011051897

About AMA

American Management Association (www.amanet.org) is a world leader in talent development, advancing the skills of individuals to drive business success. Our mission is to support the goals of individuals and organizations through a complete range of products and services, including classroom and virtual seminars, webcasts, webinars, podcasts, conferences, corporate and government solutions, business books, and research. AMA's approach to improving performance combines experiential learning—learning through doing—with opportunities for ongoing professional growth at every step of one's career journey.

.

Printing number
10 9 8 7 6

To the memory of
Private First Class Louis Anthony Leatherbury,
United States Marine Corps,
and all who have gone to *The Edge*
in the service of others

Contents

Acknowledgments for the Second Edition

Since the publication of the first edition of *Leading at The Edge*, two new crewmembers have been added to the book team. I would like to thank the extraordinary Jillian Murphy for her many contributions over the past three years. In addition to her invaluable support with clients, Jillian generated numerous suggestions and conducted research on new business cases for the updated edition. Jillian was particularly helpful in crafting "Resolving Conflicts: Lessons from the Martial Arts" (gamely participating in martial arts exercises). She also wordsmithed new passages to ensure they flowed with the existing text. As our Chief of Staff, Jillian is a critical member of our expedition.

Our newest addition to the team, the amazing Laura Gardner, was responsible for crafting the prose for new passages, and for developing the worksheets for the Moose Round-Up, all while keeping one steady hand on the office management helm (through the literal and metaphorical headwinds of Hurricane Irene!). In addition, Laura valiantly took on the task of securing necessary permissions, and she helped the team overcome writer's block by kicking us out of the office to go for walks.

When writing the acknowledgments for the first edition of *Leading at The Edge*, I noted that Christina Parisi (then McLaughlin) managed the complex production and editorial processes with laughter and competence. I have the good fortune of being able to use precisely the same words today. Christina's exceptional competence, and her delightful sense of humor, turn the hard work of writing a book into a pleasant experience. And when the time came to find a publisher for our new book (previewed at the end of this volume), there was really no decision involved. There is no one I would rather work with than Christina, and no publisher other than AMACOM.

Much of what I know about leadership I learned in the United States Marine Corps. I appreciate the leadership and teamwork demonstrated by Marines in the Third Battalion, Fifth Marine Regiment—the "Dark Horse" Battalion—whose distinguished combat record continues to this day. I am especially honored to recognize the Marines I fought with in Vietnam, and whose courage under fire enabled me to make it home to share my insights about leadership: Jerry Czarnowski, who—along with Napoleon—is one of the most renowned corporals in history; Bill Gleeson, who turned his back on safety and came back to fight; George "Hap" Hazzard, who keeps the memory of our fallen comrades alive; and Jim Kirschke, who demonstrated as much bravery after Vietnam as he did in combat. I continue to learn lessons about leadership from the Marines, and I appreciate General Rich Natonski's Strategy #11: "Plan and prepare, but be flexible when things change." Semper Gumby!

I have learned much from working with other exceptional leaders. Carl Allegretti showed me that you can be an inspiring leader while always remembering that family comes first. Brian Derksen and Katy Hollister taught me how to wade into tough issues with different but equally effective styles. Joe Echevarria's words, "somos quatro gatos," have helped in situations where there's no one but "us four cats" to accomplish the mission. And Byron Spruell showed me, in no uncertain terms, how to play like a champion.

It's also important to recognize the contributions made by our *Expedition Leaders*: colleagues who are certified to present our Leadership at The Edge® programs. These members of our extended team are located throughout the world, and they have continued to provide us with innovative ideas for teaching leadership in a wide range of cultures. We appreciate the work of Dave Ellis in Atlanta; Martha Miller in Washington, D.C.; Ron Jungalwalla and Mike Boyle in Melbourne, Australia; Hazel Rosin in Toronto; Piotr Wisoky in Wielkopolskie, Poland; and all of our colleagues in Seoul at the Korea Syncretics Leadership Center.

A number of other friends and colleagues provided critical help on the second expedition. I extend my sincere thanks to Deb Abildsoe, John Ball, Christine Banti, Marna Borgstrom, Jennifer Chobor, Dana Diamond, Andy Errato, Neftaly Fernandez, Joshua Hasbani, Reggie Higgins, Ted Hoff, Michele Johnson, Carol Just, Mike Kennedy, Su Lim, Erroin Martin, Dennis Mette, John Michalak, Camille Murphy, Ryan O'Malley, Michael Rubenstein, Matt Schenkman, Barry Schlosser, Jim Schmaltz, Edgar Smith, Carl Swope, Mike Useem, Jesse Villanueva, Howard and Rosy Whelan, Carole Lyn Woodring, and David Young.

Finally, I express my deepest appreciation for the support and counsel of my wife, Susan. As our inside joke goes: I have a PhD, and thus the title of a doctor, but some may question whether I'm the kind of doctor who can actually help anyone! I can say unequivocally, however, that Susan—a physician with years of experience in the emergency room—can help people. I watched while she Heimliched my Aunt Dottie at her ninetieth birthday party, and Susan has patched me up after a number of my adventures at *The Edge*. Not only has my beautiful wife done all those things, but she has also helped me face the challenges of life with love and laughter. I am so thankful that I found her.

Acknowledgments for the First Edition

The experience of writing this book seemed, at times, to be something like mounting a polar expedition. There was, of course, less physical hardship, and little risk of life. But the process did involve venturing into the unknown and dealing with some fairly formidable obstacles. I was fortunate to have with me in this adventure a number of colleagues who made it possible to face these challenges with a spirit of creativity and camaraderie.

I deeply appreciate the enormous contributions made by each member of the original Book Team: Peggy Holtman, Paul Kessler, and Catherine McCarthy. Although I had been using the *Leading at The Edge* approach for a number of years, the challenge of translating these concepts into a readable book was not a straightforward matter. The Book Team met regularly from the proposal stage forward, debating every major decision involved in structuring the book. Peggy and Paul drove long distances to my office in Connecticut, while Catherine participated by phone from Chicago. These meetings were often extended affairs, and I sometimes worried that Catherine would carry a permanent imprint of a telephone earpiece.

Each member of the Book Team wrote initial drafts of chapters, critiqued my work, and searched for business examples that would illustrate key lessons of the book. Peggy Holtman was tireless—a whirling dervish—in searching for factoids and ensuring that the key concepts of the book were bridged to practical organizational applications. Paul Kessler emanated optimism and demonstrated an awesome knack for catching errors that no one else could find. Catherine McCarthy exhibited an impressive "can do" spirit and—at the same time—played an important role in challenging the team's assumptions and keeping us focused.

In addition to these contributions, each member of the Book Team also showed a willingness to practice the leadership strategies highlighted in the book. One of my great satisfactions in this effort is the belief that we, as a team, did our best to practice the principles we espoused.

Words can never fully express my appreciation for the contribution of Anna Gianitsos, my office manager and assistant. The name *Gianitsos* means "loyal warrior," and Anna embodied the spirit of her family name. Through month after month of the most demanding work, Anna demonstrated an extraordinary level of dedication and breadth of skills. She was conscientious in proofreading and fact checking. She made substantive suggestions about the content of the book. When I was stuck on a small detail, Anna pointed at the "countdown" chart that she had made showing the number of days until the manuscript was due—and I got the message. Through late nights, weekends, and stress-filled days, Anna retained her determination, resilience, and winning smile. She and her family can be justly proud of her critical role in making the book a reality. Anna—*S'efharisto apo ta vathi tis cardias mou.*

Steve Elliott not only helped with editorial decisions but also served as navigator (my own "Frank Worsley") in steering through the uncharted and often turbulent waters of the publishing world. Ellen James provided valuable editorial assistance. Nick Appelby expertly created the graphics, including the map of the *Endurance* expedition. Marya Holcombe's counsel was critical in the beginning stages of the writing process as she helped me break the ice off the runners of my writing sledge. And Becky Hoffman, of Knowledge=Power, deserves special recognition for her resourcefulness in finding business illustrations of the ten strategies.

I am grateful to Bob Headland of the Scott Polar Research Institute for his timely fact checking, and for helping me avoid any errors that would qualify as major "howlers." I should emphasize that I am responsible for any remaining discrepancies, and that any conclusions—particularly those concerning Robert Falcon Scott—are my own.

The contributions to the book made by David Nadler and my colleagues at the Delta Consulting Group were invaluable. David has been a friend for more years than I care to remember and has taught me much about the art of helping organizations achieve their full potential. My friends at Delta have shared their time and expertise generously, and I thank them for their valuable assistance.

I appreciate the steadfast encouragement of Jeff Heilpern, who has been a tremendous source of support, and who helped me maintain a healthy perspective on the process of writing and on the process of living. Virginia Herndon showed an unwavering belief in the book and its message, Martha Miller beamed support from far corners of the globe, and Dave Ellis was an important source of inspiration.

Donna Gianini deserves special mention for her early work in developing the *Leading at The Edge* approach, and for her continuing innovation in applying the concept. Donna first coined the phrase, "Onward through the hummocks"—a rallying cry that helped us move through many daunting ice fields. I appreciate the ongoing encouragement of Diane Russ, my long-haul partner in exploring the frontier.

I would like to acknowledge the editors at AMACOM, who helped bring the book from proposal to print. Adrienne Hickey saw the potential of the concept, acquired the book, and provided suggestions about its structure. Christina McLaughlin managed the complex production and editorial processes with laughter and competence, and Karen Brogno's thorough copyediting of the manuscript is greatly appreciated.

A number of other individuals were important in the writing of this book, and each made a unique contribution. I thank and acknowledge Deborah Ancona, Nancy Cardwell, Fred Courtright, Jack Creighton, Anthony D'Albero, Mark Edinberg, Aaron Feuerstein, Jo-Ann Fleishman, Peg Gilliland, Lois Grady, Andrew Greatrex, Gordon Hellman, Diana Ho, Joan Imhof, Randy MacDonald, Leslie Margolin, Naoko Matsunaga, Chuck Miceli, Phil Mirvis, David Montross, Steve Moran, Renee Murphy, Robert Ostroff, Prakash Patel, Jonathan Patrick, Bill Reinsmith, Gail Robinson, Gayle Rohrbasser, Darien Roseen, Pat Russo, Barry Schlosser, Harold Shapiro, Tom Sheehan, Jane Sheppard, Paul Siegel, Scott Sklar, Lon Smith, Ken Stellar, Jim Tullos, and Grant Withers.

I am grateful to Dr. Elias Marsh, who first gave me a copy of Lansing's *Endurance*, and who exemplified the spirit of exploration. And I thank Bill Gleeson, whose courage and presence under fire helped ensure that I would be around to write this book.

Finally, I thank the members of my family who have supported me through the years, and who have taught me a great deal about leadership and overcoming obstacles. My daughter, Holly, showed me that it is possible to ride a bucking horse with a smile on your face. My son, Jonathan, showed me that it is possible to negotiate tough whitewater in a kayak with no spray skirt—and still have a good time. My brother, Bob, kept the supply chain intact throughout the expedition. I thank the "Magic Girls," Meghan and Melisa, for their smiles and courage in the face of adversity; and I appreciate Joe Hernandez's help in carrying the load. Most of all, I express my deepest gratitude to Bernadette Bialczak Perkins, who supported my quest, and whose love and compassion helped me make it home from *The Edge*.

Preface

On August 3, 1913, a Canadian expedition led by Vilhjalmur Stefansson set out to explore the frozen Arctic, between the northernmost shores of Canada and the North Pole. On December 5, 1914, the British Imperial Trans-Antarctic Expedition, led by Sir Ernest Shackleton, sailed from the island of South Georgia in the Southern Ocean. Its goal was the first overland crossing of Antarctica.

Both ships, the *Karluk* in the north and the *Endurance* in the south, soon found themselves beset in solid pack ice. Trapped by the ice, each crew was engaged in a fight for survival. But the outcomes of these two adventures—and the ways in which the two leaders dealt with the obstacles they faced—were as far apart as the poles each leader set out to explore.

In the north, the crew of the *Karluk* found themselves transformed in the months that followed into a band of self-interested, disparate individuals. Lying, cheating, and stealing became common behaviors. The disintegration of the team had tragic consequences for the eleven members who died in the Arctic wasteland.

In the frozen south, the story of the *Endurance* could not have been more different. Shackleton's expedition faced the same problems of ice, cold, and shortages of food and supplies. The response of his crew to these hellish conditions, however, was in almost every respect the obverse of that of the *Karluk*'s crew. Teamwork, self-sacrifice, and astonishing good cheer replaced lying, cheating, and rapacious self-interest. It was as if the *Endurance* existed not just in a different polar region, but in a different, contrary, parallel universe.

What Can Today's Leaders Learn from Explorers at the World's Edge?

There were many variables at play in the *Endurance* and *Karluk* adventures. I believe, however, that these two cases reflect something far different from a simple twist of fate. Having studied numerous situations in which teams faced the edge of life and death—the physical limits of human endurance—I have found that there are systematic differences between those that succeed and those that fail.

While developing the concepts for the first edition of *Leading at The Edge*, I examined numerous stories of groups that found themselves at the edge of survival, including accounts of shipwrecks, airplane crashes, mountain-climbing expeditions, and polar exploration. From this research, ten leadership principles emerged as the critical factors that distinguished groups that triumphed from those that failed. These core leadership strategies form the backbone of this book.

When *Leading at The Edge* was first published in 2000, my goal was to show how these ten strategies, employed by Shackleton and others who have succeeded in the face of extreme adversity, could help leaders reach the limits of individual and organizational performance. At the time, some questioned whether lessons drawn from such extraordinary circumstances could be applied to everyday business concerns. Granted, the typical executive does not struggle with the prospect of starvation or hypothermia. But my experience working with leaders convinced me that many organizational challenges shared similar characteristics with the survival stories I had studied.

Since the publication of the first edition, we've been brought to *The Edge* during the first decade of the twenty-first century with the terrorist attacks of 9/11 at the beginning and the economic meltdown at the end. Now more than ever, leaders need to know how to navigate the rough waters of today's business environment.

Leading at The Edge demonstrates how leadership lessons from the edge of survival can be applied to organizations confronting such contemporary challenges as competition; economic uncertainty; and the need for constant innovation, growth, and change.

Each chapter in Part One of the book illustrates how one of the ten strategies has been used under life-and-death conditions. It also includes specific tactics for implementing these strategies and uses brief case examples to show how these concepts can be applied to any organizational challenge. Finally, each chapter poses a set of questions for reflection in the form of a personal Expedition Log.

In Part Two, I share my perspective on learning the art of leading at *The Edge*, and I compare Shackleton's leadership capabilities with those of other well-known polar explorers. Finally, Part Three offers an updated expedition toolkit, which includes instruments for individual assessment, a creative framework for identifying and resolving conflicts, and suggestions for further reading.

Origins of the Leading at *The Edge* Concept

A major part of my life has been spent trying to understand what it really means to be a leader—particularly under conditions of adversity, ambiguity, and change. My passion to understand the art of leadership began at the United States Naval Academy. As a midshipman at Annapolis, I looked at the discipline of leadership as the foundation of a military career.

My quest to understand leadership began in earnest after graduation, when I was commissioned as a second lieutenant in the Marine Corps. As a platoon commander, I found myself in the sand dunes of Camp Lejeune, North Carolina, faced with the challenge of leading some thirty-five young Marines.

As a platoon leader I tried to apply what I had learned at Annapolis, and I watched other leaders to see what worked and what did not. I was naively amazed to find that—although we had all gone through the same training—the actual practice of leadership varied tremendously. Mostly, I saw good leadership; sometimes I saw exceptional leadership.

The differences between good and exceptional had effects on the attitudes and behavior of the troops, but the consequences in peacetime were not profound. Mistakes were simply mistakes, and no one died. The troops might grumble, but it was the Marine Corps and everyone followed orders.

My leadership "postgraduate education" continued off the coast of Vietnam with the Third Battalion, Fifth Marine Regiment. As part of the Special Landing Force, we sailed along the coast, launching amphibious operations to relieve units that got into trouble near the demilitarized zone. Later, I went "in country" and experienced the war in many roles. As a civil affairs officer, I saw it from the perspective of the Vietnamese. I helped build wells, distribute food and supply packages, and bring medical and dental care to the local villagers. Later, as the commanding officer of a rifle company, I saw Vietnam through a different set of lenses.

In Vietnam, the stakes were higher and blind obedience was not something to be taken for granted. Under combat conditions—in an unpopular war filled with Kafkaesque absurdity and contradiction—asking a group of people to move into harm's way required more than just giving orders. It was here that I really began to understand the nature of exceptional leadership.

I saw that some leaders were able to inspire exhausted, wet, tired, and discouraged Marines under the most grueling conditions. They were able to exercise leadership in a way that called on deep reserves of endurance and comradeship. They did things that motivated scared, anxious troops to "saddle up" and move into the dark—to venture beyond the relative safety of the concertina-wire perimeter into the face of death. It was more than the discipline of the Marine Corps. It was something else.

After Vietnam, my passion to understand leadership continued in graduate school—first, at the Harvard Business School, then later as a doctoral student in psychology at the University of Michigan, where I discovered that what I had done in Vietnam was called *experiential learning*. My ideas about leadership really began to converge, however, when I joined the faculty of the Yale School of Management. There, as a professor, I was confronted with two central questions:

> ➤ What can I tell students about the qualities and behaviors that distinguish truly exceptional leaders and teams?

> ➤ How can I help students display these qualities and practice these

behaviors when they leave the classroom and move into positions of leadership?

As I began to reflect on the academic research that I had studied—*the literature*, as we affectionately called it—I still felt that something was missing. It was not that the theories were wrong. It was just that academic theories about leadership seemed far removed from the challenges I had faced as a leader, particularly those I experienced in Vietnam. Furthermore, I found it difficult to present these leadership concepts in a way that I thought students would remember after graduation.

In my teaching and consulting outside the university, I was faced with an even more difficult challenge. Working with a diverse array of organizations, I found that leaders were often stretched to the limits and pressured to achieve the impossible in short order. They were totally unconcerned about getting a passing grade on a management-theory exam. They searched for solutions that answered their problems. They required help in identifying the critical steps that they could take to lead their organizations. They demanded ideas in a form that they could remember.

So, a series of life experiences, plus the immediate challenge of teaching and consulting about leadership, led me to blaze a new path. I thought about the power of the leadership lessons learned in Vietnam, and I decided to take a different route: to look for leadership insights in stories of groups that have been to the outer limits of human endurance—the place I call *The Edge*.

This path has led me to believe that the essence of leadership can be found in this ultimate crucible of human endeavor. I am convinced that by understanding the things that work when survival is at stake—when financial incentives or promotions become irrelevant, and when fear and self-interest surface—we can understand how to lead under other conditions. By studying *The Edge*, we can learn the things needed to lead organizations to their full potential, and we can remember these principles when we ourselves are stretched, stressed, and challenged.

In this book, then, *The Edge* is a concept with two dimensions. The first edge is the *Survival Edge*: the limits of human endurance. The second edge is the *Performance Edge*: the limits of individual and organizational potential. Throughout the book, I take lessons from the first and apply them to the second.

Contemporary organizational challenges are not, of course, exactly the same as the life-and-death situations I experienced and studied. I have, however, often observed people reacting to everyday events as if they were life-and-death matters. I have seen people more upset about missing deadlines or giving presentations than Marines under automatic-weapons and mortar fire. In one notable episode, I watched a distraught executive charge down a runway, briefcase in hand, attempting to catch a departing plane. He was apparently prepared to risk his life rather than miss an important meeting.

The challenges that you face as a leader may not involve physical survival, but you will need to deal with the human reactions that are common to any stressful situation. By understanding the leadership practices that work in extreme situations—conditions in which normal or even above-average performance means failure and even death—you will increase your ability to lead and flourish in the face of adversity.

Overview of the Ten Strategies

In my search to find compelling examples of what can be accomplished when people work together to overcome adversity, the saga of Shackleton's Trans-Antarctic expedition stood out. Although there are many other accounts of triumph at *The Edge*, the story of the *Endurance* was unique. Better than any other, the Shackleton saga encapsulated the strategies I had found to be absolutely essential for success. Consequently, I will use Shackleton's story as the primary vehicle for exploring leadership at *The Edge* and for illustrating key ideas about extraordinary leadership and teamwork.

What are these critical factors that determine success at *The Edge*? What are the core elements that made the outcome of the *Endurance* expedition so different from that of the *Karluk*? There were, of course, a number of forces that affected the ending of these two stories: weather, ice conditions, and even luck. Shackleton's luck, however, was not limited to good fortune. He had a boatload of bad luck as well, and it started at the outset of the adventure.

I am convinced that the safe return of Shackleton's expedition can be attributed to much more than luck. I believe that the leadership strategies that enabled Shackleton's crew to beat the odds can be found in a set of principles common to many other stories of survival. The underlying ingredients of triumph are expressed in these ten strategies:

1. *Never lose sight of the ultimate goal, and focus energy on short-term objectives.*

2. *Set a personal example with visible, memorable symbols and behaviors.*

3. *Instill optimism and self-confidence, but stay grounded in reality.*

4. *Take care of yourself: Maintain your stamina and let go of guilt.*

5. *Reinforce the team message constantly: "We are one—we live or die together."*

6. *Minimize status differences and insist on courtesy and mutual respect.*

7. *Master conflict—deal with anger in small doses, engage dissidents, and avoid needless power struggles.*

8. *Find something to celebrate and something to laugh about.*

9. *Be willing to take the Big Risk.*

10. *Never give up—there's always another move.*

The ten strategies are closely interwoven. A single leadership action might include several strategies, in much the same way that an athlete might employ several techniques such as balance, focus, and dynamic relaxation to hit a ball or score a goal. A chapter will be devoted to each of the ten strategies, but it is important to remember the interconnectedness that exists among them all.

The chapters that follow show how each strategy is critical to the success of groups and organizations at *The Edge*. Most important, they outline ways in which these strategies can work for you as a leader. First, however, let us look more carefully at Shackleton's extraordinary adventure.

Expedition Log

1. Before we begin our explorations at *The Edge*, you might want to reflect on a situation in which you were stretched to your own limits of performance or endurance. The situation can be one that involved leading others, or it can relate to a personal obstacle or goal.

> ► What were the qualities that enabled you to succeed or persevere—your behaviors, values, or personal characteristics?

> ► If the situation involved others, what was the nature of the teamwork or support that you were able to inspire? How did you work with others to achieve your goal?

2. If you have difficulty thinking of a personal experience, you might want to reflect on a leader who has taken a team or an organization to *The Edge*—to the highest possible limits of performance.

> ► What were the qualities that made this individual so exceptional—behaviors, values, or personal characteristics?

> ► What was the nature of the teamwork that this leader was able to inspire? How did the group work together to achieve its goals?

LEADING
AT THE EDGE

Second Edition

The Shackleton Saga

The saga of Shackleton's Imperial Trans-Antarctic Expedition has been told many times. I first encountered the story some fifteen years ago when a friend—knowing my interest in survival accounts—gave me a copy of Alfred Lansing's *Endurance*. I was so captivated by the story that I simply could not put it down. I knew that the account, while an engaging tale of adventure, was something more. It was a powerful metaphor that I could use to help leaders who were taking their organizations to *The Edge*.

A number of other excellent books on Shackleton are listed in Part Three, including Caroline Alexander's volume with superb photographs. My goal in writing *Leading at The Edge* is not to duplicate these historical accounts, but rather to examine the story in a different way using the lenses of leadership and teamwork.

Later chapters will highlight important aspects of the story, each one illustrating how Shackleton and others used the ten *Leading at The Edge* strategies. These illustrations will have more impact, however, if they are understood in the context of the overall story. This account, therefore, provides an overall chronology of key events, many of which will be explored in more detail in subsequent chapters.

Setting the Stage

The Shackleton expedition's extraordinary tale is one of the most exciting adventure stories of polar exploration. It is a story about a leader and a group of explorers who endured conditions of hardship and deprivation more extreme than most of us can even imagine.

To help frame the story, consider this question: Have you ever been cold? I mean really, really cold? Try to recall the coldest, most miserable time in your entire life. It might have been on a camping trip when you got caught in a hard rain and had to spend the night in a wet sleeping bag. It might have been while waiting for a tow truck in the winter with a dead battery.

Now, hold that feeling and imagine that someone said to you: "You're going to live this way for the next 634 days. You'll be out of touch with the rest of the world, your family will have no idea whether you are dead or alive, and you will be hungry to the point of starvation."

If you can conjure up that feeling of coldness and desolation, it will give you some sense of the conditions faced by Ernest Shackleton and the members of his Trans-Antarctic expedition.

The adventure began with an advertisement, perhaps apocryphal, that appeared in the London papers:

> Men wanted for Hazardous Journey. Small wages, bitter cold, long months of complete darkness, constant danger, safe return doubtful. Honour and recognition in case of success.[1]

Who in the world would volunteer for this journey? Some of you reading this book might feel that this is your job description, and that you have already volunteered. Amazingly, thousands of would-be explorers came forward, each wanting to join Shackleton's expedition.

But what were they signing up for? Shackleton's mission was the first overland crossing of the Antarctic Continent. He had a clear vision and a plan for how to achieve it. Shackleton intended to sail from London to Buenos Aires and then to the island of South Georgia. From South Georgia, the expedition would enter the Weddell Sea, cross Antarctica, and exit on the other side, where a ship would be waiting. Having calculated the times and distances, Shackleton believed the transcontinental journey could be completed in 120 days.[2] One way of understanding what he was trying to accomplish is to imagine walking from Idaho to Texas, except the geography is dramatically different.

The terrain of Antarctica is depicted well in a passage from Stephen Pyne's *The Ice*:

> Ice informs the geophysics and geography of Antarctica....Out of simple icy crystals is constructed a vast hierarchy of ice masses, ice terranes, and ice structures. These higher-order ice forms collectively compose the entire continent: the ice bergs: tabular bergs, glacier bergs, ice islands, bergy bits, growlers, brash ice, white ice, blue ice, green ice, dirty ice; the sea ices: pack ices, ice floes, ice rinds, ice hummocks . . . ; the coastal ices, fast ice, shore ices, glacial-ice tongues, ice piedmonts; the mountain ices: glacial ice, valley glaciers, cirque glaciers . . . ; the ground ices: ice wedges, ice veins, permafrost; the polar plateau ices: ice sheets, ice caps, ice domes . . . ; the atmospheric ices: ice grains, ice crystals, ice dust, pencil ice, plate ice, bullet ice.[3]

This description makes it clear: The surface of Antarctica is nothing but ice. The continent's perimeter begins with an ice shelf, in places as tall as a ten-story building. Once past the shelf, there are other obstacles. There are ice hummocks—jagged ridges thrust upward like so many small mountains. Crevasses that can swallow a dog-sled team abound. And, then, there is the climate. The coldest temperature on Earth has been recorded in Antarctica: −128.6°F.

The Leaders and the Crew

Crossing Antarctica was a formidable undertaking. What kind of a person would attempt a feat such as this? Ernest Shackleton believed he was the person to do it.

Shackleton was an explorer who had already gained fame in Britain in 1909, when he came within ninety-seven nautical miles of the South Pole before he was forced to turn back because of physical exhaustion and a shortage of food.[4] On that expedition, in a characteristic gesture, he gave one of his last biscuits to a comrade, Frank Wild.

The South Pole was reached in 1911 by Norwegian Roald Amundsen and then early in 1912 by the ill-fated expedition of Robert Falcon Scott. No one, however, had traversed the continent by 1914, and this frontier of exploration remained. Shackleton yearned for a challenge, and this was one of the few remaining arenas in which to test his skills.

Much has been written about Shackleton, but I believe the essence of his character can be found in the values transmitted by his family. The Shackleton family's Latin motto, *Fortitudine Vincimus* (By endurance we conquer), was his rallying cry, and the expedition put his motto to the test.

Because he was the leader of the expedition, and because of his forceful personality, much emphasis has been placed on Shackleton. As in any complex enterprise, however, leadership was exercised by many individuals. In fact, a key theme of this book is the importance of mobilizing leadership from multiple sources.

One of the most important sources of leadership came in the form of Frank Wild, Shackleton's old companion. Wild's low-key style balanced Shackleton's bold temperament, and they were so close they would finish each other's sentences. This partnership, born of deep respect and shared hardship, would serve them well when both would be stretched to their limits to maintain the integrity of the expedition.

Wild and Shackleton selected twenty-five other explorers for the expedition. Complex and diverse, the group was composed of men with a range of temperaments; personalities; and technical skills, including medicine, navigation, carpentry, and photography. The team was also diverse in social class, ranging from university professors to fishermen, and in age. The oldest, McNeish, the carpenter, was fifty-seven.

Officially numbering twenty-seven, the full complement of the ship proved to be twenty-eight with Blackborow, the stowaway. When Shackleton discovered that there was a stowaway aboard, he was furious and declared, "If we run out of food, and anyone has to be eaten, you will be first."[5] Despite this inauspicious start, Blackborow eventually became fully integrated as a member of the expedition.

Shackleton was also faced with the task of finding a seaworthy vessel to carry them south. He chose a barkentine-rigged ship, which he named *Endurance*, after his family motto. Built by a famous Norwegian ship-building yard, the vessel was powered by both steam and sail.

Endurance was specifically designed for polar travel, constructed of carefully selected wood to withstand the pounding of the ice. Unlike modern icebreakers, however, *Endurance* was not designed to ride over the ice but was constructed with a V-shaped keel.

The Adventure Begins

While Shackleton stayed behind to raise money, *Endurance* sailed at the end of August 1914 under the command of Frank Worsley. Shackleton joined the expedition in Buenos Aires, and they all set out for Grytviken, a whaling station at rugged South Georgia (Figure SS-1, map position 1 at the end of this chapter).

At the whaling station, Shackleton received disturbing reports that the ice had moved much farther north than usual. With these warnings, and knowing that wintering aboard was a distinct possibility, they sailed on December 5, 1914, with extra clothing and a great deal of apprehension. Shackleton portrayed the scene:

> The ship was very steady in the quarterly sea, but certainly did not look as neat and trim as she had done when leaving the shores of England four months earlier. We had filled up with coal at Grytviken, and this extra fuel was stored on deck, where it impeded movement considerably. . . . We had also taken aboard a ton of whale-meat for the dogs. The big chunks of meat were hung up in the rigging, out of reach but not out of sight of the dogs, and as the *Endurance* rolled and pitched, they watched with wolfish eyes for a windfall.[6]

As the ice thickened, the going became more and more difficult. As

Worsley enthusiastically rammed the ship through the floes, Shackleton became increasingly worried by the lack of progress. They wormed their way through the "gigantic and interminable jigsaw puzzle devised by nature."[7]

Trapped in the Ice

On January 19, 1915—forty-five days after their departure from South Georgia—disaster struck. The ice of the Weddell Sea closed around *Endurance* like a vise. The expedition was stuck, sixty miles from the Antarctic Continent (Figure SS-1, map position 2).

Working with picks, saws, and other hand tools, the expedition made two attempts to break free. The first time, with all sails set and engines on full ahead, the crew tried for hours and never moved a foot. In a second attempt, working from 8 A.M. to midnight, they advanced 150 yards. But they were still hopelessly stuck. The "elastic" sea ice prevented a solid blow from ramming a passage, and *Endurance* was trapped.[8]

On February 24, sea watches were canceled, and the crew resigned themselves to wintering on board. The men moved to a warmer between-decks storage area that they called "the Ritz." Their only entertainment was a hand-cranked phonograph and Leonard Hussey, the geologist, who played his banjo and a homemade violin. As the days wore on, *Endurance* became caked with snow and ice. It would be difficult to imagine a colder, bleaker scene. In these extreme conditions, members of the expedition became closer than ever.

How did this happen? I believe the answer lies in Shackleton's understanding of the absolute importance of managing the dynamics of his crew. He had learned from accounts of previous expeditions of the severe morale problems that could arise, and he made a number of conscious decisions to ensure the cohesion of the team. Foremost, as *Endurance* sat securely on the ice, Shackleton kept the crew fairly busy until the end of July 1915. At that point, deep in the Antarctic winter, high winds caused the ice pressure to increase. The ship heeled, the bilge pumps began to fail, water poured into the ship, and the stern was thrown upward twenty feet. As the ice moved relentlessly against the hull, both the timbers of *Endurance* and the crew's sense of security began to crack. Worsley, the captain, recalled:

> Two massive floes, miles of ice, jammed her sides and held her fast, while the third floe tore across her stern, ripping off the rudder as though it had been made of matchwood. She quivered and groaned as rudder and stern-post were torn off, and part of her keel was driven upwards by the ice. To me, the sound was so terribly human that I felt like groaning in sympathy, and Shackleton felt the same way. It gave me the horrible feeling that the ship was gasping for breath. Never before had I witnessed such a scene, and I sincerely hope I never may again.[9]

Endurance Goes Down

Day 327 of the expedition—October 27, 1915—marked the end of *Endurance*. The masts toppled and the sides were stove in, as shards of ice ripped the strong timbers to shreds. Frank Wild made a last tour of the dying vessel and found two crewmembers in the forecastle, fast asleep after their exhausting labor at the bilge pumps. He said, "She's going boys, I think it's time to get off."[10]

Imagine yourself in Shackleton's position. Your ship is crushed, and you are 346 miles from the nearest food depot on Paulet Island (Figure SS-1, map position 3). You have lifeboats and sleds, but they weigh almost a thousand pounds. Now what?

Shackleton proposed to head toward open water by undertaking a march across hundreds of miles of solid pack ice. Men in harness began pulling the lifeboats on sledges. The task was grueling, and after two days of hauling, the team had covered less than two miles.

Ocean Camp

Realizing that it was futile to go on, the men found a large floe more than half a mile in diameter, made camp, and came to a decision. They agreed to stay on the floe until the drift of the ice carried them closer to Paulet Island. They sat at Ocean Camp from October 30, 1915, until the end of December. So far, Shackleton's leadership had kept the team intact. Now, however, it was more than a year from the time they had set sail from South Georgia. Morale was understandably low, and Shackleton knew that something had to be done to combat the growing sense of futility. On day 384, although they were still a long way from the sea (Figure SS-1, map position 4), they once more attempted to drag the boats across the ice to open water.

The Mutiny

This second sledge march was no more successful than the first, and it set the stage for what has come to be called the "one-man mutiny." McNeish, the carpenter, refused to go on. He argued that the articles he had signed specified serving "on board" and, since *Endurance* had sunk, they were no longer binding. Despite a special clause in the articles that bound him "to perform any duty on board, in the boats, or on the shore," McNeish stood his ground.[11] He defied orders to march, so Shackleton was summoned, defused the mutiny, and enabled the expedition to move forward.

Patience Camp

Exhausted and discouraged because the ice was still impassable, the expedition crewmembers again made camp and waited. The men knew they had to get off the ice, but they had no sense of controlling their fate. Reginald James, the physicist, summed it up this way: "A bug on a single molecule of oxygen in a gale of wind would have about the same chance of predicting where he was likely to finish up."[12]

They continued to deal with the anxiety of waiting, hoping to drift to open water. As their food supply dwindled, they stayed alive on a diet of seal steaks, stewed penguin, and their favorite: penguin liver. There were some moments of excitement, including a near-fatal encounter between

Thomas Orde-Lees, the storekeeper and former Royal Marine, and a sea leopard.

By the beginning of April, the floe had shrunk from a half mile to 200 yards wide. With the floe literally cracking out from under them, the men wanted to launch the boats. But they knew that abandoning the floe prematurely might mean disaster: The unstable ice could close, crushing the boats and their only hope of survival.

Escape from the Ice

Finally, on April 9 (Day 491), the pack opened and the boats were launched (Figure SS-1, map position 5). The men tumbled into the three lifeboats, put out every available oar, and pulled with all their strength for open water. The temperature was so cold that when the waves broke over the boats, the water froze to the rowers' clothes in an instant. The men bailed furiously, but the water rose quickly to their ankles and then to their knees. Blackborow, who was wearing leather boots, soon lost all feeling in his feet.

They were all emaciated, suffering from diarrhea, and desperately craving fresh drinking water. The first night they camped on a flat, heavy floe and fell asleep. Late that evening, "some intangible feeling of uneasiness" moved Shackleton to leave his tent. He stood in the quiet camp, watching the stars and the snow flurries. Suddenly, the floe split under his feet, and from the darkness he could hear muffled, gasping sounds. Shackleton ran to a collapsed tent and threw it out of the way, exposing a member of the crew who was struggling in his sleeping bag in the frigid water below. With a tremendous heave, Shackleton pulled him onto the ice, just as the two halves of the broken floe came back together with a crash.

As the winds and currents changed, the group was forced to change its destination four times during the five-and-a-half-day voyage. Finally, they found respite on a rocky, barren speck of land known as Elephant Island. The beach was only 100 feet wide and 50 feet deep, but for the first time in 497 days they were on solid ground.

Elated, but on the verge of collapse, the men ate their first hot meal in almost six days. Given their enfeebled condition, even the most basic tasks were painful. They built shelters out of lifeboats, sails, and clothing. Unfortunately, the shelters were constructed on snow that had been mixed with hundreds of years of penguin guano. Body warmth and the heat from a blubber stove melted the guano, and the crew soon found themselves wallowing in a foul-smelling yellow mud of penguin guano. So they had made it to safety—sort of—but what now? There was only a small food supply on the island—a few penguins, some seagulls, shellfish, and some elephant seals. Still, the chance of rescue was slight and another decision loomed: whether to stay and wait for rescue, or to sail for help. If you sail, where do you go?

The Scotia Sea

There were no good options, and the danger of running out of food also weighed heavily on Shackleton. He confided in Worsley: "We shall have to make the boat journey, however risky it is. I'm not going to let the men starve."

Shackleton decided that part of the crew would sail for help. Because the region's gale-force winds blew from west to east, he elected to make the 800-mile run to South Georgia, sailing through the most treacherous stretch of water on the planet, with winds of hurricane intensity and enormous waves.

Shackleton chose the *James Caird*, the one lifeboat that was the most seaworthy, and attempted to create a vessel that would survive the voyage. Although McNeish was a troublemaker on occasion, he was also a skilled and creative carpenter. His ingenious solution for decking and outfitting the lifeboat for this risky journey proved invaluable. Shackleton selected five members of the expedition to sail with him. After a farewell breakfast, all hands mustered to launch the *James Caird* on Day 506 (Figure SS-1, map position 6).

The next sixteen days were even more harrowing than the journey to Elephant Island. The boat was constantly pounded by immense waves known as Cape Horn Rollers. Each watch, one of the men was forced to risk his life to chip away ice that was constantly forming on the deck and lines.

On May 10, 1916, the exhausted sailors sighted South Georgia. As they made their landing, the rudder fell off the *James Caird*, but by late afternoon Shackleton and his companions were standing on the island they had left 522 days earlier (Figure SS-1, map position 7).

Across the Glaciers

A safe landing was the good news. The bad news was that they were on the wrong side of South Georgia, an island abounding with uncharted and treacherous glaciers. Shackleton and the two best able to travel proceeded overland to reach the whaling station of Grytviken at Stromness Bay. It took the men three days and nights—each filled with danger and enormous physical challenge—to reach the station.

The men left behind on the far side of South Georgia were soon rescued. Shackleton and five others were finally safe. Back at Elephant Island, however, conditions were desperate. Frank Wild, whom Shackleton had left in charge, worked desperately to keep up the crew's spirits. After four months of waiting, however, the men were wondering if they would ever be found.

The Rescue

Shackleton struggled to get help for the rest of his crew, making three attempts in three different ships. Finally, at the end of August—128 days after the launching of the *James Caird*—he succeeded on the fourth attempt. The timing was providential: The pack ice opened for only a few hours, just enough time to get a boat ashore and to complete the rescue.

Captain Worsley's final journal entry reads:

Rescued! August 30, 1916
All well! At last! All ahead full.
Worsley[13]

With that entry, the saga of Ernest Shackleton and the men of the Trans-Antarctic expedition ended, 634 days after their departure from South Georgia.

Every time I relive this story, I want to give these explorers a round of applause. I want to applaud them not just because they made it to safety, but because of the extraordinary leadership and teamwork they exhibited. Not only did they survive, they all survived with a unique level of caring and camaraderie.

What was it, exactly, that made Shackleton such a great leader? What was it that enabled Shackleton and his team to overcome such seemingly insurmountable obstacles? The chapters that follow provide answers to these questions.

Figure SS-1. Map of the *Endurance* expedition.

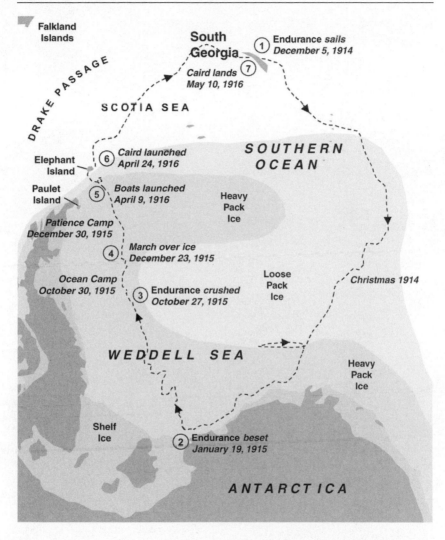

PART ONE

Ten Strategies for Leading at *The Edge*

1

Vision and Quick Victories

Strategy 1:
Never lose sight of the ultimate goal, and focus energy on short-term objectives.

> ...I feel sure that it is the right thing to attempt a march.... It will be much better for the men in general to feel that even though progress is slow, they are on their way to land, than it will be simply to sit down and wait for the tardy northwesterly drift to take us out of this cruel waste of ice.[1]
>
> —Ernest Shackleton

Leaders who take their organizations to *The Edge* must channel energy toward two equally important goals. First, they must continually be aware of their ultimate destination—their longer-term, strategic objective.

This ultimate goal, however, may be distant and uncertain. So while pursuing this long-term target, leaders also must be vigilant in focusing the scarce resources of the organization on the critical short-term tasks that create momentum and ensure survival. Ernest Shackleton demonstrated an almost uncanny mastery of these two essential, but very different, leadership skills.

Be Willing to Find a "New Mark"

It is hard to imagine a bleaker scene than the one surrounding the demise of *Endurance*. Shackleton and his crew had suffered as the ship was slowly, inexorably crushed by millions of tons of ice. For days, they watched the death agony of the ship, waiting helplessly as their floating home disintegrated plank by plank.

Even with the uncertainty of the shifting ice, wind, and ocean, life aboard ship had followed a relatively predictable routine. The crew had warm food and the comforting security of a familiar environment. Now, marooned on the ice and snow, their familiar, stable world had been turned upside down.

With the end of *Endurance*, Shackleton saw his dream of crossing the Antarctic Continent die as well. And he faced more than failure: Shackleton was not expected by the world to reappear until February 1916, and his chances of rescue were nonexistent.

In this wrenching moment of personal challenge, however, Shackleton was able to shift quickly his long-term goal from the crossing of the continent to bringing every man back alive. Refocusing his efforts, he wrote, "A man must shape himself to a new mark, directly the old one goes to ground."[2] With no prospect of rescue, facing an unknown future with little chance of survival, he turned to his crew and simply said: "So now we'll go home."[3]

How was Shackleton able to exercise this kind of tenacity in the face of such overwhelming adversity? He certainly had his private doubts, writing in his diary, "I pray God I can manage to get the whole party to civilization."[4] Acutely aware of his responsibilities as the leader, Shackleton let go of his original plan, shifted his focus, and devoted himself completely to this new mission. By the intensity of his conviction and the force of his will, he instilled in others the deep belief that they would achieve their new goal: returning safely, without loss of life.

Lessons for Leaders

Efforts to explore the unknown are inherently filled with unexpected events. Changing environmental conditions and shifting opportunities are part of any truly innovative, challenging adventure. This means that, as a leader, you need to be willing to shift both long- and short-term goals without clinging to the past. Additionally, you must be able to commit to these new goals with as much passion and energy as you did to the original mark.

A classic business example of this is CEO Andy Grove's decision to alter Intel's direction. Intel, a company known for microprocessors, was once primarily a maker of memory chips. In the mid-1980s, Japanese chipmakers moved to win away Intel's chip business by undercutting its prices by 10 percent. The Japanese were successful, and Intel lost $173 million in one year.

After considering many options, Grove determined to take Intel out of the memory-chip business and make a commitment to microprocessor manufacturing. In coming to this decision, Grove asked his colleague and former Intel CEO Gordon Moore a hypothetical question: "If we got kicked out and the board brought in a new CEO, what do you think he would do?"[5]

Moore told Grove that this new CEO would take the company out of the memory-chip business. Grove decided that rather than wait for his successor to change things, he would do it himself. Thereafter, resources were redirected into developing Intel microprocessors, a business sector then secondary to chips. This new direction provided the foundation for Intel's future success.

Intel continued to adapt to changing demand by looking beyond the microprocessor market. While projections for PC sales fell, Intel boldly acquired assets in the cable-modem chip, wireless chip, and security software businesses. It redirected resources to new product lines: Intel chips for tablet computers and smartphones.[6] With each of these moves, Intel was finding a new mark and forging ahead in Shackleton style.

Do Something!

When *Endurance* went down, the crew's anxiety might have been overwhelming. Instead, their energy was focused and channeled. Although many of their activities did not produce positive results, Shackleton was tireless in finding ways to capture the free-floating anxiety that permeated their situation. Shackleton looked for every opportunity to do something concrete, to take decisive action.

The initial attempt to drag *Endurance*'s heavily laden lifeboats was a complete failure. Their goal was to head northwest for Paulet Island, hoping to reach the emergency food stores that Shackleton knew had been left some twelve years before. This trek of 312 miles was an unbelievably ambitious undertaking. Even Shackleton had expressed doubts that it could be accomplished at the projected rate of five miles a day—the best they could hope for, dragging sleds and lifeboats across the jagged ice. The boats were essential, since their plan was to reach open water and then to sail to safety.

In spite of the dangers, Shackleton understood the need to try. The task was nearly impossible, but this immediate activity shifted attention from the loss they had just suffered to the clearly defined task ahead. After recovering supplies from the ship and packing the sleds, the journey began. Shackleton and three others forged ahead, searching for a passable route.

Their route was obstructed by a series of pressure ridges, each of which required heavy chopping with shovels and mountaineering pickaxes. The advance party was forced to perform the mind-numbing work of clearing a level trail, and the rest of the expedition followed, man-hauling the sleds in relays. After three hours on the trail, the expedition had gone only a mile from the ship in a straight line.

Ironically, the rising temperatures of the next day made things even worse. The expedition members were now plowing through snow stew, bulldozing their way inch by inch, foot by foot. The men sweated profusely, swore at the snow, and made little progress. At the end of the day, they had bulled their way just one more mile. Realizing that it was impossible to go on, Shackleton faced reality and called a halt to the march.

Not surprisingly, this change of plans created no small measure of disappointment. After all, this was to be a march to the open ocean, and eventual rescue. Once more, Shackleton defused a potentially destructive mood, turning the crew's attention toward salvaging any remaining food, clothing, and other supplies from the wreckage of *Endurance*. Frank Wild and six others returned to retrieve gear and—most important—the third lifeboat. Then, all hands focused on the new task of establishing Ocean Camp.

Shackleton's first decision after *Endurance* went down was in some ways a glaring mistake. They had no chance of covering the vast distance to Paulet Island, and precious energy was wasted on an unreachable goal. Or was it?

Shackleton had discovered the absolute importance of sustaining psychological momentum on an earlier adventure, the British Antarctic expedition of 1907–1909. Marooned in McMurdo Sound, he sensed growing frustration and anxiety among the expedition members. To create an outlet, he proposed climbing Mount Erebus. The ascent was marked by days of suffering, sickness, and fatigue, but it concluded with a major achievement: the first ascent of an Antarctic peak.[7]

The "sledge march," like the ascent of Mount Erebus, served its purpose. The march kept the crew from dwelling on its misfortune and redirected their energy toward concrete action. Perhaps most important, the effort forced the members of the expedition to work together toward a common goal.

Lessons for Leaders

Leading at *The Edge* means seizing every opportunity for decisive action and refusing to be discouraged when some efforts prove unsuccessful. The very act of doing something concrete creates a sense of momentum, and a series of small victories will lay the foundation for eventual success.

James Burke, CEO of Tylenol-maker Johnson & Johnson, faced a difficult (and now iconic) decision in September 1982, after an unknown person laced Extra Strength Tylenol capsules with cyanide, causing seven deaths. His handling of the Tylenol danger is a powerful illustration of the value of decisive action in a crisis situation. He had to choose between waiting for conclusive evidence of a nationwide threat or incurring the cost of recalling all the capsules.

The public had come to equate Johnson & Johnson's products with health and safety; now people were panicking. The company's response would be critical to restoring trust in Tylenol, the company's top-selling product, and the rest of the firm's product line.

The way in which Burke and J&J responded is now regarded as the gold standard of crisis management. Burke's and the firm's actions were guided by the company credo: "The first responsibility is to the customer." Burke quickly formed a strategy team to deal with the crisis, posted a $100,000 reward for finding the killer, ran full-page newspaper and television ads offering consumers an exchange of capsules for tablets, set up a toll-free hotline to field questions, and established public programs to reach doctors and other significant constituencies.

The company redesigned its packaging and eventually retrieved some 31 million capsules from stores and homes around the country. Three months after the crisis, thanks to the company's quick action, tablet sales had returned to 80 percent of the precrisis level. The Tylenol capsules were eventually replaced with more tamper-resistant caplets. Decisive action saved the company's market and—more important—its reputation.[8]

The problems faced by Continental Airlines did not involve loss of life, but the company and its leaders faced a similarly daunting situation. Greg Brenneman, former president and COO, described the state of the airlines during one crisis:

> Managers were paralyzed by anxiety. The company had gone through ten presidents in ten years, so standard operating procedure was to do nothing while awaiting new management. The product, in a word, was terrible; the company's results showed it. . . . And the company hadn't posted a profit outside of bankruptcy since 1978.[9]

On the verge of an unprecedented third declaration of bankruptcy, and with employee morale in shambles, Brenneman and former CEO Gordon Bethune devised a strategy for Continental that they called the "Go Forward Plan"—then they went forward. Brenneman remembers:

> If you sit around devising elegant and complex strategies and then try to execute them through a series of flawless decisions,

you're doomed. We saved Continental because we acted, and
we never looked back.[10]

These decisive actions by Continental's leaders enabled the airline to survive another sixteen years. It weathered the terrorist attacks of 9/11 and
the economic plight of the airline industry until merging with United
Airlines. While he was at the helm, Bethune's leadership had a major impact on the airline: Continental went from receiving dismal customer re-
views to winning prestigious awards for excellent quality and customer
service.[11]

The spirit of moving forward is exemplified in a story recounted by
my friend Bob, a senior manager in a large federal agency based in Washington, D.C. Bob was given the task of revitalizing two regional offices,
one located in New York, the other in Boston. Although he was in constant contact with the two offices by phone, he was often required to be
physically present to troubleshoot. He did this by using the New York–
Boston airline shuttle.

During one particularly hectic week, Bob ran to the airport and
boarded the shuttle for Boston. As the plane was taxiing down the runway, he realized, panic-stricken, that he was not absolutely sure he had
boarded the right plane. He could be going to the wrong city. Then, he
took a breath and said to himself, "Don't worry, Bob, it's not such a big
deal. You have so much to do that either city will work!" He kept his
nerve, kept his momentum after the plane did land in Boston, and the
revitalization effort succeeded.

There is a caveat here. A few years ago, I worked with a leading technology organization to try to discover why it expended so much time
and resources and accomplished so little in the marketplace. What we
found was a culture that valued activity over results.

A cultural icon within the company was the belief that it was important to be seen working late and on weekends. As I interviewed a
number of senior executives, it became clear that many of them were
more concerned about the appearance of working hard than they were
about the work's outcome. This focus on activity over results diverted
energy from more important tasks and was a significant barrier to the
company's economic success.

Look Beyond Your Own Needs for Action

Shackleton's focused vision and decisive team actions contrast dramatically with those of Vilhjalmur Stefansson on the *Karluk*. The tragedy of the *Karluk* expedition resulted, in part, from a leader who failed to understand the distinction between individual actions and team motivation. Conceived by Stefansson, the Canadian Arctic Expedition of 1913 was intended to explore the possibility that there might be an undiscovered continent somewhere beneath the polar ice.

The expedition was, from the beginning, a flawed effort. Stefansson was an anthropologist and a self-promoter, not a seaman. Short of time, he chose the only available vessel, a twenty-four-year-old wooden barkentine known as the *Karluk*. It was a sailing vessel with an auxiliary engine designed for fishing. The ship was capable of limited speed, only five to seven knots. *Karluk's* main assets were her cheap price and her availability.

The captain, Robert Bartlett, was a better choice. He, too, was selected at the last minute, but at least he was a distinguished mariner. A native of Newfoundland, he had sailed with Admiral Robert Peary in his historic Arctic exploration in 1909. Captain Bartlett was disappointed in the ship and knew that it would never survive a winter trapped in the ice.

Confusion reigned from the start. Having left preparations to others, Stefansson reached Victoria, British Columbia, just three days before the *Karluk* was to sail. He arrived to find the boat a shambles and the crew anxious about their safety. Already, Stefansson had made incredible public statements that *Karluk* would press northward as far as possible and would probably be crushed and sink. Understandably, the crew was nervous about its uncertain fate.

The *Karluk* sailed from Vancouver Island on June 17, 1913. After fog, engine failure, and five broken hawsers, she finally reached Nome on July 8. On July 26, she sailed from Point Clarence, only to encounter an early blizzard and unusually heavy field ice.

The *Karluk* was not designed for these ice conditions, and Bartlett advised turning back while there was still time. Stefansson refused, and they plowed ahead. On August 13, the ice pack closed around the *Karluk*.

No one was particularly concerned, since they expected the sea conditions to change. In fact, they "cavorted about on the ice for hours," enjoying the scenery.

After sitting for five weeks waiting for the ice to open, Stefansson became impatient. He was a leader who thrived on activity, and the delay hardly suited him. He concluded that "the *Karluk* was not to move under her own power again, and that we were in for a voyage such as that of the *Jeanette* or the *Fram*, drifting for years, if we had the luck to remain unbroken."[12]

Having reached that conclusion, and dreading the prospect of inaction, Stefansson set out on a personal expedition. On September 19, he abruptly announced that he was going to hunt for caribou. Caribou were apparently extinct in the region, so this appeared to many as simply an excuse to leave the ill-fated ship. Stefansson loaded two sledges with food and ammunition and, after posing for photographs, set out with four others for Point Barrow. He left a letter with Bartlett promising to be back to the ship in ten days "if no accident happens."

In September 1913, with the expedition trapped and separated from its leader, the *Karluk* drifted into the realm of "ultimate inaccessibility," into the frozen Arctic Sea. When the *Karluk* was carried out to sea, Stefansson made an effort to follow, but by then it was too late. Apparently reconciled to the loss of the ship, Stefansson went on with his plans for mapping and geographic discovery. He was not seen again until 1918, when he suddenly reappeared after five years of exploration.

Stefansson later rationalized his decision to abandon the expedition, and he minimized the plight of the crew. He was, as he later reported, convinced that the destruction of the *Karluk* would take place slowly and that the crew would be able to salvage their critical supplies and reach safety. He was partly right. They were able to retrieve most of the stores and equipment. What he did not foresee, or apparently care about, is that many would not reach safety and would die in the ice.

Stefansson left behind a leadership vacuum that was never filled, but one thing is clear: If the energy of the crew had been focused and directed, the story of the *Karluk* expedition might have had a very different and much happier ending.

Lessons for Leaders

Vilhjalmur Stefansson did a good job of focusing anxiety—but only his own. Stefansson's caribou hunt is a glaring example of a leader who focused on his own needs for action while neglecting the rest of the organization. This sort of self-involved activity is not, of course, unique to polar explorers.

I observed one senior executive at a leading aerospace firm whose behavior under stress paralleled that of the *Karluk* leader. Whenever this executive was faced with a financial downturn, he closed his door, sat behind his computer, and stared at spreadsheets for hours. By endlessly running the numbers, he focused his own anxiety. This self-absorption left the rest of the management team adrift, wondering who was steering the company.

Leaders at *The Edge* need to maintain a balance between their own needs and the needs of the team, and they must concentrate on engaging the whole organization. By doing so, they will channel their own anxiety and simultaneously ensure that the expedition maintains momentum and focus.

Overcome Uncertainty with Structure

There are times at *The Edge* when it is simply not possible to take proactive, decisive action. But there are other ways of focusing team energy, even when direct forward movement is blocked. Shackleton's ability to create structure and order was effective even when there was little to do but wait. These routines provided a sense of stability, and they helped quell the ever-present anxiety about the future.

To understand just how important these structures were to the stranded crew, picture the inherent chaos of their environment. Adrift on the ice, they were a sorry collection of castaways. Their equipment was primitive at best, with reindeer-skin sleeping bags and rudimentary tents. Their new home was a seesaw of shifting, grinding ice that moved without warning.

In the middle of the first night, a crack opened in the middle of their encampment. The men were awakened by Shackleton blowing the alarm whistle. Tents and stores were moved to the larger section of the floe, but the incident made it clear that their temporary refuge was not a safe home.

While the environment had changed for the worse, the crew's routines had not. From the outset, Shackleton had understood the importance of these essential systems; the necessity of organization had been underscored by the state of his crew after the voyage from London to South Georgia.

Shackleton had stayed behind in England to deal with the perpetual problem of raising money for the expedition. There were harbor and coal bills to contend with and wages to be paid to the crew's families while they were away.[13] This left Frank Worsley, the captain, to take *Endurance* on the first leg of the journey, from London to Buenos Aires, Argentina.

Worsley would later show himself a brilliant navigator, but his initial command was a disaster. He was a leader who shared Shackleton's ebullience but lacked an understanding of the importance of order and organization. Early on, the captain's erratic nature gave Shackleton reason for concern, and he expressed his doubts in a letter to Ernest Perris of the *Daily Chronicle*. Shackleton wrote that Worsley "was not the type to hold men well together," and that he was eager to have "the whole show under my own eyes."[14]

The effects of this inconsistent, haphazard leadership were apparent when Shackleton arrived in Buenos Aires. He found the crew surly, fragmented, and often drunk.[15] With Shackleton's arrival, everyone breathed a sigh of relief. His very presence restored a sense of order and security. As Orde-Lees put it, it was "splendid having Sir Ernest on board. Everything works like clockwork & one knows just where one is."[16]

Unlike Worsley, Shackleton demonstrated fiery enthusiasm that was complemented by an ability to make order out of chaos. From the start, he established routines that continued after their original purpose had evaporated. Sea watches were kept even after *Endurance* was locked in the ice, and the daily chores of living together proceeded effortlessly. Ice was hauled on board for water, seals were hunted, and the radio watch was maintained.[17]

This tactic of "business as usual" went a long way toward offsetting the bitter disappointment and frustration that everyone felt. Scientists did their work, even if the work was restricted to identifying stones from penguin stomachs. Frank Hurley, the photographer, recorded the changing panorama of ice and sky, and a routine was established for training the dogs.

Shackleton had learned from a previous journey the critical importance of managing the dogs, and he still held out hope that the transcontinental journey could be achieved. So each dog-team leader was assigned the task of producing an effective "work group" through regular practice and exercise.[18]

The stabilizing role of structure became even more important after *Endurance* had been crushed and the expedition was cast out on the ice. Given the strain he was under, Shackleton demonstrated astonishing attention to detail. He realized, for example, that they might be forced to abandon their makeshift quarters in a hurry. He wrote up a detailed plan of just how that would be accomplished and pinned a copy of it to each tent. After reviewing the plan with the crewmembers, he warned them that an evacuation drill could be called at any minute—a sort of "pop quiz" to test their ability to respond.[19]

These stabilizing structures, then, provided a foundation of organized activity that had vital, positive effects on the morale of the team. In his diary, Worsley summed up the sense of security and confidence that this contributed to the expedition:

> I don't think we have a genuine pessimist amongst us. Certainly a good deal of our cheerfulness is due to the order & routine which Sir E. establishes. . . . The regular daily task & matter-of-fact groove into which everything settles inspires confidence in itself, & the Leader's state of mind is naturally reflected in the whole party.[20]

Lessons for Leaders

When leaders move into unexplored terrain, ambiguity and uncertainty are inevitable. Establishing critical organizational structures—a "matter-of-fact groove"—can give people the sense of order they need to be productive. Larry Bossidy's leadership when he was at AlliedSignal (now Honeywell) illustrates the power of this approach.

Lack of confidence throughout the organization was the glaring concern for Bossidy when he took over the reins as CEO. "People were downtrodden, disillusioned, and disappointed. So the essential thing was to try to lift all boats, to communicate things that we could specifically do."[21]

Bossidy's solution was to design a rigorous structure for the company's key processes. He reorganized human resources, detailing systems for selection, reward, development, and motivation. He established structures for strategic planning, including a process for identifying the obstacles that blocked AlliedSignal's success and for deciding how these barriers would be overcome. He revamped the operating plan and developed contingencies—"preconsidered options"—that could be implemented in response to changing external events. He also put in controls to ensure that the company would maintain a focus on its customers.

Bossidy's campaign of systematization extended to manufacturing. He made sure, for example, that the Six Sigma Quality Process—defined as 3.4 defects per million parts—was deeply embedded in the organization. He also instituted an employee-education program called "forever learning" in which every employee—including the operators on the floor—received forty hours of training a year.

The investment in these core processes halted AlliedSignal's drift, and it paid off in financial performance. These efforts also changed the personality of the organization. As former COO Fred Poses stated: "[Larry] can be relentless, but he also gives us a burning desire to win."[22]

Create Engaging Distractions

At times during the twenty-three-month ordeal, the Shackleton expedition members, as a practical matter, had very little to do. Naturally, attention often turned to thoughts of home and, of course, food. Shackleton was always on the alert to find distractions that also made real contributions to the expedition. In one notable instance, a crewmember was so discouraged that he literally wanted to lie down and die. Shackleton fixed the problem: The despondent man was given the job of cook, and he became so preoccupied with his new role that he snapped out of his depression. Shackleton later recalled:

> The task of keeping the galley fire alight was both difficult and strenuous, and it took his thoughts away from the chances of immediate dissolution. In fact, I found him a little gravely concerned over the drying of a naturally not over-clean pair of socks which were hung up in close proximity to our evening milk. Occupation had brought his thoughts back to the ordinary cares of life.[23]

The transformation was remarkable. When challenged with a demanding task, a crewmember waiting to die became a valuable contributor.

Lessons for Leaders

Winning leaders cultivate the ability to monitor the condition of each person on the team and to sense when individuals are becoming overwhelmed. They need to direct negative energy toward activities that divert people's attention from their problems and harness this energy for positive results.

I recently came upon a contemporary example of an engaging distraction. I was discussing human behavior under stress with a friend who is an airline pilot. He had just returned from an intensive training course on dealing with emergency water landings, and he shared an interesting observation.

The lifeboat section of the course dealt with procedures for instructing surviving passengers on a process for setting up a shelter over their rafts. The cover provided, he admitted, very limited protection from the elements, and the assembly task was complicated. The central purpose of the task, however, had little to do with physical protection. Instead, it was designed to give people a concrete activity that would occupy their minds while waiting for rescue.

There is nothing quite like responsibility—especially a role in which others depend on you—to focus your attention. As a leader at *The Edge*, you must continually scan for people who exhibit nervousness and anxiety. When you find them, figure out a way to capture that free-floating energy. Assign them a special project. Give them added responsibility. As a martial arts instructor of mine used to say, "Anxiety is energy without a goal."

Expedition Log

Before you can communicate a long-term vision to others, you need to be clear in your own mind about your goals. This clarity needs to exist on two levels: a personal vision for you as a leader and a vision for the organization.

Defining a Long-Term Vision

1. What is your personal leadership vision? What are the qualities and behaviors that will be required to lead your organization to *The Edge*?

2. What is *The Edge* goal for your organization—the ultimate destination for the expedition you have undertaken? Is there a "new mark" that you should consider?

Focusing Energy on Short-Term Goals

1. What are the key opportunities for action? What concrete things can you do to create a sense of momentum and forward movement?

2. What are the structures and routines that you use to create a sense of stability? What other things might you do?

3. Can you think of any "engaging distractions" that would contribute to the morale of your organization?

4. What are your short-term milestones? How are you measuring success on the journey your expedition has undertaken?

2

Symbolism and Personal Example

Strategy 2:

Set a personal example with visible, memorable symbols and behaviors.

> Speaking with utmost conviction, Shackleton pointed out that no article was of any value when weighed against their ultimate survival, and he exhorted them to be ruthless in ridding themselves of every unnecessary ounce, regardless of its value. After he had spoken, he reached under his parka and took out a gold cigarette case and several gold sovereigns and threw them into the snow at his feet.[1]
>
> —Alfred Lansing

Chapter 1 stressed the vital importance of keeping energy flowing toward short- and long-term goals. This chapter highlights a set of specific leadership tactics for mobilizing that energy through personal example and with clear, concrete images and symbols.

Particularly under conditions of stress and discouragement, visible leadership can mean the difference between success and failure. Shackleton understood this well. He knew just how important it was for the crew to *see* him as the leader—and to outline the work to be accomplished with unmistakable clarity. We do not all have to be Ernest Shackleton, but leaders need to be aware that their personal presence is a unique source of energy and power. They need to draw on this power to lead their organizations to *The Edge*.

Give the Right Speech

When the situation is dire, the power of the right words is striking. It is impossible to exaggerate the devastation the men felt when *Endurance* was crushed by the ice. As Captain Frank Worsley wrote:

> Actuated by an invisible force countless miles away, the rigging tautened and sang like harp strings, then snapped under the strain as the ship was twisted and wrung by the giant hands of ice that grasped her....To talk was impossible. Each man knew that it was the end of the ship. We had lost our home in that universe of ice. We had been cast out into a white wilderness that might well prove to be our tomb.[2]

The loss of the actual ship, dramatic though it was, was made more poignant by the men's sure knowledge of its consequences. They had only a four-week supply of food; their linen tents were so flimsy that they provided minimal protection; the lack of tent floors meant that the crew were sleeping in pools of water as the heat from their bodies melted the ice. Even though *Endurance* would not sink immediately, everyone knew that, as Frank Worsley wrote, "Many of our stores were irretrievable.... A shortage of food was not a pleasant prospect."[3]

The explorers were standing on an ice floe, in the middle of the Weddell Sea, listening to the beams of their ship snapping in two, knowing they could never get to their stores, and wondering what would happen next. Despite Worsley's quaint Victorian understatement, their anxiety must have been palpable. At this point, Shackleton made a speech. Frank Wild remembered:

Shackleton made a characteristic speech to hearten our party, the sort of speech that only he could make. Simply and in brief sentences he told the men not to be alarmed at the loss of the vessel, and assured them that by hard effort, clean work, and loyal cooperation, they could make their way to land. This speech had an immediate effect: our spirits rose, and we were inclined to take a more cheerful view of a situation that had nothing in it to warrant the alteration.[4]

The crew knew that nothing had physically changed. But Shackleton used precisely the right words and tone. He chose words that gave members of the expedition a sense of control over their fate. Shackleton later recalled:

After the tents had been pitched I mustered all hands . . . and stated that I propose to try to march with equipment in the direction of Paulet. . . . I thanked the men for the steadiness and good morale they have shown in these trying circumstances, and told them I had no doubt that, provided they continue to work their utmost and to trust me, we will all reach safety in the end.[5]

It is axiomatic that people who do not believe they can influence their destiny become anxious and fearful. Shackleton's words gave them the belief that they could influence their own survival and that of the expedition.

In addition, Shackleton chose the right tone—calm, confident, and reassuring. It might have been tempting to dramatize the situation, but Shackleton chose a calm demeanor, probably using his characteristically solid stance with his hands on his hips. His speech was not a pep talk or a locker-room rallying exhortation. That would have been incongruent, given the gravity of the situation. Shackleton's speech provided a balanced, realistic look at the situation and assured the men of his confidence that they would survive through their own efforts.

Lessons for Leaders

I have worked with a number of senior executives who are uncomfortable in large group settings. As a result, they exercise leadership in their most natural style, emphasizing one-on-one or small-group interactions.

Establishing strong individual relationships is an important part of leadership. But there are times when the role demands something different, when the energy of the entire group or organization needs to be mobilized. On these occasions, the leader needs to face his or her team and communicate a message to the team as a whole—to make a speech.

I have seen speeches take the form of "get one for the Gipper" motivational addresses. I have also seen speakers deliver extended, dry remarks filled with complex financial projections, or sermons filled with dire predictions about the future—and admonitions to work hard or else.

There are occasions for financial projections and times when a standard set of motivational remarks will suffice. There are other times at *The Edge*, however, when something more is needed. These are the times that call for *the right speech*.

The right speech needs to be more than a recital of remarks written by a staff member given the job of coming up with something clever. The right speech needs to be authentic, and it needs to be delivered with sincerity. But it need not be filled with histrionics. It is more important for the message to be delivered from the heart than with flowery language, and there are times when a cheerleading speech is counterproductive.

When the situation is grim—when people are fearful and obstacles loom large—an excessively cheerful and overly emotional message is the wrong speech. What is called for is calm reassurance, straight talk, and unmistakable resolve.

Mary Jane Fortin was appointed as CEO of American General Life Insurance in August of 2009. Fortin assumed the role of chief executive the same month that Robert Benmosche came out of retirement, leaving his Croatian vineyard to lead the beleaguered parent company, American International Group.

It is difficult to overstate the grimly chaotic circumstances surrounding American General and AIG at that time. The world was still recoiling from the fall of Lehman Brothers and the subsequent collapse of the credit markets. AIG had posted a $100 billion loss the year before, and its stock prices had plummeted. Newspapers were filled with headlines predicting the worst, including a *Wall Street Journal* article by Arthur Laffer declaring that "The Age of Prosperity Is Over."[6]

The fall of the insurance giant AIG was, in many ways, similar to the sinking of the *Endurance:* A vessel that all had thought was secure had, astonishingly, imploded. It was the biggest banking crisis in seventy years. Jim Millstein, the Treasury Department's chief restructuring officer, recalled that AIG "was totally toxic, and nobody really wanted to be identified with it. . . . It looked like it was going to collapse."[7]

Many taxpayers were infuriated by the $182.3 billion government bailout and eager to point fingers at anyone connected with AIG. Their anger was sometimes directed at employees of American General, who had nothing to do with the people at AIG Financial Products unit who had taken big bets on complicated credit products. Everyone—including clerical workers—had to face the possibility of being accosted in public, or even physically threatened.

It was in this atmosphere that Mary Jane Fortin agreed to take the helm of American General. Although she was described as a "rising star" by insurance industry publications, Fortin had no prior experience as a chief executive. She had developed a strong reputation as a CFO, but this role was different. The organization was enveloped in fear, and the future was uncertain.

Fortin called American General's corporate officers together at a meeting to discuss their situation. Most were physically present in Houston; others watched the videocast in locations throughout the country.

With her petite stature and sense of style, Fortin did not fit anyone's preconception of an insurance industry executive. Nevertheless, she projected a compelling ebullience that filled the room.

Fortin began by talking about the rich history of American General and how it had repeatedly demonstrated resilience. Fortin expressed confidence that the company had worked through change many times before and every time had become stronger and better. She then recounted a personal story:

I, like you, have been wrapped up in many of the AIG events. I read the horrible media stories that we were working for the most hated company in America. It has been a tough time, but I received a call from my parents telling me that my 47-year-old cousin had died unexpectedly. He left behind two 9-year-old children, and a stay-at-home mom.

What struck me, as I reflected on the call when I took the plane ride home to Connecticut, were two things. One was that what I thought was a crisis was, quite frankly, not that much of a crisis compared to what had struck my cousin's family. And, second, I said to myself, "I hope he took care of the kids, I hope he had life insurance."

It hit me, at that moment, that I had forgotten the importance of what we do on a day-to-day basis. We help people protect their families. We help them save for retirement. We help them out during one of the most profound and difficult moments in their lives. We do good work, we do necessary work, and we should be proud of what we do. We can never forget that.[8]

It was clear that Fortin had spoken from the heart. But the fact that their work was important work didn't change reality. They had been downgraded by the rating agencies, the AIG brand was toxic, and the parent company was not flush with excess capital. They were no longer the 800-pound gorilla.

Fortin went on to recognize these realities but argued that—despite the obstacles—the American General team could still be successful and rebuild the organization. She then asked the group to indulge her while she shared another story:

In June of this year, I traveled to Italy with my husband and my 12-year-old daughter. For those of you who don't know, my parents were born in Italy and immigrated to the United States a couple of years before I was born.

I was fascinated to learn that Venice, which is built on a series of islands, was developed by refugees fleeing a barbarian invasion. They sought refuge on these deserted islands, leaving behind their homes and their belongings.

Instead of giving up, these refugees—through incredible vision, innovation, creativity, hard work, and sheer courage—built Venice into a major thriving city. This city, over time, became a huge strategic European region. Even today, thousands of years later, it is a true marvel for all of us.

As the local expert was explaining all this, I couldn't help but think about what we were going through here. And I realized that the refugees had made a choice in the face of adversity: They chose to rebuild, and they chose to win. They chose to make themselves better, and to create a lasting legacy. And then I thought about us, and that we have choices to make as well.

I have chosen to look forward, to rebuild, and to win. And I need you to make that same choice. There is no question that we have suffered a setback, but at the core we have not changed. We are a resilient organization that prides itself on innovation. This is not gone, and no one has taken this away from us. We need to get the message out: American General is open for business.

I want to thank you for your talent and your energy and your perseverance during what I know has been an incredibly difficult time. I'm looking forward to making this organization as extraordinary as it can be, and I'm looking forward to having your help in doing that. So let's go![9]

Like Shackleton, Fortin acknowledged the severity of their circumstances; she used powerful metaphors to capture the importance of their work and the task that lay ahead; and she painted a vivid image of success. Finally, like Shackleton, she expressed appreciation for the hard work that had been done to survive the crisis that had engulfed them.

Fortin's remarks were met with thunderous applause. And with that, Fortin and her team began their own "sledge march" to open water.

Use Vivid Symbols

Although Shackleton deliberately took a low-key tone in describing the expedition's situation, he was far more dramatic when he outlined the work to be done to reach the expedition's goals. Not an alarmist about things he could do nothing about, he was a genius at drawing on drama, even theatricality, when he needed to mobilize the expedition to overcome extraordinary obstacles.

Shackleton had demonstrated his ability to use symbolic behavior earlier—in Buenos Aires—when First Officer Lionel Greenstreet fouled the propeller while attempting to maneuver *Endurance*. Greenstreet expected to be called on the carpet, perhaps even disciplined. Instead, Shackleton helped him repair the damage and never again spoke about the incident. The message he had visibly demonstrated was clear: We will all make mistakes; fix them and move on. This public act became a symbolic gesture for the whole expedition.

When *Endurance* was crushed by the ice, Shackleton again acted symbolically. He was convinced that a successful sledge march to the ocean could be accomplished only if every nonessential item was discarded. He had to communicate to the crew that anything that would not contribute to the success of the expedition—no matter what the emotional attachment or how intrinsically valuable elsewhere—had to be left behind.

Shackleton realized that some personal items, though they did not necessarily contribute to physical survival, were essential for psychological well-being. He struggled to find a balance between weight and speed:

> I rather grudged the two pounds allowance per man, owing to my keen anxiety to keep weight at a minimum, but some personal belongings could fairly be regarded as indispensable. The journey might be a long one, and there was a possibility of a winter in improvised quarters on an inhospitable coast at the other end. A man under such conditions needs something to

occupy his thoughts, some tangible memento of his home and people beyond the seas.[10]

So mementos of home were indispensable, while other items that might have had great value in a different situation were expendable. After issuing the order that each man could carry only two pounds of personal gear, Shackleton set the example for traveling light with a dramatic gesture. He reached inside his parka, took out a handful of gold sovereigns, and threw them to the ground at his feet. Again, he reached into his parka and found a gold cigarette case. This too he threw to the ground.

The message, as Worsley recalled, was clear:

> Shackleton now determined to cut down every ounce of superfluous weight, in the hope that we could sledge to Graham Land, the most northerly part of the Antarctic Continent. He himself set the example, throwing away, what a spectacular gesture, a gold watch, a gold cigarette case, and several golden sovereigns. Naturally, after witnessing this action, which brought home to me at any rate the shifting values in life and the knowledge that there are times when gold can be a liability instead of an asset, we all discarded everything save the barest necessaries.[11]

In this dramatic gesture, Shackleton personally demonstrated that only items that had value in terms of survival were important. He provided a focus for the expedition that was unmistakable and unambiguous: We must jettison anything that will not directly enable us to accomplish our goal.

Lessons for Leaders

It is one thing to tell people that a task needs to be done, and it is another to dramatize the challenge with visible, memorable symbols and behaviors. These symbols can be as dramatic as throwing gold sovereigns into the snow, or they can be more prosaic. Whatever the symbol, it needs to be vivid and memorable.

One airline—ranked last in customer service among the ten largest airlines—was stifled with a bureaucratic set of rules that specified everything from the color of pencils to be used on boarding passes to the kind of fold used in a sick-day form. The problem was that these rules had tied the hands of airline employees to the point that they had no real discretion to solve problems—and they were punished for disobeying the rules.

If a plane was canceled, for example, a full-fare passenger might get a hotel room, whereas a next-in-line bargain-fare passenger could get a meal voucher. Naturally, this sort of rigid decision making did little for the company's public image. It also subjected gate agents to the wrath of irate customers, practically making gate agents eligible for hazardous-duty pay.

The policy manual—the "Thou Shalt Not Book"—was an icon for this rigid system. To symbolize the need for change, the CEO took a group of employees into the parking lot. They threw the manual into a fifty-five-gallon drum, poured gasoline onto it, and set it afire. By burning the manual, they sent a message to the organization: Do not blindly follow the book—use your ingenuity and do what is right for the company and for the customer.[12]

Be Visible: Let People See You Leading

Shackleton understood the importance of demonstrating through action as well as words that he was a leader doing his duty. He was a visible presence throughout the experience, yet one of the most striking examples took place during the open boat voyage from Patience Camp to Elephant Island.

This grueling journey was one of their most physically exhausting, demoralizing experiences. The men were soaked by constant rain, and the cold was so severe that sleep was often impossible. The tiny boats were surrounded by the hisses of killer whales, and the men dealt with the fear that they could capsize when the creatures came up to blow.

The winds and currents were so strong that—after hours under sail—they were sometimes dismayed to discover that not only had they made no forward progress, they were actually farther from their destination than when they had begun. Exacerbating the situation, they lacked fresh water and could relieve their thirst only by chewing raw seal meat and swallowing the blood. Finally, to cap it off, many of the men suffered from seasickness as the small boats wallowed in the heavy swells.

Shackleton described the scene:

> The temperature was down to four degrees below zero, and a film of ice formed on the surface of the sea. When we were not on watch we lay in each other's arms for warmth. Our frozen suits thawed where our bodies met, and as the slightest movement exposed these comparatively warm spots to the biting air, we clung motionless, whispering each to his companion our hopes and thoughts. Occasionally from an almost clear sky came snow-showers, falling silently on the sea and laying a thin shroud of white over our bodies and our boats.[13]

Conditions were so severe that there were times when Shackleton doubted that all hands would survive the night. If ever there was a time for visible, inspiring leadership, this was it. Understanding the importance of his role, Shackleton made a point of standing erect in the stern of the lifeboat *James Caird*, "conning the course," showing that he was keeping vigil and inspiring the men.

When Hurley, the photographer, lost his mittens, Orde-Lees observed Shackleton's response:

> At once [he] divested himself of his own, and in spite of the fact that he was standing up in the most exposed position all the while he insisted upon Hurley's acceptance of the mits, and on the latter's protesting Sir Ernest was on the point of throwing them overboard rather than wear them when one of his subordinates had to go without; as a consequence Sir Ernest had one finger rather severely frostbitten.[14]

Shackleton's presence as a leader and his example of self-sacrifice were critical to the crew's success in reaching the safety of Elephant Island.

A more recent example, one from the Vietnam War, confirms the power of visible leadership. Phil Caputo was a Marine lieutenant in Vietnam. In his personal memoir, *A Rumor of War*, Caputo describes the way his platoon sergeant, "Wild Bill" Campbell, dealt with the panic of an ambush. Caputo and his platoon had come under heavy automatic-weapons fire. Bullets were smacking into trees, shredding leaves, and snapping twigs. The Marines panicked, emptying their magazines and wasting ammunition by firing at targets they could not see. Caputo recalled:

> I wasn't frightened, just confused. Or maybe I was confused because I was frightened. Then I heard Campbell's voice booming above and behind us. "Cease fire, you silly shits! Cease fire!" Several enemy bullets walked up the trail behind him, splattering dust, the last round striking less than an inch from his heel. He kept walking as casually as a coach at the rifle range. "Cease fire, Second [Platoon]. Can't see what the hell you're shooting at. Let's have a little goddamned fire discipline."[15]

Encouraged by the sergeant's calmness while under intense enemy fire, the Marines came to their senses and stopped wasting ammunition. The gunfire halted, and Lieutenant Caputo climbed out of the trench in which he had taken cover. When Caputo complimented the sergeant on his presence of mind, Campbell brushed off his heroism, attributing it to a back injury he'd sustained jumping off the chopper. Most likely, the veteran Marine knew that his platoon was spooked and out of control and needed reassurance. His personal example turned the platoon around in a tough situation.

Lessons for Leaders

Leaders can be quietly competent, but they must be visible. The open boat journey to Elephant Island was physically demanding and one of the most extreme stress points that the expedition had encountered. It was stressful for everyone, but especially for Shackleton, who bore the principal burden of leadership.

In spite of the personal hardship, Shackleton recognized the importance of being in the forefront and was willing to face the freezing ocean spray. "Wild Bill" Campbell also understood the importance of visible leadership and stood conspicuously under fire to stabilize his platoon.

This type of action is all too easy to talk about in the abstract, when one is warm and dry, or in a case study discussion of leadership. It is quite different to be a visible leader when you are exhausted and facing danger—whether the threat comes from weather, sniper fire, or angry customers, analysts, or shareholders.

These difficult situations, however, are those during which it is most important to let people see you "standing in the stern sheets." If you are conscious of this necessity, you can create opportunities for visibility that allow you to use the power of your role as a leader to provide assurance, direction, and inspiration.

The power of visible leadership is not, however, restricted to turnarounds and crises. Ray Kroc, the founder of McDonald's, had a penchant for stopping unannounced at the McDonald's restaurants near the company's headquarters in Oakbrook, Illinois. He relayed this story of what happened on one such occasion:

> One sunny July afternoon, I pulled into a McDonald's parking space and noticed that the flowering bushes were littered with shake cups, Happy Meal boxes, napkins, and other trash. Inside, I asked for the manager. Only the assistant manager was there, so I had him call the manager and waited for the anxious man to rush in after a speedy drive from his nearby home. "What can I do for you, sir?" the manager asked me. I led him to the parking lot, pointed at the shrubbery, and said, "Look! We don't want trash around our sites!" In a matter of minutes, I, my driver, and the manager had picked up all the garbage out of the bushes.[16]

By working side by side with this manager, Kroc conveyed that it is more important to fix a problem than to establish blame, and he also set an example that no one is above doing the work that needs to be done. This story has become part of the corporate lore at McDonald's and has helped to establish a culture where attention to detail and collaboration are valued.

The point of these stories is clear: You, as a leader, have a unique role and a special power. Chart your course and—with presence, symbolism, and personal example—use that power to lead your organization to *The Edge*.

Expedition Log

1. As you look at and think about the things your team needs to do to reach *The Edge*, what are the most critical priorities?

2. How can those priorities be dramatized with vivid, memorable symbols or images? Is there a story or metaphor that portrays the work to be done? What is your equivalent of throwing gold sovereigns into the snow?

3. Have you given the right speech to mobilize the power of the team? Do you need to address your team members again, to reenergize the organization?

4. What is your visibility plan? That is, what are you doing to ensure that you are visible as a leader? How much time do you spend out of the office or in situations that allow you to project your presence?

3

Optimism and Reality

Strategy 3:
Instill optimism and self-confidence, but stay grounded in reality.

> Shackleton had a wonderful and rare understanding of the men's at-
> titudes towards one another and towards the expedition as a whole.
> He appreciated how deeply one man, or a small group of men, could
> affect the psychology of the others. Therefore he almost insisted
> upon cheeriness and optimism; in fact his attitude was, "You've damn
> well got to be optimistic."[1]
>
> —Frank A. Worsley

Keen intellect, business competence, and strong interpersonal skills are essential leadership qualities. But if there is one quality that makes the difference at *The Edge,* it is the ability to remain optimistic in the face of daunting adversity. It is the capacity to look at odds that are impossible, to believe that it is still possible to win, and to convince others that you are right.

Some critics might say that Shackleton's entire plight came about because he was too optimistic and never should have embarked in the first place. After all, the Norwegian whaling skippers had warned him that ice conditions were treacherous, and yet he elected to continue when a more prudent course might have been to turn back.

This is an issue I will pick up in this chapter and later in the book. Nevertheless, the fact remains that the expedition was able to prevail against enormous obstacles largely because of Shackleton's dogged optimism—and his superb skill in spreading this positive outlook to others.

Cultivate Optimism in Yourself

Before you can instill optimism in others, you first need to find it in yourself. Shackleton's family motto—*Fortitudine Vincimus* (By endurance we conquer)—sums up the explorer's personality. His indomitable spirit, however, was more than a family legacy. It was a quality that he worked to develop.

Shackleton spent time nourishing his own spirit of optimism. It seemed to pervade everything he did, especially his reading. For example, he was fond of quoting Robert Browning's "Prospice":

> I was ever a fighter, so—one fight more,
> > The best and the last! . . .
> For sudden the worst turns the best to the brave
> > The Black minute's at end . . .[2]

Shackleton framed the world in an invariably optimistic way. On his first expedition to the South Pole, when the march was stopped by a blizzard, he spent time reading Darwin's *Origin of Species*. He embraced Darwin's belief that natural selection leads to perfection and felt buoyed in spite of his ill health.[3]

The spirit of the times was unflaggingly optimistic, of course, but Shackleton took it to a new dimension. He was more than just a salesman, although his salesmanship was revealed by his dogged refusal to take no for an answer when he was gathering financing for his expedition. Shackleton believed he would succeed, and his belief spread to others.

Lessons for Leaders

A reasonable question to ask is whether optimism like Shackleton's is something you either have or not. He was, after all, a charismatic leader with special qualities. Shackleton and other great leaders often seem to have been born with a special belief in their own ability. General George Patton, for example, grew up with a belief in the inevitability of his place in history.

Some may have a difficult time identifying with Shackleton's boundless optimism and his enthusiastic belief that things would somehow work out in the end. Few of us grew up in families whose mottoes were as inspiring as "By endurance we conquer." I have one client, for example, who—after reading accounts of the *Endurance* expedition—volunteered that his family motto was "We meant well." Not quite so inspiring. Another leader quipped, "It's easy for me to be an optimistic leader anytime except when I'm depressed."

For many leaders, questions remain. Is this capacity for optimism an innate characteristic? Can optimism really be acquired or cultivated? How can I develop a more optimistic personality if I do not already have that predisposition?

Optimism is not a natural act for everyone, but there is reason to believe that it is an ability that can be learned and greatly improved. The key lies in the inner dialogue that goes on, often unnoticed, almost all the time for all of us.

I will sometimes ask a group the question, "How many of you talk to yourselves?" Usually, about half of the group members raise their hands. The other half say (to themselves), "I don't talk to myself."

The reality is that this self-talk is part of human nature, and the first step in cultivating optimism is to pay close attention to what you say to yourself. If you are aware of this inner dialogue, especially during times of adversity or setback, you will be conscious of the messages you are sending yourself about failure or success. The right messages are energizing; the wrong ones are deflating.

The way to develop a feeling of optimism is to consistently send positive messages that override voices of discouragement and pessimism. Some of the mechanics of sending these positive messages may sound hokey or contrived. I agree: They may seem contrived—but they often work.

One of my clients had the task of leading a team with an extremely difficult assignment. The task was to complete a thorough report in a business field in which no one on the team had prior direct experience. Progress was glacially slow. Operating under a tight deadline, everyone was discouraged, even the leader. The goal seemed unreachable.

Then one day the team leader was looking at a magazine ad that stated, "You can do it!" emblazoned in color across the page. He cut out the words and taped them to the mirror in his bathroom. Every morning, the first thing he saw was his face with the caption, "You can do it!" This optimistic image literally changed the way he began the day. Contrived, yes—but effective, because the team completed a well-received report by the deadline.

There are more complex ways of thinking about how to change these self-messages. Psychologist Martin Seligman pioneered one systematic approach called *learned optimism*.[4] Seligman studied the effects of optimistic self-talk, or *explanatory style*, in real-world conditions ranging from selling insurance to surviving plebe (freshman) year at West Point. His conclusions are that optimists do better than pessimists and that their success rate is greater than objective data (such as SAT scores) would predict.

Seligman argues that his ABCDE model is more effective than simply sending positive messages. His process, which I have simplified, involves five concepts and related actions:

1. *Adversity.* Identify the adversity you have encountered (e.g., a computer crash in the middle of an important project).

2. *Beliefs.* Note your thoughts and beliefs about the event—that is, your interpretation (e.g., "I'll never get the report done").

3. *Consequences.* Recognize the consequences of your belief (e.g., you feel discouraged).

4. *Dispute.* Dispute the negative belief with a sound argument based on evidence (e.g., "I have overcome other technology disasters through persistence").

5. *Energy.* Generate the energy and feelings needed to overcome the adversity (e.g., "I feel more relaxed and confident that I can deal with the problem and finish the report").

The learned optimism approach can be a valuable tool, but the process requires rehearsal. Practice using the method to deal with minor setbacks so that it will become second nature under conditions of more serious adversity. And, whatever approach you use, be aware of your inner dialogue. As Henry Ford once said, "Whether you think you can, or whether you think you can't, you're right."

Spread the Spirit of Optimism

Shackleton did more than cultivate optimism in himself. He was able to communicate his positive outlook in a way that had a profound influence on every member of the expedition, even the cynics. He exercised this remarkable power in a number of ways.

Shackleton's fundamentally ebullient personality was a contagious force that infected others. In large measure, he believed so completely in success that it was difficult not to subscribe to his cheerful outlook. Shackleton also established the attitude that "you've damn well got to be optimistic" as a core operating principle of the expedition. It was a discipline to be learned and cultivated.

There were also times in which Shackleton's ability to inspire confidence lay in his ability to put on a good face—the traditional British stiff upper lip and steely self-control. This was illustrated by his behavior at a ship's "party" that was held before the other members of the expedition realized the extent of their predicament.[5]

These festive events, held in the below-deck area known as the Ritz, were in keeping with a tradition of polar exploration. They consisted of skits, songs, and whatever makeshift costumes the crew could devise. While the crew was preparing for the fun of the masquerade party, Shackleton met with Frank Wild and Captain Worsley to deliver his grim assessment of their situation. He had become convinced that the ship was doomed, and he gave Worsley the news with no equivocation:

> The ship can't live in this, Skipper. . . . You had better make
> up your mind that it is only a matter of time. It may be a
> few months, and it may be a question of weeks, or even
> days. . . . But what the ice gets, the ice keeps.[6]

Immediately after this dire prophecy, First Officer Greenstreet
knocked on the cabin door and announced that the crew was ready to
begin the party. Minutes later, Shackleton was laughing with "the boys"
in the Ritz. No one ever would have guessed the thoughts that must have
lain heavy on his mind.

There were times, of course, during which even Shackleton's dogged
optimism flagged under the enormous stresses of responsibility. This was
especially true during the time before their escape from Patience Camp
to the relative safety of Elephant Island. It was a difficult time for the
leader, with his expedition sitting on a dwindling cake of ice, buffeted by
wind and weather and threatened by collision and heavy swells. Shackleton recalled his feelings at the time:

> I confess that I felt the burden of responsibility sit heavily on my
> shoulders; but, on the other hand, I was stimulated and cheered
> by the attitude of the men.[7]

Shackleton took heart from the optimistic spirit of the team and, in
return, Shackleton's presence and demeanor engendered optimism among
his crew. But the Boss did not simply exhort people to be hopeful. He was
masterful in the subtle ways in which he created a pervasive spirit of future possibility and positive energy.

He kept the group engaged, for example, with a lively discussion
about—remarkably—the prospect of an expedition to Alaska![8] For a
group stranded in the middle of a frozen Antarctic sea, the idea of another polar undertaking could have seemed preposterous. But the prospect
provided an engaging alternative to dwelling on their predicament or
thinking about the potential dangers that lay ahead. Captain Worsley recounted:

> We look up all the maps & books on the subject that we can
> lay our hands on, & are enthusiastic about our next trip before
> we can definitely settle how the devil we are going to get out
> of this one.[9]

Planning an expedition to Alaska was clearly a method for entertaining the expedition during the long empty hours. In this sense, it was an "engaging distraction." But it was more than that. It provided a future focus and a promise that there would be other adventures—with the obvious implication that they would triumph over their present situation. It represents just one way in which the whole culture of the expedition encouraged confidence and hope.

Lessons for Leaders

Leaders who are successful at *The Edge* are able to instill in others the belief that the organization will achieve its goals. But just how does a leader radiate optimism? How does a leader spread "the spirit" when survival is not at stake?

Leaders must convince their teams that success is both necessary and possible. They must challenge people's beliefs without personal criticism, and—when change is called for—demonstrate that it is feasible to change course. Finally, they must find a way to create a sense of personal connection throughout the organization. These are the critical ingredients of inspiration.

Shackleton often used a personal approach with members of his crew, and was tenacious in winning them over. This persistent approach worked for Shackleton, but there is another question that surfaces for me as I think about optimism at *The Edge*: Just how candid should leaders be in sharing their uncensored doubts and inner feelings when faced with adversity?

There are those who believe that personal authenticity demands complete openness, and that leaders should reveal the depths of their emotional inner life. They argue that anything other than this level of disclosure is patronizing—and that openness creates space for others to be similarly revealing.

My perspective is different. I believe there are times in which leaders need to maintain their composure, despite the natural inclination to express feelings of discouragement, fear, or even despair. This is not to say that they should shield others from reality or withhold basic information about the situation. Rather, it is to say that there are times at *The Edge* in which the perceived attitude of the leader is a powerful force that can create energy and optimism or fear and pessimism: It becomes a self-fulfilling prophecy.

When fears and doubts are expressed openly, it may be difficult or impossible to rekindle the optimism that is so important for success. Therefore, I believe the role of the leader demands that personal fears are best controlled or dampened until negative information is digested. Then a discussion of concerns can be coupled with potential solutions and a positive message of hope for the future.

Build the Right Team "Optimism Quotient"

After hearing the story of the Trans-Antarctic expedition, some people conclude that the success of the expedition can be traced to the initial selection process and Shackleton's ability to assemble such a capable team. In fact, Shackleton's interviews were often cursory and haphazard. But he did succeed in filling several critical roles with extremely competent individuals and in making the best use of those finally selected.

His knack for putting the right team members in the right job showed itself in technical tasks, but Shackleton was also sensitive to having the right mix of temperaments and outlooks. In particular, he seemed to have a sense of the threshold level of what might be called the "OQ"—the optimism quotient, or ratio of optimistic to more pessimistic team members—needed to take on arduous tasks.

Probably the most important team choice Shackleton made was his second in command, Frank Wild. Shackleton had endured extreme hardship with Wild on their previous expedition to the South Pole and, consequently, had a complete grasp of the man's character. Wild was not only steadfast and loyal. He also shared Shackleton's fundamental belief that obstacles existed to be overcome.

Wild's optimism was important on numerous occasions. After Shackleton's jarring pre-party announcement about the fate of *Endurance*, for instance, Wild saw that Captain Worsley was shaken. Wild immediately rose to reassure the captain with softly spoken but confident words: " . . . We are not going to let the ice get us. Poor little *Endurance* may go, but we won't."[10]

It was the perfect remark, and Worsley was comforted. Worsley later remembered:

> . . . [Wild] had said just [the] right thing. To an old seaman like myself, the very idea of giving up a ship is something like having an arm or leg amputated; but Wild's words made me realize that in spite of the importance which the ship might have in my eyes, there were human lives at stake . . . and that our job was to see that the ice didn't get them—even if it got my ship.[11]

This was not an isolated event. Wild's ability to maintain an optimistic spirit was an anchor that remained solid throughout the ordeal. And it was a quality tested dramatically after Shackleton sailed with the *James Caird* for South Georgia. Shackleton left Wild in full command of the twenty-two men left behind on Elephant Island. Managing the emotions of the "castaways" was an enormous leadership challenge. In fact, it may have been even more difficult than that faced by the Boss in his run to South Georgia.

Shackleton's fate was unknown for 128 days, and Wild had the daily challenge of maintaining hope in the face of the obvious possibility that disaster might have overtaken the rescue party. There were also other potential sources of despair. Orde-Lees, ever the pessimist, predicted that their supply of penguins would disappear, and conditions continued to become more and more desperate. They all suffered, especially Blackborow, the stowaway, whose foot had to be amputated from the ball joint forward.[12] Given all this (along with the extreme dismay when the tobacco supply ran out), an atmosphere of doom easily could have prevailed.

Shackleton's confidence in Wild's ability to hold the party together was well founded. Wild not only maintained the routines that had served the group so well in the past but also kept the men infused with the positive attitude that they had exhibited under Shackleton.

In the absence of the Boss, it became clear that Shackleton's optimism had become embedded in the ethos of the team, and it was nourished constantly by Frank Wild. He refused to entertain even the slightest possibility that they would not be rescued. As an unwavering symbol of his conviction, Wild roused the men every day with a cheery shout of, "Lash up and stow, boys, the Boss may come today."[13] Even the morose Orde-Lees was forced to admit that Wild's ability to maintain the spirits of those likely to be despondent was "a fine thing."

Shackleton's choice of Wild was central to the crew's successful return, but there were other instances in which optimism seemed to be an explicit selection factor. When choosing a crew for what was to be the most arduous and dangerous part of the journey thus far—the voyage to South Georgia—Shackleton looked for men with a number of qualities. He seemed to have an innate understanding of the importance of having someone he could rely on to keep up the spirits of the team.

Shackleton filled one of the five scarce billets on the *James Caird* with Timothy McCarthy, an "able seaman" whose good-natured personality had endeared him to everyone on the expedition. True, McCarthy could contribute physical strength, but his most important contribution was probably his ability to maintain a positive outlook under the worst sea and weather any of them had ever experienced.

"Macty" maintained his cheery outlook throughout the sixteen-day journey. Worsley recalled one vivid example:

> Macty [McCarthy] is the most irrepressible optimist I've ever met. When I relieve him at the helm, boat iced and seas pouring down your neck, he informs me with a happy grin, "It's a grand day, sir, I was feeling a bit sour just before. . . ."[14]

McCarthy's indomitable good spirits undoubtedly buoyed the morale of the soaked sailors. He was a good choice for such an arduous voyage.

Lessons for Leaders

When selecting people for key roles, it is natural to think about the knowledge, skills, and abilities needed for top performance. Other personal qualities, such as the ability to work with others, and values, such as integrity, are often considered carefully. But it is less obvious that an individual's characteristic tendency toward optimism or pessimism might be an important—in some cases, the most important—factor in a particular role.

This is not to suggest that everyone take a personality test as part of the selection process. But it does argue for looking carefully at the way individuals respond to adversity and for explicitly including those with optimistic attitudes in difficult team assignments.

From my perspective as a frequent flyer, one of the most difficult assignments I can imagine is contending with exhausted, weary travelers. At Southwest Airlines, building the right optimism quotient starts with the hiring process.[15] As Herb Kelleher, the former CEO of Southwest Airlines, once said, "We want people with positive attitudes, who enjoy helping others."

To foster optimism, training exercises are structured so that everyone must contribute in order to complete the exercise. In discussions following the exercise, the trainer points out how each person contributed and notes differences in personality and temperament. By hiring employees who have positive attitudes and building on that through training and acknowledgment, Southwest has been successful in fostering both diversity and optimism in its workforce.

Exactly what should the team OQ be? The answer is not a team composed solely of individuals who view the world through rose-colored glasses. As I will discuss later, there is value in diversity in this dimension. However, the team OQ should be high enough to sustain the belief in success, even when the task seems insurmountable. Every team needs a McCarthy!

Know How to Reframe a Tough Situation

Optimism can be sparked by leaders who reframe disastrous events in positive, empowering ways. An example comes from the survival story recounted in the book *Alive.*

On October 13, 1972, a group of Uruguayan rugby players and their families crash-landed high in the Andes Mountains. In their struggle to survive, there were many setbacks and challenges. One of their consolations was the daily radio broadcast on the progress of the rescue effort. After eight days, however, the search was called off. Three of the group, upon hearing this news, discussed whether to tell the rest of the group. Finally, Gustavo Nicolich, one of the emergent leaders of the group, insisted that they must tell the rest of their predicament:

> He climbed through the hole in the wall of suitcases and rugby shirts, crouched at the mouth of the dim tunnel, and looked at the mournful faces which were turned toward him. "Hey boys," he shouted, "there is some good news! We just heard it on the radio. They've called off the search." Inside the crowded cabin, there was silence. As the hopelessness of their predicament enveloped them, they wept. "Why the hell is that good news?" Paez shouted angrily at Nicolich. "Because it means," he said, "that we're going to get out of here on our own."[16]

The optimism and confidence exhibited by Gustavo Nicolich helped the group get through one of the most depressing and potentially debilitating events since the crash. By reframing the situation in an empowering way, he was able to rally the group. Then, they, as a whole, began to take responsibility for their own rescue.

Lessons for Leaders

I had read that the Chinese character for crisis, Weigee, incorporates two figures: The upper character represents "danger," the lower one "opportunity" (see Figure 3-1). I first doubted this was true, so I asked a Chinese student at Yale what the real story was. He hesitated, drew the figure, and looked at me with a smile. It was true, he confirmed, although he hadn't really seen it until I asked him the question.[17]

Effective leaders are able to look at adversity and see the opportunity, even if others see only the danger. This perspective may be resisted. A standing joke in one organization I worked with is that people were

Figure 3-1. Chinese character for crisis.

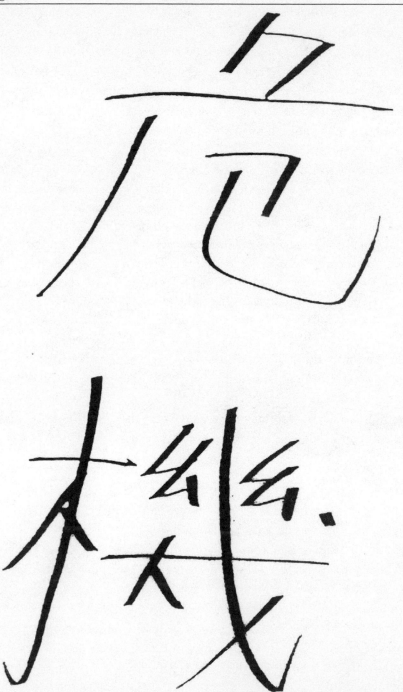

tired of "major opportunities" and would be satisfied just to have a few "minor problems." Nevertheless, a leader who is able to reframe events in a positive light, and stick by that point of view, can turn the tide.

Lieutenant General Lewis B. "Chesty" Puller was a master of reframing tough situations. Often adding a healthy dash of humor to encourage his troops, Puller served in the U.S. Marine Corps for forty years and is the most decorated U.S. Marine in history. He led Marines in some of the most important engagements of the twentieth century, including the legendary battle at Henderson Field Guadalcanal in World War II, and the Chosin Reservoir Campaign during the Korean War.

In the fall of 1950, General Douglas MacArthur pressed for a decisive end to the Korean War. Vowing to crush the North Koreans, MacArthur sent the forces of the United Nations, including Puller's First Marine Regiment, across the Thirty-Eighth Parallel toward the Yalu River. MacArthur was convinced that the Chinese would not intervene and that victory was at hand.[18]

As MacArthur was optimistically predicting a swift end to the war, the PLA Ninth Army Group, consisting of some hundred thousand men in ten divisions, crossed the Yalu. Marching at night to avoid detection, they were intent on stopping the advance of the Marines.[19] The Chinese were following Mao Tse-tung's playbook, luring their enemy to penetrate deeply because it was their most effective move when faced with a strong opponent.[20] The tactic worked: Puller's regiment, and the entire First Marine Division, were trapped in the bitter cold of the North Korean mountains.

The Chinese army had resolved to destroy the American Marines. A pamphlet distributed to the Chinese troops declared, "Soon we will meet with the American Marines in battle. We will destroy them. When they are defeated, the enemy will collapse and our country will be free from the threat of aggression. Kill these Marines as you would snakes in your homes!"[21]

The Chinese attacked at night, without regard for casualties. With bugles blaring, their human wave attacks were repelled only by hand-to-hand fighting, and it was clear that the Marines were surrounded. Caught in −40°F temperatures, heavy snow, and wind, the division was isolated from air cover and in danger of being overrun. The situation was grim, and the outcome potentially disastrous. Puller, however, was not discouraged. When he realized enemy forces were on all sides of his men and outnumbered his troops eight-to-one, Puller famously said, "We've been looking for the enemy for several days now. We've finally found them. We're surrounded. That simplifies our problem. . . ."[22]

The Chinese attacks continued for days. Each evening, Puller would disappear—going from hole to hole, checking on his Marines to make sure that they had enough food, that they were prepared for the next assault, and that they knew the "Old Man" was looking out for them. He continued to reframe their dire situation. In one radio conversation, when asked how things were going, Puller remarked: "Fine. We have contact with the enemy on all sides."[23]

When Puller finally left his position at Koto-ri, he walked alongside his troops for miles before climbing into a jeep. He wanted to make absolutely sure that his Marines had escaped the trap set by the Chinese. When the breakout was complete, Puller spoke with reporters before boarding a ship in Hungnam Harbor. His framing of the situation was the same as it had always been: "Remember, whatever you write, this was not retreat. All that happened was that we found more Chinese behind us than in front of us so we about-faced and attacked."[24]

It is important to note that the concept of reframing is not simply saying blithely that things will be all right. There are three steps to the process. The first step is to take a difficult situation and envision all the possible outcomes, both positive and negative. The second step is to focus on a positive way of thinking that is consistent with the reality of the situation. This positive view may not, in a statistical sense, be the most likely outcome. But it must be a conceivable scenario. Finally, this positive outlook must be maintained in spite of resistance and cynicism.

Stay Grounded in Reality

Shackleton's insistence that "you've damn well got to be optimistic" was one of his most admirable qualities as a leader. But the relentless optimism that Shackleton exuded also had its costs. There were times when this singular focus seemed to blind him to reality, and it created dissension among the crew.

One such occasion was Shackleton's conflict with his crew over stockpiling food. First Officer Greenstreet was convinced that the expedition needed to be prepared for an extended time on the ice. Shackleton thought that a month's supply was sufficient and was content when a hunting party returned with four seals. When Orde-Lees skied into camp and announced that he had killed three more, Shackleton refused to allow additional slain seals to be brought into camp. Greenstreet wrote:

> ... [T]he present shortage of food is due simply and solely from the Boss refusing to get seals when they were to be had. . . . His sublime optimism . . . being to my mind absolute foolishness.[25]

Shackleton was recklessly optimistic, and he was also angered by Greenstreet's argument, interpreting the first officer's behavior as an act of disloyalty. Had this become a habit—had Shackleton continued to reject people's alternate views of reality—he might have lost the confidence of the expedition.

Lessons for Leaders

A *Fortune* article titled "CEOs in Denial" sounds an ominous note:

> There's something in the nature of CEOs—pride, vanity, a primal need for control, an obsession with success, good old-fashioned idealism—that makes many smart, well-regarded chief executives into idiots when the world turns against them. They rationalize. They justify. They circle their wagons, build their bunkers, mollify their troops. They claim themselves "victims" of their "situations." In these trying times for executives, denial is more popular than ever.[26]

Optimism is an important leadership quality, but denial is deadly. Harvard Business School professor Richard S. Tedlow explores the problem of excessive optimism in his book *Denial: Why Business Leaders Fail to*

Look Facts in the Face—and What to Do About It. He argues that now—
more than ever—CEOs need a realistic outlook: "What is different today
is that the cost of denial has become so high. We are living in a less for-
giving world than we once did."[27] With stakes this high, leaders must balance optimism with reality checks.

One way of thinking about the paradox is that leaders at *The Edge*
need to engage in Janusian thinking.[28] Janus, the Roman god of gates,
was able to look in two directions at the same time. Effective leadership
in demanding situations means being able to see the optimistic view and,
at the same time, deal with stark reality.

This duality is often difficult to achieve. Under stressful conditions, no
one wants to hear bad news. Movie mogul Samuel Goldwyn Jr. once
commented, "I don't want any yes-men around me. I want them to tell
me the truth, even if it costs them their jobs."[29] Leaders often send similar messages.

Refusal to hear contrary points of view can have disastrous consequences. The story of Robert Haas and Levi Strauss & Company controlled by his family provides a compelling example.[30] Following an
organizational restructuring, Haas became accountable only to three people, his uncle and two cousins. Haas invested time and energy in creating
a socially conscious, values-driven organization. The goals were admirable.
The business results were not. Although programs designed to create an
enlightened workplace flourished, product innovation lagged, costs soared,
internal battles raged, customer service dropped, and competitors en-
croached. In three years, Levi Strauss's market value shrank by some $6
billion.

How could this happen to a great American brand such as Levi's? It
appears that Haas simply had the power to ignore reality. A *Fortune* article argues, "Levi Strauss is a failed utopian management experiment. It's
a story of what can happen when well-intentioned but misguided managers run a private company answering to no one."[31] Free from account-
ability, Haas lost touch with the business focus needed to achieve
commercial success.

Fortunately, in recent years Levi Strauss has successfully reinvented
itself and recaptured market share. By facing reality, and using such tac-

tics as courting more sophisticated customers, recruiting executive talent, and aggressively opening new stores, the company recovered from its slump.[32]

The lesson is clear: Resist the temptation to exclude contrary ideas; stay in touch with reality. Find people who will tell you the truth, and reward them for doing so.

Expedition Log

1. How do you typically react when faced with adversity or potential setback? What do you say to yourself—what goes on in your inner dialogue?

2. Are there changes that you can make to this "self-talk" that will create a more optimistic view and enable you to bounce back more quickly?

3. Think about a current business challenge you are facing. What are you doing to instill optimism in your team or organization? Does your language communicate confidence and hope? Have you been able to reframe this situation in a convincing way?

4. Think about your most difficult individual or team assignments. Is the optimism quotient high enough to ensure success?

5. What are your mechanisms for staying in touch with reality and getting the full picture? Are people comfortable in giving you bad news? How do you know?

4

Stamina

Strategy 4:
Take care of yourself: Maintain your stamina and let go of guilt.

> I had not slept for eighty hours. . . . I had been steering for nine
> hours while leading the other boats and found it almost impossible
> to keep awake. Greenstreet—a fine seaman—continually urged
> me to hand over the tiller and have a nap. I had, however, become
> so obsessed with steering for the island . . . that I kept on when I
> should have handed it over to him. The consequence was that at
> intervals I fell asleep for a few seconds and the *Docker* . . . sheered
> off course. Everyone through fatigue and loss of sleep had slightly
> lost his judgment.[1]
>
> —Frank A. Worsley

Those who choose to lead at *The Edge* are often individuals gifted
with high energy and drive. At the same time, pursuing lofty
goals places heavy demands on physical and psychological reserves.
These demands are most obvious under extreme survival conditions,
but they are endemic to any tough organizational challenge. There is
an inherent tension between taking care of one's self—of preserving one's
own well-being—and accomplishing the mission at any cost.

Some choose to ignore the dilemma. I recently heard a senior executive remark, "A leader needs to be there 100 percent or not at all—even if it means sacrificing your health; that's what it means to be a leader." I disagree.

The tension is real, of course, and it needs to be acknowledged. Strategy 2, for example, highlights the importance of personal example, and there are times in which setting an example means making personal sacrifices. When Shackleton gave Hurley his "mits" on the journey to Elephant Island, he wound up with a frostbitten finger. Sacrifices can take a physical or psychological toll, and there is a trade-off to be recognized.

There might be times when you choose deliberately to make this sacrifice—but be careful. As the leader, you are the foundation of your expedition. If you fail to maintain your own stamina, then you will be unable to summon the energy needed to reach *The Edge*. Furthermore, taking care of yourself is essential because others on your team will take their cues from your behavior. If you want others to have the reserves of energy they will need to do their jobs, you need to reinforce that message by personal example.

This chapter explores the critical importance of taking care of yourself and your team so that you will have the stamina needed to reach your goal. It addresses the burden of responsibility often experienced by leaders at *The Edge*, and suggests ways of dealing with feelings of guilt that can accompany mistakes and errors of judgment.

Look Out for Yourself as Well as Your Crew

Polar exploration calls for individuals who can withstand almost continuous physical and emotional challenges: extreme temperatures; lack of sunlight; possible starvation; painful snow blindness; social isolation; and physical hardships, including frostbite. Shackleton was a man who yearned to explore the outer reaches of the Earth, where he pushed himself to the physical and psychological edge.

Surprisingly, Shackleton was not blessed with good health. A boy who always dreamed of being a sailor, he was able to convince his parents to let him join the merchant marines at the age of sixteen. On his first voyage, he became ill with what Shackleton called the "Mauritius fever." Biographer Roland Huntford suspects that this illness, which has no mention in medical diagnostic history, was malaria, or perhaps even rheumatic fever that caused irreparable damage to the young explorer's heart.

Possibly because of his health problems, Shackleton deliberately avoided the physical examination before joining the *Discovery* expedition when he, Robert Scott, and Edward Wilson attempted to reach the South Pole in 1902. It was a grueling journey, and after ninety-four days in the bitter cold of the Antarctic, the twenty-eight-year-old Shackleton was close to death. Delirious, having difficulty breathing, and unable to walk, he was lucky to make it back to the *Discovery* in time to receive shelter, food, and medical attention from the ship's physician. Shackleton was diagnosed with a severe case of scurvy and what might have been pneumonia.[2]

Shackleton was devastated by Scott's decision to send him home early from the expedition to recuperate. This event seemed to reinforce the need for Shackleton to keep himself at arm's length from the medical profession, and he developed a pattern of avoiding the physical evaluations necessary for joining future expedition crews. Huntford observes:

> Exactly what ailed Shackleton, however, remained an enigma . . . but Shackleton shied away from doctors. Perhaps he was afraid of what he might find. If for no other reason, in the Edwardian cult of manliness, sickness was a stigma. In any case, his health remained part of the secret core of himself he shared with nobody at all.[3]

In spite of these physical limitations, Shackleton never complained either to his men or in his personal diaries about the physical difficulties he experienced while exploring. He seemed to deal with what must have been intense discomfort and, sometimes, excruciating pain by denying its existence and willing himself to continue.

In the light of this, it is somewhat ironic that Shackleton placed tremendous importance on the physical and psychological needs of his men. He constantly monitored the crew's condition. For example, Shackleton was aware of the toll of moving everyone onto the ice floes from the crushed *Endurance*. He watched closely for signs of trouble and wrote, "I took a final survey of the men to note both their mental and physical condition, for our time at Ocean Camp had not been one of unalloyed bliss."[4]

Shackleton was also known to let the men sleep late after a night in which the weather had made it difficult to get any rest. When the sun would shine and the temperature was warm enough to allow them to be outside safely, Shackleton would order the sleeping bags and other gear to be hung out to dry to make things more comfortable. He encouraged everyone to eat until they were full before or after days when they overextended themselves. He noted:

> Although keeping in mind the necessity for strict economy with our scanty store of food, I knew how important it was to keep the men cheerful, and that the depression occasioned by our surroundings and our precarious position could be alleviated by increasing the rations.[5]

His vigilance for the well-being of others was maintained with consistency as the days dragged on. Reflecting on Shackleton's leadership toward the end of the expedition, during the 800-mile sail to South Georgia, Worsley wrote:

> Looking back on this great boat journey, it seems certain that some of our men would have succumbed to the protracted strain but for Shackleton. So great was his care for his people that, to rough men, it seemed at times . . . even to the verge of fussiness. If a man shivered more than usual, he would plunge his hand into the heat of the spare clothes bag for the last sodden pair of socks for him.[6]

Shackleton was also consistently willing to put the well-being of others above his own. He would unselfishly volunteer to stand extra watches and to stay at the helm for extended periods—often three times longer than the other men.

His self-control, lack of self-pity, and ability to care for others are admirable qualities. But his disregard for his own health undoubtedly contributed to his early death. On his last expedition, while attempting to circumnavigate Antarctica, he suffered a massive heart attack. He called Macklin, the surgeon, who had joined the expedition to be with the Boss again. But Shackleton refused to be examined and, against medical advice, stayed on the bridge four nights in a row, keeping his vigil during a storm.[7]

Days later, while anchored at the whaling station where *Endurance* had been moored some eight years earlier, he suffered a second heart attack. The indomitable leader, who had cared so much for others, was gone, just over a month shy of his forty-eighth birthday.[8]

Lessons for Leaders

There is considerable evidence showing that effective leaders have high levels of energy, stamina, and the ability to deal with stress. This makes sense, since leadership—especially at *The Edge*—typically means putting in long hours, making decisions under ambiguous conditions, and dealing with adversity. And we sometimes think of exceptional leaders as superhuman beings who have been blessed with perfect health and boundless energy.

As Shackleton demonstrated, however, the idea that every leader is a picture of health is clearly a misconception. Shackleton was physically flawed, but in spite of his limitations, he was able to summon the courage and the stamina to overcome his physical limitations.

Unfortunately, the care that Shackleton extended to his own crew was never turned inward. Certainly, if any one of his men had exhibited these symptoms, the Boss would have been the first one to ensure that he got adequate treatment. Shackleton's denial of his own health problems, and perhaps his feelings of invincibility, prevented him from doing the things that would have enabled him to extend his days of exploration. This attitude is not unique to polar explorers, and it extends beyond the behavior of an individual leader.

I spoke with a senior executive at Texas Instruments (TI) after the sudden death of the company's leader many years ago. He described the shock that hit the organization when Jerry Junkins, the company chairman, chief executive officer, and president, died unexpectedly on a business trip to Germany.

Junkins's obituary described him as a relaxed leader who was not a workaholic and who had no history of heart disease. Yet the TI culture was one that rewarded heroic efforts, long hours, and machismo. The death of their leader prompted many in the organization to reexamine their values and to think carefully about the limits of extended performance pressures. As a result of this shock, an intensive effort was made to examine the expectations placed on leaders and to promote wellness throughout the workplace.

Junkins's death is an extreme case, but I have observed other instances in which leaders pushed too hard and lost their effectiveness. In one case, a newly appointed CEO felt that he needed instantly to "get his arms around" his new role. This meant long hours and relatively little sleep. Unfortunately, this also meant that he was bone-tired in meetings.

The problem came to a head when he started dozing during presentations. Many times presenters had worked for weeks in preparation for the event and were looking forward to their moment in the spotlight. Understandably, the sight of their leader nodding off was a deflating experience. The CEO, fortunately, was able to hear my feedback in a coaching session and changed his behavior. The problem was easily solved. He stopped trying to do more than was humanly possible and became more effective as a result.

Strong leadership extends beyond monitoring one's own health, and many companies are beginning to realize how important it is for employees to be healthy.[9] In one recent study, 73 percent of companies surveyed reported having programs to promote healthy behavior. Encouraging healthy lifestyles makes economic sense: With premiums doubling for American employees in the past ten years, smart organizations aim to prevent avoidable health issues.[10]

Pitney Bowes is one company leading the way in employee health initiatives. Focused on rewarding positive choices rather than punishing unhealthy behaviors, Pitney Bowes offers wellness programs to help employees lose weight and quit smoking. Employees can save money on drugs to manage chronic conditions, which has ultimately saved the company 8 percent and 15 percent on spending for employees with diabetes and asthma, respectively.[11] These programs, combined with providing a pharmacy at World Headquarters, healthy options at cafeterias, and fitness centers and medical clinics at several facilities, are helping Pitney Bowes employees to improve their stamina and performance.[12]

The message here is clear. At *The Edge*, leaders need to demonstrate concern for others and monitor the health of those who work for them. They also need to extend this awareness to themselves and to recognize that even the most energetic individual has limits.

There is a nautical expression that applies to this dilemma: "One hand for the sailor and one hand for the ship." In other words, do what you need to do to accomplish your work—but make sure that you keep one hand free to keep yourself from being washed overboard.

Beware of "Summit Fever"

How is it that smart people can completely lose sight of their physical limits? One cause is a psychological phenomenon known in mountaineering as "summit fever." The individual becomes so fixated on reaching the summit that all else fades from consciousness.

The ill-fated 1996 Everest expedition, recounted in Jon Krakauer's *Into Thin Air,* provides one such example. Of the twenty climbers who fought their way to the summit, five would die. One survived with such severe frostbite that his right forearm, his nose, and most of his left hand had to be amputated.

Although some elements of Krakauer's account have been disputed,[13] one conclusion stands out. While a "rogue storm" was the immediate cause of the disaster, attributing the death of the five climbers to bad weather misses the point. The underlying causes are complex, but it is clear that—in their relentless drive to reach the summit—both the guides and their charges completely lost sight of their physical and psychological limits.

Scott Fischer, who died on the mountain, was a world-class climber. His strength and stamina were legendary. In 1994, he had climbed the

29,028-foot peak without oxygen. But on the day of the 1996 ascent, Fischer had gone beyond the limits of his strength. As Krakauer wrote:

> "That evening," recalled his tent-mate Charlotte Fox, "I couldn't tell that Scott might have been sick. He was acting like Mr. Gung Ho, getting everyone psyched up like a football coach before the big game." In truth, Fischer was exhausted from the physical and mental strain of the preceding weeks. Although he possessed extraordinary reserves of energy . . . by the time he got to Camp Four they were nearly depleted.[14]

Fischer was strong, but he was not invincible. Although he concealed his inner turmoil, the strain and worry of the ascent, coupled with physical exhaustion, took its toll.

The proclivity to ignore all but the goal is not limited to mountain climbers. Pilots on dive-bombing missions have been known to fly their aircraft into the ground trying to find their target. The label *target fixation* is different, but the phenomenon is the same. It is a human tendency to be so concerned about the goal that all else fades into oblivion. At the *Survival Edge*, this obsession can mean death.

Lessons for Leaders

In work situations, the emotional fever to meet deadlines, complete projects, or accomplish business goals can be dangerously analogous to that experienced by mountain climbers and pilots. Leaders need to be aware of this threat and build in safeguards to ensure that they maintain a sense of perspective and recognize when it is time to make camp, turn around, or pull out of a dive.

Periodic process meetings, for example, can be devoted to reviewing the physical and emotional health of the team. Leaders can help ensure that team members schedule regular downtime—even if only fifteen minutes a day—to regroup, reassess, and relax. Leaders can also sense when target fixation is setting in and intervene with something "completely different."

During a push to redesign a popular SUV, for instance, pressure was extremely high.[15] The deadline was looming, and the design team had yet to submit a promising concept sketch. The current president could have turned up the heat, but he took another path. He chose to close up shop and take everyone—designers to secretaries—to the movies!

The decision not only enhanced the team's health—it had a direct business payoff as well and was worth the cost of movie tickets and a long lunch break. Shortly afterward, ideas began to flow and the project got back on track. As the president put it, "The cost . . . for our truancy was fifty movie tickets, fifty bags of popcorn, and about fifty extra minutes of lunchtime. The payoff was a flood of ideas for an international product representing hundreds of millions of dollars in development investment."

Find Outlets for Your Own Feelings

Shackleton was amazing in his ability to maintain the morale and psychological health of his expedition. What was not obvious to most of the other explorers, however, was that Shackleton was dealing with his own fears at the same time he was managing others' anxieties.

He dealt with these potentially destructive internal forces in a number of ways. For one, he talked to Frank Wild, a partner in whom he had complete trust. He could confide in Wild in a way that he could not with others.

He also shared private feelings with Frank Worsley, the captain. At one point during the open boat journey, exhausted and anxious for the safety of his men, Shackleton became discouraged and worried and was close to depression. In a rare moment, he said to the captain one day: "I will never take another expedition, Skipper."[16]

Shackleton also kept a private journal in which he recorded doubts that he could not share with others. These entries revealed, for example, just how much the loss of the *Endurance* had affected him. After the ship went down, he wrote:

> The end of *Endurance* has come. . . . It is hard to write what I
> feel. To a sailor his ship is more than a floating home, and in

the *Endurance* I had centered ambitions, hopes, and desires. Now, straining and groaning, her timbers cracking and her wounds gaping, she is slowly giving up her sentient life at the very outset of her career.[17]

As painful as this experience must have been, the ability to write down his feelings provided some relief from despair.

Finally, he wrote letters home. After his third unsuccessful attempt to rescue the castaways on Elephant Island, Shackleton was so distraught that his misery was palpable. Worsley observed: "So deep were his emotions that, in contradistinction to his behavior after the first two attempts, he did not even speak of the men on the island now."[18] In the depths of his despair, he found an outlet in a letter to his daughter, Cecily:

> I am very anxious about . . . our men for they must have so little to eat now. . . . We are very short of water, and have not been able to wash since we left South America . . . but that is nothing for I had no wash from October last year until 25th May this year. . . . I will have many stories to tell you . . . when I return, but I cannot write them. I just hate writing letters but I want you to get this to know I am thinking of you my little daughter.[19]

Thus, although he could not share his doubts publicly, he was able to express his feelings in a poignant letter to his daughter.

Lessons for Leaders

Leaders need not be completely stoic, solitary figures. They can, and should, enlist the support and guidance of those around them to assist them in taking the right next steps for the team.

Shackleton's approaches to dealing with his inner fears suggest ways in which leaders in other situations can find outlets for their own anxiety:

▶ *Talk to friends.* Find a Wild or a Worsley—someone you can trust who understands the challenges you face and can deal with your candid thoughts.

➤ *Keep a journal.* Shackleton expressed many of his private doubts in his journal. The simple act of recording one's emotions can provide relief.

➤ *Write letters home.* Communicate with others you care about, even if they may not fully understand the conditions you face. Shackleton wrote letters, even though there was no way to send them. Of course, we have access to technology not available in the days of early polar exploration, including email and voice mail. Use whatever works. The point is to find effective outlets to ease the weight of leadership.

➤ *See a counselor or coach.* Periodic meetings with a professional can be valuable both as a forum for leaders to express their feelings and as a way to get an independent perspective on the challenges they face. The expression "It's lonely at the top" may be old, but it's also true—and it's especially true for leaders who ascend to the highest levels. These leaders are often surrounded by others who have their own agendas, however benign. And they frequently find themselves in situations in which spontaneous expression of feelings would be inappropriate. For these leaders, counsel from a trusted advisor outside the organization is an excellent option.

Let Go of Guilt (But Learn from Mistakes)

Those at the *Survival Edge* are often placed in positions that require split-second decisions that can have disastrous consequences. One such instance occurred when Joe Simpson and his climbing partner, Simon Yates, found themselves on a 21,000-foot peak in the Andes Mountains. Attempting to negotiate an ice wall, Simpson fell to the slope below. He hit the base of the cliff with both knees locked, felt his bones splitting, catapulted backward, and slid screaming down the slope, headfirst on his back.

Yates somehow checked Simpson's slide and Simpson came to a violent stop. Simpson's right knee, which had literally exploded in the fall, had been shattered beyond repair. He was alive, but just barely.

In the hours following the accident, Yates attempted to lower Simpson down the mountain to safety. Each movement was agonizingly painful. It appeared that they might succeed in their painful progress until Simpson slid unexpectedly into space, spinning helplessly as an avalanche of snow poured over him.

Above, Yates clung to the cliff, as immobilized as Simpson. He had two choices. He could hold on indefinitely, lose consciousness, and be pulled from the mountain. Then he and Simpson would both fall to their deaths. Or he could cut the rope.

Yates cut the rope, but was consumed with guilt:

> It wasn't until I had descended half the rope's length that I glanced down and saw the crevasse. I jammed the belay plate shut, and stopped abruptly. I stared at the endless black depths at the foot of the cliff, and shuddered in horror. Joe had undoubtedly fallen into the crevasse. I was appalled. The idea of falling into that monstrous blackness yawning below me made me grip the rope tightly. I shut my eyes and pressed my forehead against the taut rope. For a long nauseous moment feelings of guilt and horror flooded through me. It was as if I had only just that minute cut that rope. I might as well have put a gun to his head and shot him. . . .
>
> If I hadn't cut the rope I would certainly have died. Yet, having saved myself, I was now going to return home and tell people a story that few would ever believe. No one cuts the rope![20]

Yates finally overcame his remorse and—certain that Simpson had died—returned to their base camp.

Simpson had fallen 100 feet into the crevasse and was badly injured. But he summoned enough strength to make four attempts to escape before giving up hope of climbing out. After lying trapped in the dark for seven hours, Simpson rappelled to the bottom of the crevasse. Then, energized by the light of a sunbeam, his outlook was transformed:

> In seconds, my whole outlook had changed. . . . I could do

something positive. I could crawl and climb, and keep on doing so until I had escaped from this grave. Before, there had been nothing for me to do except lie on the bridge trying not to feel scared and lonely, and that helplessness had been my worst enemy. Now I had a plan. The change in me was astonishing. I felt invigorated, full of energy and optimism. I could see possible dangers, very real risks that could destroy my hopes, but somehow I knew I could overcome them.[21]

This confidence enabled Simpson to overcome the pain of his broken leg and continue his descent. Using his ice axe to cut his yellow foam sleeping bag, he constructed a crude splint using straps from his crampons and rucksack. Then, bent over and using his short ice axe as a cane, he developed a pattern of movement: "Place the axe, lift the foot forward, brace, hop, place the axe, lift brace-hop, place-lift-brace-hop."

Simpson knew that time was running out. Since Yates would be convinced Simpson had died in the fall, his partner would soon be breaking camp. If Yates left, Simpson was a dead man. Spurred on by that knowledge, he hopped, then crawled and—in the final stages—dragged himself backward down the mountain.

Three days later, Joe Simpson crawled into base camp, just as Yates was preparing to break camp. Simpson was crippled, starving, and frostbitten, but he was alive. If Yates had refused to cut the rope, or lost his will to survive through guilt, both climbers would almost certainly have died on the mountain.

Lessons for Leaders

The very act of exploring at *The Edge* puts leaders in situations that call for tough decisions. Some of those decisions will be the wrong ones, mistakes in judgment, and those mistakes can create feelings of self-recrimination.

Although mistakes are to be avoided, leaders who dwell on them only compound the problem. Feelings of guilt can be distracting, causing a loss of focus and an inability to deal with the next challenge. Instead of fixating on the past, leaders should identify the critical issues at stake and develop solutions to deal with them.

In *Reputation Rules*, Daniel Deirmeier recounts how a luxury car-maker made an impressive turnaround from a well-publicized public relations fiasco. After investing in an extensive ad campaign for a car designed for young women and families, the company was contacted by a journalist who said the car had flipped over during a safety test. Rather than rush to assure its customers—and the media—of its commitment to safety, company leaders handled the fallout badly, at first issuing no statement and then making remarks that focused on faults with the crash test. Although the test was indeed flawed, the public recoiled at the cold response to a car that was marketed to carry children, and the media lambasted the company as its stock fell sharply.

Company leaders finally owned their mistake and developed an aggressive strategy to regain public trust. No longer criticizing the imperfect safety tests, the carmaker recalled the vehicle and fitted it with technology that fixed the issue. To rebuild its reputation with the media, the company invited journalists to submit the new model to rigorous tests and also launched an ad campaign with a famous athlete describing the times he learned from his own mistakes. These tactics worked, and the model ultimately became the number one seller in the country.[22]

As Deirmeier points out, when handled well, efforts to reframe public relations problems can actually improve a company's standing.[23] Make decisions, make mistakes, and move the expedition forward.

Expedition Log

1. Step back and take stock of your physical health. Are you taking care of yourself, as well as those who work for you? What more can you be doing to maintain your stamina as a leader?

2. Think about a current challenge, change, or "summit" that you are facing. What, specifically, can you do to keep your perspective and avoid summit fever?

3. Assess your emotional well-being and stress resistance. Whom do you turn to when you need to vent? Identify a person, a process, or an activity that will alleviate stress and reenergize you.

4. Reflect on a time when you have made a significant mistake or faced a disappointment. Did you let your feelings of guilt or frustration distract you? If so, what changes did you make to get yourself back on track? Do you need to alter the way you characteristically react to mistakes—especially those "massive learning opportunities"?

5

The Team Message

Strategy 5:

Reinforce the team message constantly: "We are one—we live or die together."

> Shackleton was always opposed to splitting the party, and he very wisely refused to consider such a move ... although the temptation to explore ... was almost overwhelming.[1]
>
> —Frank A. Worsley

*T*eamwork has become something of a modern rallying cry in today's high-performing organizations. Sometimes the word appears so often that it seems to be just another corporate buzzword, and leaders invoke the teamwork mantra whether or not the task calls for collaborative effort. Or, as happens in many academic organizations, teamwork is preached but individual achievement is rewarded.

Why is teamwork so popular? Although the concept of teamwork can be faddish, the reality is that the challenges faced by most organizations can be overcome only through unified effort. It is not surprising that in *Fortune*'s "All Star" list of the world's most admired companies teamwork consistently appears as a critical part of the organizational culture. Whether in the wilderness, the classroom, or the corporation, sustained success turns on cohesive effort. This chapter explores tactics for creating a solid team and sending a strong message of unity.

Establish a Shared Identity

There was no question in Ernest Shackleton's mind that survival depended on exceptional teamwork. Under the conditions faced by the Imperial Trans-Antarctic Expedition, a fracture in the group would mean energy wasted. This disharmony might well mean the difference between life and death.

Since Shackleton so consistently emphasized teamwork in everything he did, it is curious that he does not mention the subject more explicitly in *South*—his story of the expedition. Perhaps the importance of a solid team was so clear to him that it needed no special notice. He had certainly seen the potential danger of fragmentation on his earlier expedition with Scott, when interpersonal frictions were rampant. Or, perhaps, solid teamwork was simply something whose importance he instinctively understood—and that he had a knack for instilling in others.

The ability of individuals to work with others was clearly on his mind from the beginning. For example, when interviewing Reginald James, who later became the expedition's physicist, he asked whether the prospective scientist could sing. He was not, however, probing for vocal ability. In asking whether James could "shout a bit with the boys,"[2] Shackleton was undoubtedly looking to see if James could live and work with others in close quarters under difficult conditions.

With some notable exceptions, Shackleton seemed to have largely succeeded in selecting a group of people who had the capacity to work together. But he clearly did not select a homogeneous group that could be expected to gel of its own accord. There was a diverse mix of temperaments: some cheerful and gregarious, others introverted and reserved. There were physicians, scientists, seamen, and artists. Shackleton did not simply assume that teamwork would happen.

Almost everything that he did was designed to promote the message of team unity. Before *Endurance* went down, for example, Shackleton brought all hands together in the wardroom after evening meals. These gatherings served to promote spontaneous discussion and to build the social bonds that would become so important later in the journey.

As the days wore on, Shackleton proposed a ceremonial haircutting for all, and he volunteered to be the first shorn. As Worsley described the scene:

> [Rickenson] gloatingly seized the clippers & plies them till not a vestige of hair longer than a bristle is left, & his victim looks like one of the Roman Emperors. But it is when the roles are reversed, that we [are] all clipped . . . & looking like a group of convicts. When the commotion was over, an official group photograph was taken "to perpetuate this evening & to cure us, where necessary, of conceit."[3]

The incident, although comical, was much more than entertainment. The ceremony and the haircuts themselves were also vivid statements of the men's common identity.

This shared identity was only to grow as their adventure continued. Later, during sledge marches, the group advanced in relays to ensure that the party would remain together if cracks appeared in the ice. On Patience Camp, the tents were kept together. Still later, during the open boat journey to Elephant Island, the three lifeboats stayed in constant contact.

As a result of this continuous affirmation of team unity, near the end of the expedition, when Shackleton was forced to split the party and sail for South Georgia, the sense of cohesion remained intact. There was no fear that their comrades would abandon the "castaways"—they were as one.

Contrast this episode at *The Edge* in Antarctica with that of the Everest expedition described by Jon Krakauer. On May 9, 1996, dozens of climbers camped side by side, preparing for their assault on the summit. Judged by the standards of their equipment, the Everest climbers were much better prepared than any of Shackleton's team. Instead of reindeer-skin sleeping bags and linen tents, they relied on ripstop nylon and the finest cold-weather clothing.

Thanks to the backbreaking work of a Sherpa, New York socialite Sandy Pittman was equipped with a thirty-pound satellite telephone that would enable her to file Internet dispatches from 26,000 feet. They had everything money could buy, but they lacked the one thing money could not buy on Everest—teamwork.

Krakauer describes the scene:

> There were more than fifty people camped on the Col that night, huddled in shelters pitched side by side, yet an odd feeling of isolation hung in the air. The roar of the wind made it impossible to communicate from one tent to the next. In this godforsaken place, I felt disconnected from the climbers around me—emotionally, spiritually, physically—to a degree I hadn't experienced on any previous expedition. We were a team in name only, I'd sadly come to realize. Although in a few hours we would leave camp as a group, we would ascend as individuals linked to one another by neither rope nor any deep sense of loyalty. Each client was in it for himself or herself, pretty much. And I was no different.[4]

At another time, this fragmentation, isolation, and lack of unity might not have been fatal. After adding the elements of an unexpected storm, exhausted guides, and the cognitive deterioration that occurs in the oxygen-depleted "death zone," however, the concoction was deadly.

Climbers came upon others who were lying close to death in the snow and simply moved on without offering food, water, or oxygen. They passed the other climbers without a word, and as one later explained: "We were too tired to help. Above 8,000 meters is not a place where people can afford morality."[5]

Lessons for Leaders

I have seen organizations that operate like the Everest expedition. One global financial institution, for example, was known as "the lumberyard." In an effort to establish a presence in the United States, it hired a number of investment bankers with contracts that took the dimensions of lumber, such as two-by-fours and three-by-tens. In economic terms, this translated into assured compensation contracts of $2 million annually for four years, $3 million annually for ten years, and so forth.

The reward structure created an individualistic culture in which institutional loyalty was almost nonexistent. The problem was that the financial success of the organization depended on making money "between the boxes"—that is, between the institution's different divisions. It required collaboration of investment bankers, commercial and institutional bankers, and others throughout the organization. With no common identity or loyalty, this teamwork often failed to occur.

Success at *The Edge* demands a different outlook, and this sense of identity can be fostered in a number of ways. Values statements, for example, can be used effectively to create a common culture and identity. The effects are not automatic, and there are instances in which corporate values statements are little more than superficial window dressing. They make attractive wall hangings, but little else. In consulting to one organization, for example, I was once asked to create a corporate values statement because the senior management team was too busy to participate in the process. As one remarked, "You're the expert, you take care of it." Faced with this lack of engagement, I declined.

I have seen other organizations, however, in which statements defining organizational values were taken seriously and used with great impact. At Johnson & Johnson, I was asked to help create a survey that would measure the extent to which its Corporate Credo was practiced throughout the organization.

I interviewed employees throughout the company and found that they not only knew the Credo but also used it as a guide for making business decisions. The Credo was cited, for example, as an important source of guidance during the Tylenol crisis. It was a foundational building block for the culture of the firm, and it helped define the shared identity of every member of the organization.

Maintain the Bonds of Communication

Establishing a shared identity is an essential first step in creating unity, but more is needed to reinforce the team message. To maintain a sense of connectedness, the bonds of communication need to be nurtured in every way possible.

On January 25, 1990, a Boeing 707 carrying 159 passengers on Avianca Airlines Flight 52 crashed on a wooded hill in Cove Neck, Long Island, after running out of fuel. On impact, the plane sheared into two sections, with the nose of the aircraft resting on the house deck of a terrified elderly couple.

The scene was horrific. Debris and wreckage were scattered everywhere. Oxygen masks hung from the trees, screams filled the air, children were crying, and there was little light to aid the rescuers.

The seventy-three who had died in the crash were mixed with survivors, children were separated from parents, and many of the passengers spoke only Spanish. The potential for confusion was enormous. In spite of the danger that the aircraft would explode, police, firefighters, physicians, paramedics, and local volunteers worked together to pull the passengers from the wreckage. Joan Imhof, a key figure in the rescue effort, vividly described the scene:

> The focus was on saving lives. Ordinary people were doing things they had never done before, working side by side with surgeons in this nightmarish environment, applying tourniquets, and comforting survivors as best they could. Words are just so inadequate to explain the situation. People pushed away all other thoughts and focused on doing what needed to be done.[6]

The rescue effort worked almost seamlessly. For hours, workers pulled people out of the aircraft, separated the dead from the survivors, and tried to reunite terrified children with their parents. The teamwork was extraordinary, but it was also physically demanding and emotionally wrenching. As she worked to save lives, Joan was struck by the way the rescuers were interacting:

People would pass each other, reach and take a hand for a moment. Or they would look at each other, make a brief comment, and then move on. Sometimes they would embrace or nod, then continue applying bandages or moving bodies to the makeshift morgue. People needed that brief, but meaningful, contact to continue working with determination. It rejuvenated us.

Afterward, she met with a surgeon to discuss the events of the night. They stood in the hospital hallway talking about the rescue, how many limbs had been saved, and what the experience was like. At the end of this animated conversation, she realized that they had been talking in the middle of the hallway, oblivious to the traffic that went on around them, never breaking eye contact, and holding hands.

This spontaneous contact, whether it took the form of an embrace, a comment, or simply eye contact, served as the connective tissue that held the team together as its members worked successfully to save lives. It was an extraordinary rescue effort, made possible—in part—by the ability of each individual to maintain contact with the other members of the team.

Members of the Avianca rescue effort could look at each other, talk to each other, and even embrace. But the bonds of communication can be used to bind a team together even when human touch or face-to-face contact is impossible.

American POWs held in the Hanoi Hilton prison in North Vietnam were isolated, placed in solitary confinement, tortured, and subjected to systematic efforts designed to fragment the group. The prisoners maintained their integrity and sense of solidarity, however, using what became a second language known as the "Tap Code."[7] Tapping on the thick walls between prison cells, the POWs communicated with an alphabet matrix consisting of five rows and five columns of letters, as shown in Figure 5-1.

"A"—the first row, first column—was sent with a *tap, tap*. "B"—the first row, second column—was sent with a *tap,* (pause) *tap, tap*. Each letter of the alphabet thus had its own unique code. "K" was omitted and "C" substituted.

Figure 5-1. The Tap Code.

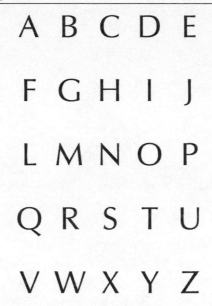

| A | B | C | D | E |

| F | G | H | I | J |

| L | M | N | O | P |

| Q | R | S | T | U |

| V | W | X | Y | Z |

Tapping went on throughout the day and night. As one POW described it, "The building sounded like a den of runaway woodpeckers, with everyone tapping." To signal another prisoner, a POW would tap the sequence familiar to every American—"Shave and a haircut"—and wait for the response: "Two bits." The North Vietnamese tried to intercept the messages but, unfamiliar with the tune, they invariably tapped the wrong response and could not figure out what they did wrong.

The prisoners tapped the equivalent of *War and Peace* several times over during their time in captivity. They built up speed, tapping at rates of five or six words per minute. They were also ingenious in finding different ways to use the Tap Code. They swept in code with brooms. They shoveled in code. They flashed pans across holes in code. They coughed, sniffed, spit, and sneezed in code. Since they often had colds, the communication went unnoticed.

The code was used to pass information, of course, but it was much more than that. Prisoners would tap to other prisoners for years without ever seeing each other's faces. Yet the POWs were so intimately connected they knew each other's moods, simply by sensing the sound of the taps. Anger, sadness, and happiness were all interpretable through prison walls by strangers who had never met.

Their captors tried repeatedly to split the prisoners so that they would be unable to gain strength from each other. They never succeeded, though, and the bonds of communication held.

Lessons for Leaders

Few organizational challenges are as emotionally demanding as coordinating an aircraft rescue or maintaining team integrity in a prisoner of war camp. But the need for frequent communication is always important in maintaining a sense of team unity.

Traditionally, we have had the luxury of working in close proximity with other team members. This means having the ability to look others in the eye and communicate face-to-face. Increasingly, however, teams are geographically dispersed entities that rely on other means of communication: email, letters, phone calls, and videoconferencing.

We are just learning how to use these media effectively. I have frequently heard the lament that electronic media are depersonalizing the workplace, draining organizations of the personal quality that is such an important part of human connection. There is growing evidence, however, that people can work together effectively in ways that were never thought possible before the advent of these new technologies. The effectiveness of the Hanoi Hilton Tap Code in communicating nuances of mood suggests that there is nothing inherent in electronic communication that makes it ineffective for bonding. In fact, the burgeoning of romance on the Internet makes it clear that a form of intimacy can flourish at a distance.

The challenge in all this is to ensure that the efficiency of technology is linked with the personal dimension so important for team cohesion. In addition, since different people are more comfortable with different media, multiple channels are needed. A handshake is, after all, a time-honored way of connecting with other humans.

Barry Salzberg, Global CEO of Deloitte Touche Tohmatsu Limited, is one leader who has been recognized for his exceptional communication skills. Salzberg's ability to connect with Deloitte employees has undoubtedly contributed to his success: first, as the head of Deloitte's U.S. Tax Practice, next as U.S. Managing Partner, then as Chief Executive Officer, and now in his current role. Salzberg describes his approach to communication this way:

> In the end, it's all about how people feel. So much of the job is making people feel connected, with real access to leadership—making them feel like part of a community that truly has their best interests at heart. True, we can't accommodate every request, and we don't always get it right. But this is definitely the idea [and the spirit behind the approach].[8]

For Salzberg, communicating with employees is especially important during financial downturns, when many are concerned about layoffs.[9] By talking honestly and openly about issues, Salzberg has helped reduce anxiety while setting a positive example for other leaders at Deloitte.

Salzberg uses a number of different channels to communicate with colleagues. His *Ten Things* books, available to all employees, provide lessons from his thirty-plus years in business. Each volume reveals ten insights into a wide spectrum of topics including leadership, diversity and inclusion, client service, and leading in "tough times."

Recognized for his ability to interact directly with Deloitte employees, Salzberg has held "Straight Talk" Town Hall sessions around the country. Participants are given the option to attend in person, phone in to listen, or gain access via the Deloitte website. Salzberg answers any questions posed by his employees: No topic is off limits.

There is evidence that these tactics have paid off. Within Deloitte, employees give Salzberg exceptionally high marks for his candid answers, and for his willingness to be unguarded and available.[10] He has received external acclaim and, as U.S. CEO, was named Executive of the Year (Services) in the American Business Awards competition.[11]

We live in the Age of Social Media, but for Barry Salzberg—as it was for Ernest Shackleton—there is nothing quite like personal contact for strengthening the bonds of a team. As Salzberg sees it:

Trust is like oxygen for a business. When it's in short supply, the effect—for employees and customers alike—can be like a loss of cabin pressure on an aircraft. And never has the danger been higher than it is now in the viral conditions of the Twitter Age.

Against these seemingly unstoppable high-tech forces, I am heartened that even today, trust and transparency still can emanate from the ultimate in low-tech: a leader standing flat-footed in a room, listening and offering, as best he or she can, the plain, unvarnished truth.[12]

Keep Everyone Informed, Involved, and Thinking About Solutions

A unified team is one in which every member understands the task to be done and feels a sense of deep personal responsibility for the success of the group's efforts. For this to happen, each person must have a clear picture of the challenges faced by the team. This implies the open sharing of information, options, and potential consequences of choices. The unity of the Trans-Antarctic expedition reflects, in many ways, Shackleton's ability to create this broad sense of active engagement.

Shackleton was a proactive leader who took on a great deal of personal responsibility. He was intimately involved in almost every aspect of the expedition, including the routine details of food preparation and how they would live together. He thought through how they would deal with emergencies, such as their plans for quickly striking camp. He wrestled with the life-and-death issues of how they would obtain their rescue—deciding, for example, who would make the open boat journey through the Scotia Sea.

It is remarkable, then, that he was able to sustain this level of personal involvement while creating a strong sense of empowerment and encouraging personal initiative in others. A key element to this duality lay in his ability to keep people psychologically engaged and continually thinking about potential solutions to the obstacles they faced. Undoubtedly, he had dual motives: One was to maintain morale, the other to solicit practical ideas that would contribute to their survival.

How was he able to express his own ideas strongly and, at the same time, keep people thinking about solutions? One of his actions was to create the Directive Committee, an inner circle of key advisers. The Directive Committee—comprising Frank Wild, Frank Worsley, and Frank Hurley—acted as a sounding board for all major decisions.

The Quorum, as Hurley described the group, had unanimously agreed to establish Ocean Camp after the failed sledge march. The committee also weighed the difficult alternatives it faced. These choices were grim ones and the outcomes uncertain. As Worsley described it, the Directive Committee debated and prepared:

> . . . for the worst eventuality of having to stop on the Pack for another winter. . . . On the other hand if by the end of January we have, as is probable, drifted near enough to Graham's Land, or the S. Orkneys, we may make one or the other by aid of the leads we hope to have come to. . . . The third alternative is a risky but a necessary dash to the West at the end of Jan, abandoning boats but sledging the small punt the Carpenter has made. This we would only do if the drift became arrested . . . so . . . that we were fairly certain we would otherwise have spent the winter on the floe running the risk of it opening and crushing the boats some dark winters midnight.[13]

Although Shackleton had strong ideas about the right course of action, he listened to the counsel of the Directive Committee, and these meetings influenced his views. In addition, this advisory group helped build the strong core of support that Shackleton would need later when the odds against their survival grew, along with the potential for mutiny and resignation.

As important as the Directive Committee was, Shackleton's willingness to consult with others was not restricted to this inner circle. As he made the rounds, Shackleton continually asked "whether there was anything we might be doing that we aren't doing."[14]

He did not, of course, make decisions by majority vote or act on all suggestions. Shackleton was approachable, however, and he gave each person the feeling that he had a role in affecting the course of events. Especially when plans changed—as often happened—the Boss encouraged open discussion and comment. As a result, everyone was made to feel that his opinion counted.[15]

Lessons for Leaders

Information really is power. It can be shared openly or it can be closely held and doled out reluctantly. In one case, a culture of financial transparency and open communication enabled a boutique consulting firm to avoid turning a potential acquisition into a divisive issue.

With the CEO nearing retirement age, he was concerned that the transition could be disruptive. He had watched another founder–entrepreneur sell his consulting firm with no employee preparation or involvement and no distribution of profits. The CEO appeared the morning after the sale wearing an expensive Rolex watch and a self-satisfied grin. Shortly after that abrupt transition, the firm fell apart.

Determined to avoid this scenario, the thoughtful CEO worked hard to involve each member of his team in candid discussions concerning their shared future. Everyone had access to the firm's financial information, including salaries, and everyone was expected to contribute ideas to best position the firm for acquisition. The CEO also met with other former business owners who had successfully sold their firms and then shared his findings with his team. As a result of the CEO's strategy of open communication and inclusive action, the team was fully aligned in preparation for the sale.

This is not to argue that every detail of a developing situation need be instantly shared and without interpretation. There were times when Shackleton waited until the crew was rested to announce bad news. Every leader needs to be sensitive to the timing and context in which information is shared. However, for a group to succeed at *The Edge*, all of the essential facts of the situation must be understood and integrated into the collective consciousness of the team.

Leverage Everyone's Talents—and Deal with Performance Problems Constructively

Shackleton displayed a unique ability to understand each person's temperament and skills, and then to match those qualities with the needs of the expedition. As a result, all crewmembers contributed as best they could, and Shackleton avoided many performance problems that might have otherwise arisen. There were, nevertheless, times at which he had to bring people back into line. His ability to manage poor performers is somewhat surprising, given his unusual sensitivity to the feelings of others.

This sensitivity is illustrated by one incident that occurred in the perilous journey to South Georgia. The plug tobacco carried by the crew eventually disintegrated through the constant pounding of waves. The leaves washed around in the ballast and mixed with hair from the reindeer-skin sleeping bags, creating an odiferous concoction.

An ingenious seaman collected the leaves, dried them with the Primus stove, and created cigarettes using soggy toilet tissue for rolling paper. When the creator offered this special treat to the Boss, Shackleton would take a few obligatory puffs, then quickly pass it on as soon as the donor's back was turned.[16]

As much as he took great pains to avoid hurting others' feelings, Shackleton was quick to act when corrective measures were needed. The eccentric Orde-Lees, for example, took to riding his bicycle out onto the ice, amusing himself with feats of trick riding. On one ride he became hopelessly lost and had to be rescued by a search party. Thereafter, he was sternly ordered never again to leave the ship by himself.[17]

Orde-Lees's odd disposition and eccentric ways caused repeated conflicts with others, and he could easily have been scapegoated by the rest of the crew. He even managed to antagonize the agreeable Wild—but he never became the outcast he could have been. As a result, he was able to contribute when and where he could. Thus, on the sail to Elephant Island, Orde-Lees took Blackborow's frozen feet and warmed them against his chest.

The principal factor in keeping Orde-Lees within the team was

Shackleton's unerring dedication to maintain team unity and his ability to avoid even the appearance of favoritism. He was acutely sensitive to the possibility of splintering and took great pains to ensure that fragmentation was nipped in the bud. Worsley observed:

> When there are twenty-eight men herded together in partially enforced inactivity, with nothing but snow and ice to look upon, life is bound to become irksome. The irritation of trying to drift north and knowing ourselves powerless to combat the inexorable laws of nature . . . was bound to result in a certain fraying of nerves and consequent ebullitions of temper. Little cliques and factions grew up, but Shackleton's tact and diplomacy soon destroyed that spirit. He would redistribute the occupants of tents . . . and would remind each man that strength lay in unity.[18]

This commitment to avoid bias even extended to his relationship with Worsley and Wild. Shackleton leaned heavily on both of these key figures for counsel, and they were clearly the ranking officers in the expedition's hierarchy. But they were never seen as "cronies"—all were as one under the aegis of the team.

Lessons for Leaders

Probably no leadership task is more difficult than dealing with poor performers while, at the same time, maintaining sensitivity to individual feelings and team unity. Leading at *The Edge* involves dealing with that complicated mix, however, and team cohesiveness is never advanced by overlooking individuals who fail to pull their weight.

When it comes to performance problems, I have seldom, if ever, heard a leader say, "I acted too quickly to deal with the issue." The tendency is to do just the opposite—wait until performance has deteriorated to the point that there is no possibility of recovery or until others have been alienated by being let down by the poor performer. An unwillingness to deal with performance detracts from, rather than supports, team integrity.

As important as it is to deal with poor performers, it is equally important to act in a way that avoids isolating the individual and that gives him or her a chance to recover. Bob, for example, was head of R&D at a leading chemical company. Bob had a star performer on his team—a research chemist responsible for some of the firm's most innovative, creative, and profitable new products. In accordance with organizational goals, he rewarded Charlie (not his real name) with a promotion to senior management.

Not long afterward, however, Charlie's performance began to suffer. Accustomed to hands-on work, Charlie was lost when it came to supervising a research staff, and his administrative abilities were severely lacking. Not only was he failing to develop new product ideas, he was also hindering the ability of his staff to do so.

Bob confronted the problem, but he dealt with it in a constructive way. Rather than reprimand his colleague, Bob recognized that the company and Charlie would be better served if Charlie were freed from daily management responsibilities. Bob created a position that had comparable status to senior manager. As "senior research fellow," Charlie returned to a creative role and his management duties were assigned to an executive who was strong in that capacity.

Bob's creation of an alternate career path for Charlie not only supported organizational goals but also created an opportunity for Charlie (and other creative members of the organization) to succeed in a situation that could easily have produced resentment and fragmentation.

The best leaders are sensitive to individual needs and skills, and they find ways of using diverse talents. When corrective action needs to be taken, it is done in a way that avoids isolating or scapegoating people. Successful leaders continually drive home the team message: "We are one—we live or die together."

Expedition Log

Shared Identity

1. What have you done to promote a sense of shared identity for your team?

2. Are your team values explicit and understood by all? Are they used in making decisions?

3. What else can you do to promote identification with the team?

Communication

1. What do you do to stay in touch with the members of your team? Could you be doing more?

2. How would you assess the quality of communication among team members?

3. Are there occasions when the team is able to come together for face-to-face discussion and contact?

Information and Involvement

1. Do all members have a clear picture of the challenges faced by the team as a whole, and a sense of personal responsibility for the team's success?

2. Are there occasions for open discussion of options and decisions—and of potential consequences of different courses of action?

3. Is there anything more you might be doing to keep everyone engaged and thinking about solutions?

Performance

1. How do you assess your ability to deal effectively with individual performance problems? Are there issues you should be dealing with, but are avoiding?

2. Are there factions, or individuals, within your team that are now isolated or scapegoated? If so, what can you do to bring them into the group so they can be fully engaged?

6

Core Team
Values

Strategy 6:
Minimize status differences and insist on courtesy and mutual respect.

> Shackleton privately forced upon me his one breakfast biscuit, and would have given me another tonight had I allowed him. I do not suppose that anyone else in the world can thoroughly realize how much generosity and sympathy was shown by this: I do, and By God I shall never forget it. Thousands of pounds would not have bought that one biscuit.[1]
>
> —Frank Wild

All of the ten strategies for dealing with situations at *The Edge* are tightly interwoven, but the tactics in this chapter are most closely associated with Strategy 5, which emphasizes the importance of reinforcing the team message. In fact, many of the approaches described in this chapter could have been included in the previous one and considered simply as another set of tactics for developing a cohesive team. Strategy 6, however, plays such a vital role in success at *The Edge* that it deserves a chapter of its own.

Minimize Status Differences and Special Privileges

Robert Falcon Scott is one of the most famous explorers of all time. Scott, who reached the South Pole just over a month after Norwegian Roald Amundsen, died with his companions on their return journey. Yet Scott secured his immortality by capturing the imagination of the British public, which saw the expedition as a failed but heroic effort.

Statues throughout the world depict Scott facing death and are inscribed with his last message:

> I do not regret this journey, which has shown that Englishmen can endure hardships, help one another and meet death with as great a fortitude as ever in the past.[2]

In fact, some have argued that Scott's misadventure resulted from severe deficiencies in his personal style and leadership ability. Roland Huntford, for example, in his book on the Amundsen–Scott race, *The Last Place on Earth*, is merciless in describing Scott's flaws. The book's index entries[3] include the following list of Scott's "characteristics":

> absentmindedness; agnosticism; command, unsuitability for; depression, bouts of; emotionalism; impatience; improvisation, belief in; inadequacy, sense of; insecurity; insight, lack of; irrationality; isolation; jealousy; judgment, defective; leadership, failure in; literary gifts; panic, readiness to; recklessness; responsibility, instinct to evade; sentimentality; and vacillation.[4]

Others have charged that Huntford was excessively biased and unduly harsh in his assessment of Scott. Sir Vivian Fuchs, who led the British Trans-Antarctic Expedition of 1957–1958, has argued that Huntford used "the full force of his vitriolic pen" to pursue a personal vendetta against Scott.[5]

Huntford may have been hard on Scott, but there is little question that—as a leader—Shackleton was everything that Scott was not. Both men were products of a romantic age of exploration, and both were highly competitive ambitious individuals. But there were fundamental differences in their effectiveness as leaders and, in particular, their ability to create a sense of team unity. Why were these two individuals so different? What created these sharp contrasts?

When you look beneath Huntford's index of "characteristics" and into Scott's limitations as a leader, one thing becomes clear. There is little question that many of Scott's deficiencies resulted from the environment in which he learned to lead: Britain's Royal Navy in the latter part of the nineteenth century. This environment is worth looking at more closely, because in it there are lessons for leaders and for organizations today.

In the 1880s, when Scott attended Dartmouth—the British Naval Academy—the Royal Navy was living in the past. Still basking in Admiral Horatio Nelson's victory over the French at Trafalgar in 1805, the navy was complacent, resistant to innovation, and focused on form rather than function. It was, as Huntford put it so well, "more like an exclusive yacht club than a warlike institution."

Leadership focused on appearances—smart-looking ships with obsolete weapons, for example. Another pitfall was the Royal Navy's reliance on hierarchy, strict obedience, and centralized decision making. Scott's limited talent and personal insecurities, then, were mixed with a leadership training regimen that was as ill-suited for Antarctic exploration as it was for naval warfare.

This unfortunate combination played out in Scott's leadership in many ways. Lacking Shackleton's understanding of the positive functions of structure (described in Chapter 1), Scott put the crew to work on tasks that were ridiculously inappropriate. As the commander of the National Antarctic expedition, he directed the crew of the *Discovery* to follow the Royal Navy tradition of scrubbing the decks daily. The crew was ordered to perform this task in subfreezing temperatures. The water turned to ice instantly and had to be shoveled away.[6]

Scott was also fond of holding inspections with all hands on deck, forcing the men to stand in place until their feet were frostbitten.[7] As if this were not enough, Scott was also a terrible communicator. Instead of using information to strengthen the bonds of team unity (Chapter 5), he withheld the most basic information. Even the officers were kept in the dark about their destinations and how long they would be staying.[8]

All of these behaviors created anger, resentment, and depression among the crew. Scott's greatest flaw, however, may have been the "classist," hierarchical view of the world that he learned in the Royal Navy. It is true, of course, that other British naval officers had much the same training and were still able to be effective leaders. The combination of Scott's personality and his rigid training, though, was toxic.

In assembling the crew of the *Discovery* expedition, for example, Scott resisted the involvement of anyone who was not a member of the Royal Navy, because he doubted his ability to deal with "any other class of men."[9] The organization of the *Discovery* maintained the strict separation between officers and enlisted men, between the wardroom and the mess deck. Scott seldom even spoke to ordinary seamen, except during inspections. This caste system was wholly unnecessary on a merchant vessel and a liability in the snow and ice of Antarctica. It created a fragmented, dispirited group that could hardly be considered a team.

Shackleton's approach to leadership was a night-and-day contrast to Scott's. Shackleton's father, unable to afford the high cost of a Dartmouth education and a cadet training ship, sent young Ernest to sea on a full-rigger named the *Houghton Tower.* Shackleton literally "learned the ropes"—all 200 of them on the ship—from the bottom up.[10]

Not only did he learn basic seamanship, he also lived in a world far different from the rigid Royal Navy. To be sure, there were status distinctions between officers and seamen, but they were nowhere near as rigid as those of the navy. In this environment, the gregarious Shackleton made friends among all factions—officers, engineers, and apprentices alike.

When Shackleton joined Scott as a member of the *Discovery* expedition, he brought with him more than an outgoing, ebullient personality. He also carried a view of people and relationships that was fundamentally different from Scott's. While Shackleton was a strong leader, he saw no value in unnecessary trappings that differentiated team members. He saw the need for decision-making authority, but it did not take a form that created a superior, elite class.

On the *Discovery* expedition, the fundamental differences between the two men surfaced again and again. When expedition members were learning to ski, Scott looked on while Shackleton and the rest of the expedition floundered in the snow. When Scott bullied Hartley Ferrar—the expedition geologist and youngest member of the wardroom—Shackleton stood by Ferrar because he felt Scott's anger was misplaced.[11]

It was on the Imperial Trans-Antarctic Expedition, however, when Shackleton was given full latitude to lead, that the striking contrast became so clear. In particular, Shackleton's ability to eliminate the damaging effects of unnecessary hierarchy was clearly illustrated. On *Endurance*, everyone pitched in, regardless of station. Scientists, physicians, and seamen alike worked side by side to do the work. A photograph from the expedition, for instance, shows Macklin, the surgeon, on his knees vigorously scrubbing the deck.

Not everyone understood and initially embraced this egalitarian view. Thomas Orde-Lees, who was brought up in the Royal Navy system, wrote in his diary:

> I am able to put aside pride of caste in most things but I must say that I think scrubbing floors is not fair work for people who have been brought up in refinement.[12]

Over time, however, this caste-free system became part of the culture of the team. Unlike Scott, who observed while others labored, Shackleton was an integral part of the team.

This egalitarian spirit had two critical benefits. First, it ensured that every member of the expedition would do his utmost to accomplish whatever work needed to be done. Second, it served to minimize the resentments that inevitably arise when, under conditions of stress, hardship, and deprivation, there is a perception that some are more equal than others.

One way in which Shackleton maintained this sense of equality was in his scrupulous fairness about distributing resources. Shortly after *Endurance* broke up, for example, the crew was faced with the dilemma that there were not enough reindeer-skin sleeping bags for every member. These bags, specially made by expert furriers, were perhaps the best insulating protection against the cold available at the time. Their original plan required reindeer-skin bags only for the sledging party, so there were only eighteen. Now everyone was out in the cold, and ten of the twenty-eight would have to make do with Jaeger woolen bags. To ensure equal treatment, the desirable reindeer bags were distributed using a lottery, in which Shackleton did not participate. As an "old hand," he decided to make do with wool.

As important as protection from the cold was, food was even more central to the life of the crew. Feelings ranging from wild exuberance to deep depression would turn on the size of the rations. Even the appearance of favoritism would have created conflict and resentment. Here is how the Boss described the Solomonic process used to ensure impartiality:

> All is eaten that comes to each tent, and everything is most carefully and accurately divided into as many equal portions as there are men in the tent. One member then closes his eyes or turns his head away and calls out the names at random, as the cook for the day points to each portion, saying at the same time, "Whose?" Partiality, however unintentional it may be, is thus entirely obviated and every one feels satisfied that all is fair, even though one may look a little enviously at the next man's helping which differs in some especially appreciated detail from one's own. We break the Tenth Commandment energetically, but as we are all in the same boat in this respect, no one says a word.[13]

To reinforce this norm of equal treatment, Shackleton made sure that he, as the leader, got no special privileges. He wore the same clothing, ate the same food, and took his turn with the daily chores. He assumed, for example, the role of "Peggy," carrying the "hoosh pot" from the galley filled with their daily fare—a yellow-brown mixture of lard, oatmeal, beef and vegetable protein, salt, and sugar. When Shackleton learned that the cook had given him special treatment, he quickly put a stop to this violation of the law of equals.

Another of Shackleton's characteristics that helped him retain authority while maintaining a sense of equality was his ability to apologize, to admit when he was wrong. He had strong ideas, of course, and he could be bullheaded. But when it was clear that he had made a mistake, he was quick to own up to it.

On one such occasion, Worsley and Shackleton disagreed about the amount of ballast needed for the *James Caird* to make it to South Georgia. Knowing that the crew and stores would weigh 1,000 pounds, Worsley argued for a relatively small amount of extra weight. Shackleton, fearful that the boat would capsize in heavy seas, insisted on nearly a ton of ballast. This caused the *Caird* to ride low in the water and handle badly, making the ride worse than it needed to be. When Shackleton realized his mistake, he spoke directly to Worsley:

> Skipper, you were right. I made a mistake about the ballast. Had
> I listened to you, I think the journey would have been shorter,
> the boat wouldn't have been so stiff or so jumpy in her move-
> ments and we should have shipped very few heavy seas.[14]

This admission, made after the *James Caird* had successfully completed the passage, could have been omitted. Others might have glossed over the mistake. But Shackleton did not, and it only served to increase his credibility as a leader.

Lessons for Leaders

All organizations have hierarchy, but some are more explicit about it than others. In his thoughtful book *From the Ground Up*, Ed Lawler describes a German corporate headquarters with an unusual design.[15] The building is shaped like a pyramid, and each level of the building houses one level of management. Every employee knows his or her position in the hierarchy, and moving up in the organization means exactly that: Those who are promoted relocate to the next higher floor.

This degree of rigid stratification is hardly conducive to teamwork at *The Edge*. Hierarchy itself, however, is not the problem. People understand the need for legitimate authority and for differences in salaries, roles, and titles. What fragments a group is the perception of an elite upper class—a sense of superiority conferred on a chosen few. Thus, the critical leadership challenge is to create an environment in which each person experiences a basic sense of respect regardless of his or her role in the organization.

To illustrate this point, here's a story from my own experience: After graduating from the Harvard Business School, I continued my career journey by taking a job in Washington as an assistant to the Commissioner of the Office of Education, John Ottina. I arrived at work my first day eager to attack the problems of education in America. I found, however, that the other new assistants and I were jammed into an office area so small it was difficult to have a conversation or to think deeply enough to do analytic work. It was not a matter of survival, but it was a very poor work environment.

John saw us jammed into the office, sized up the situation, and then acted quickly. He immediately moved out of his big corner office reserved for "the Commissioner" and set up shop with a table and some filing cabinets in a much smaller space. He did not make a production of it; he did not brag about it; he just did it. That simple move said it all: We were all in this effort together and—regardless of our titles—we were going to work as one to do the formidable job faced by the team.

Willingness to admit mistakes is another way of minimizing status differences, and I am always impressed by leaders who can say they were wrong. Scott Sklar was the former co-CEO of TravelSmith, an outfitting catalog business specializing in products designed to withstand the rigors of the road. Sklar once took a career course I taught at Yale, and we met on one occasion to catch up. During our conversation, Sklar took great pleasure in recounting the story of "the little black dress."[16]

Natalie Carlson, at the time the head of women's apparel, had proposed including a black knit dress in the TravelSmith catalog. Sklar resisted the concept. It was something the company had never done before; he knew little about dresses; and TravelSmith was taking "baby steps" in women's apparel. But Carlson persisted. Her husband was working for a company in France, and she frequently spent long weekends in Paris. Without the right wardrobe, and surrounded by chic Parisian women, she often felt out of place. So Carlson went on a protracted hunt for the perfect black dress that packed well, didn't wrinkle, and looked stylish. She had so much difficulty finding the perfect dress that she designed and developed her own. Carlson knew that this was a dress that could be important—not just for her, but for other female travelers as well.

Sklar had reservations, but he listened. Persuaded by Carlson's arguments, he finally agreed. The results surprised him. As Sklar reflected:

> It was probably one of the most successful products we could have conceived of running. It's become our trademark. What it illustrated for me was that you don't have to be an expert in everything to be an effective leader. But you have to be an expert in understanding people's talents and how to motivate and manage them.

Carlson was promoted to vice president of merchandising, and the "indispensable black dress" became part of the TravelSmith culture. Through his retelling of the story, Sklar made it clear that he did not pretend to be omniscient as a leader. And he encouraged Carlson and others to stand up for what they believed in.

Insist on Mutual Respect and Courtesy

It is not possible to force one human being to have genuine feelings of concern about another. But it is possible to create an environment in which taking care of others becomes a normative behavior and—over time—these caring behaviors help forge emotional bonds.

From the beginning of the Trans-Antarctic expedition to its end, Shackleton consistently encouraged behavior that emphasized respect and caring. His extraordinary attitude of self-sacrifice, plus his ability to act in the service of others, created a foundation for teamwork. These obvious manifestations of caring for his comrades help explain why the crew felt such a strong pull of personal loyalty to Shackleton. It explains why First Officer Greenstreet would be moved to say:

> [Shackleton's] first thought was for the men under him. He didn't care if he went without a shirt on his back as long as the men he was leading had sufficient clothing . . . you felt that the party mattered more to him than anything else.[17]

This sense of connection meant more than fidelity to the Boss. It became, over time, a force that created enormously powerful bonds of loyalty among every member of the expedition.

Shackleton's nurturing behaviors—including his demonstrations of Strategy 2, setting a personal example—were often simple things. On one occasion, after the destruction of *Endurance*, Shackleton and Wild heated hot milk for the crew and went from tent to tent with the "life-giving" drink. After the sail to South Georgia, when the exhausted crew had landed, Shackleton took the first watch, which he kept for three hours instead of the usual one.

Just as Shackleton avoided scapegoating, the way in which he cared for the crew reflected his absolute commitment to team unity. Again, on the sail to South Georgia, he took great pains to avoid singling out those in special need. During the bitter night, Shackleton made sure that every four hours a drink of hot milk was served to stave off the cold. The men drank the liquid scalding hot, willing to endure the pain to get extra warmth inside their bodies.

As a result of this nurturing drink, no one died on the journey. But it was close. Worsley remembers:

> Two of the party at least were very close to death. Indeed, it might be said that [Shackleton] kept a finger on each man's pulse. Whenever he noticed that a man seemed extra cold and shivered, he would immediately order another hot drink of milk to be prepared and served to all. He never let the man know that it was on his account, lest he become nervous about himself and, while we all participated, it was the coldest, naturally, who got the greatest advantage.[18]

What is important to realize is that Shackleton's behavior as a leader had ripple effects beyond his individual concerns. Crewmembers often performed acts of caring and self-sacrifice for each other, showing a concern that rarely occurred in accounts of other expeditions I have studied.

One of the most dramatic moments in the *Endurance* story occurred at Patience Camp, just before the launching of the boats. The food supply had dwindled to dangerously low levels. Less than a week's supply of blubber remained, and the small ration of seal steak normally served at breakfast was eliminated. The waste meat generally used to feed the dogs was examined for any edible scraps, and several of the crew had tried eating frozen, raw penguin meat.

Under these desperate conditions, and after a wet sleepless night, an argument broke out among Worsley, Macklin, Orde-Lees, and Robert Clark, the biologist. Caught in the middle, Greenstreet spilled his tiny ration of powdered milk and shouted at Clark. It was a tragic moment. In his book on the *Endurance* expedition, author Alfred Lansing described the scene:

> . . . Greenstreet paused to get his breath, and in that instant his anger was spent and he suddenly fell silent. Everyone else in the tent became quiet, too, and looked at Greenstreet, shaggy-haired, bearded, and filthy with blubber soot, holding his empty mug in his hand and looking helplessly down into the snow that had thirstily soaked up his precious milk. The loss was so tragic he seemed almost on the point of weeping. Without speaking, Clark reached out and poured some of his milk into Greenstreet's mug. Then Worsley, then Macklin, and Rickenson and Kerr, Orde-Lees, and finally Blackborow. They finished in silence.[19]

Thus, others emulated the caring behaviors that Shackleton modeled. In the face of death and starvation, the bonds of teamwork held.

Another important method for creating mutual respect comes from insisting on common courtesy, even under stressful conditions in which it may seem unnecessary. Of course, conflict under extreme conditions is inevitable and—as will be discussed in the next chapter—it can even contribute to the health of the team. But living at *The Edge* does not mean ignoring civility. Frank Wild was known to remind the crew that, as Shackleton later put it, "a little thanks will go a long way." And so will "please," "excuse me," and the other familiar phrases that lubricate social interaction.

This point was brought home to me in a personal way early in my service in Vietnam. During one of our first operations, my battalion encountered heavy resistance from the North Vietnamese. One unit—India Company—walked into an ambush and was hit by devastating mortar and automatic-weapons fire from an entrenched enemy force. After the attack, a third of the company lay killed or wounded. It took only a few minutes to cripple the unit.

The company made it back to battalion headquarters, a hastily constructed command post on a just-captured, blackened ridge. The hill, still smoking from the air strikes that had preceded the American assault, looked like something out of hell. The battalion intelligence officer, or S-2, was questioning the India Company commander, who was still in a state of shock. The two officers knelt facing each other in the dirt, several feet apart, as the S-2 fired questions about the strength of the enemy, their weapons, and possible countermeasures.

Above, helicopters flew forward firing machine guns, while others flew back carrying casualties. Jet aircraft dropped napalm yards away. I had no idea whether we were about to be overrun or whether the North Vietnamese had disengaged. In the middle of this chaos, and without thinking, I ran directly between the two Marines, bent on my mission of carrying a message to the battalion commander. As I ran by, I heard the S-2 snarl, "Excuse you."

Excuse me? I thought. *Where the hell do you think we are?* Then it struck me. In this surreal situation, I had been rude. I had insulted the company commander, who was struggling to recover from shock. I had angered two members of my team. Under these conditions, common courtesy was one of the few vestigial elements of civilization left. It was an important lesson, one that I never forgot.

Lessons for Leaders

Leaders who want team members to care about each other need to model that behavior themselves. It is not something that can be delegated, and it cannot be feigned. If it is modeled and reinforced, though, over time it will become part of the culture of the team.

Michael, the CEO of a large media company, took over an organization that one close observer described as "political, competitive, and nasty."

People were regularly ripped apart in public. Insulting, abusive, and demeaning behaviors were commonplace.

Michael soon came to realize that, under these conditions, the collective intelligence of the team could not be brought to bear on the pressing competitive issues the company faced. In collaboration with other members of his senior team, he developed a code of conduct that laid out the behaviors that would be expected of leaders in the organization. Fundamental to that code were respect for others and courteous behavior.

In the beginning, skeptics suspected that this was a paper exercise, designed for appearances but without "teeth." It was not. This became clear when, after repeated, visible, and well-verified violations of the code, two senior executives were asked to leave the organization. The message soon reverberated throughout the organization, and a company once described as a "magnet for obnoxious behavior" transformed its culture. In doing so, it replaced an antiquated, individualistic society with a team prepared to move into the digital age.

Expedition Log

1. When you look at the structure of your team and organization, what are the special distinctions that create differences in class or status? Are there policies or procedures that create fragmentation? If so, are they really necessary? How can these differences and special privileges be minimized or eliminated?

2. How, specifically, are resources divided among members of your team? Are there ways the team can share resources or deploy some to others with greater need? Does the process for distributing resources support perceptions of equity and fairness? Consider making this a topic of an agenda item for a team meeting.

3. If you asked members of your team to assess your leadership, would they see you more as a Shackleton or more like a Scott? Would they describe you as "above the action," "looking on," or "in the trenches" with them? Are there physical or psychological barriers that separate you from your team?

4. Have you ever spent some time doing a team member's task? Make a plan to spend time this month actually doing some task assigned to the team. This hands-on experience can have multiple benefits. First, it will show that you are willing and able to perform the same duties as others. Second, you will have a better understanding of the challenges and kind of work that your team must perform, so you'll be empathetic to the needs of the team. Finally, it can provide insights that will contribute to process improvement.

5. When was the last time you made a personal sacrifice for the benefit of the team? Have you ever done the equivalent of "serving tea and milk"?

6. Does the culture of the team reinforce courtesy and mutual respect? Are there explicit or implicit "rules of the road" that create expectations about the way team members will deal with one another?

7

Conflict

Strategy 7:

Master conflict—deal with anger in small doses, engage dissidents, and avoid needless power struggles.

> . . . Such were the usual psychological hazards of an isolated community. Cliques, quarrels and tension hung in the background. There was the irritation of all too familiar faces, and no hope of escape. . . . Above all, however, it was essential to believe in the leader, and Shackleton possessed the power of forestalling trouble without actually appearing to do anything.[1]
>
> —Roland Huntford

*C*onflict: The very mention of the word can raise feelings of anxiety. Competent executives who fearlessly enter the competitive marketplace often go to great lengths to avoid interpersonal friction. Yet conflict is a predictable component in the volatile mix of attitudes and emotions found in organizations at *The Edge*. It comes in many forms: direct arguments, disagreements, sabotage, and passive aggression.

If handled ineptly or suppressed, unresolved tension can be incredibly destructive. At the *Survival Edge*, it can result in loss of life, either through physical attack or breakdowns in teamwork. For organizations in which physical survival is not the issue, conflict can mean decreased productivity, increased stress, wasted energy, and diminished problem-solving ability. It can also result in an unhappy workplace; loss of revenue; vulnerability to competition; and, ultimately, organizational death.

This chapter looks at cases in which conflict has spun out of control and resulted in the loss of lives, along with examples in which conflict was managed effectively under the most stressful conditions. It illustrates how proactive leaders can skillfully use conflict to their advantage in creating and sustaining higher performance.

Deal with Anger in Small Doses

The *Karluk* expedition (described in Chapter 1) suffered from a gaping leadership hole created by Stefansson's abrupt departure, and by the subsequent inability of Captain Robert Bartlett—who was left behind with the ship—to create a cohesive team. The fatal effects of this fragmentation became magnified as the months wore on and conflicts erupted unchecked among the members of the ill-fated expedition.

In a sledge march even more grueling than that faced by Shackleton, Captain Bartlett managed to lead the remainder of the *Karluk* expedition across the ice from the trapped ship to land. Having reached the relative safety of Wrangel Island, however, Bartlett saw no alternative but to leave the exhausted survivors and set out for help.

Leaving fifteen surviving members behind, Bartlett and his Eskimo guide, Kataktovik, began their journey to Siberia in a snowstorm on March 18, 1914. It was a treacherous 200-mile journey across the floating, unstable sea ice. On April 5, 1914, the two exhausted travelers reached land and were soon taken in by a party of friendly Siberian Inuits.

Bartlett and Kataktovik rested for two days with the Inuits, but—concerned about those left behind on Wrangel—set out once again with their weary dogs. On April 25, 1914—thirty-seven days after leaving Wrangel—Bartlett and Kataktovik arrived at the Siberian settlement of East Cape. They had covered about 700 miles of ice and shoreline and had averaged almost 20 miles a day, in what has been called the "most dangerous ice journey ever made by human beings."[2]

As heroic as this effort was, it was not until May 1914, when the ice had broken up, that Bartlett was able to find a ship to take him to Alaska. After arguing with a telegraph operator who refused to send a message without advance payment, Bartlett was finally able to send out messages telling of the plight of the Wrangel Island castaways.

While Bartlett tried frantically to mount a rescue effort, the already shaky community of the Wrangel Island survivors continued to deteriorate. Quarrels broke out constantly. The responsibility of leadership had passed to Chief Engineer Munro, who was placed in command on the island. Munro, who had earlier developed strained relations with a number of his shipmates, was no Frank Wild.

Further undermining a sense of unity, the party split into four subgroups, each of which was free to do as it pleased. The rationale for this arrangement was that it would increase hunting opportunities. However, it also had the effect of increasing the centrifugal forces that were pulling the group apart.

McKinlay, the expedition meteorologist, observed:

> . . . [I]n our very mixed community we had all the seeds of future disaster. In normal circumstances we might have got by as very ordinary chaps, our frailties and idiosyncrasies unnoticed by any but our nearest and dearest. A good leader might have brought out the best in everybody. . . . But on our own, the misery and desperation of our situation multiplied every weakness, every quirk of personality, every flaw in character, a thousandfold.[3]

Biscuits became a major source of dispute. The men shouted obscenities in arguments over an eighth of a biscuit. Crewmembers accused each other of plotting to hide hunting spoils. When game was shot, the fortunate hunters gorged themselves rather than share their bounty, or lied about what they had shot.

At times, conflict escalated to the point where there were threats of violence. One enraged member of the party threatened to shoot another, and Breddy, the fireman, was found shot dead. Although the incident was apparently suicide rather than murder, a search of his effects uncovered numerous items Breddy had stolen from his comrades.

Attempts to talk through the disagreements momentarily helped dampen the conflicts, but the truces were only temporary. Incredibly, people became so argumentative and preoccupied that they forgot Bartlett's last instructions: to meet a rescue ship at Rodgers Island. This oversight almost cost them their lives.

On September 7, 1914, the nine surviving members of the *Karluk* were rescued by the schooner *King and Winge*. The castaways were so dazed that they first ignored the rescuers, then—finally—stumbled across the ice to the ship. Eleven of their comrades had died: eight on the ice, two of malnutrition, and one of a gunshot. Conflict and lack of unity had destroyed the ability of the team to function at *The Edge*.

The *Karluk* is but one of many survival accounts in which an inability to deal with conflict played a destructive role. The infamous Donner Party is another tragic example in which petty disagreements escalated into violence and disaster.

In 1846, the eighty-seven members of the Donner Party left St. Louis, Missouri, for California. One of the pioneers, Milt Elliott, was driving a team of oxen and attempted to pass in front of another member of the party, John Snyder. They became entangled on a narrow path. An enraged Snyder began beating Elliott's oxen furiously with his whip. John Reed, the leader of the party, rushed over to try to stop him. Snyder was further angered by this act and lashed out at Reed and his wife with his whip. Reed, now himself overcome with rage, drew his hunting knife and subsequently murdered Snyder.[4]

The fight lasted only seconds, but the disastrous event had a terrible outcome. First, it fractured whatever sense of unity existed among the families:

> ... [T]he evil feelings that had been loosed that day ... were not to be again confined. The emigrants were no longer a "company"; they were only a number of family groups each for itself, some of them ready to cooperate only where manifest good was to be gained for themselves. Hatred and inhumanity walked beside the wagons.[5]

Second, precious time was wasted dealing with the aftermath of the murder. The train encamped. A council was created to deal with the event. Written depositions were taken. People called out for vengeance. Further shooting was threatened, as the pioneers took sides.

Finally, a compromise was reached, and Reed was allowed to leave without firearms. The resentment remained, however, and the delay was to prove tragic. The Donner Party reached the summit of the Sierras only to be trapped by blinding snow. The horror, cannibalism, and unbelievable suffering that followed can, once again, be traced to the inability of the party members to deal with conflict.

The destructive conflict seen in the Donner Party and the *Karluk* expedition stand in stark contrast to the way conflict was handled by the crew of *Endurance*. In part, Shackleton's effectiveness in dealing with conflict may have come about because he knew—at first hand—just how destructive conflict could be. On the earlier National Antarctic Expedition, Shackleton's relationship with Robert Scott disintegrated to the point that the two men barely spoke to one another. They quarreled about almost every crucial issue, including diet, discipline, and dogs. Scott's impatience and quick temper, his ineptness at decision making, and his often-pessimistic attitude were constant annoyances to Shackleton. This tension was a steady drain on their efforts to reach the pole and was only eased by the intervention of Edward Wilson, the third member of the team.

Shackleton, however, had more than direct experience. He had also studied the records of other explorers and accounts of previous expeditions, including the fate of the *Belgica*. The *Belgica*, which carried the Belgian Antarctic expedition, was caught in the ice in 1898 and drifted for more than a year in the ice of the Bellingshausen Sea. The *Belgica* was the first ship to winter in the Antarctic, and the experience was not a happy one.[6] Boredom, paranoia, hopelessness, and dissidence affected most of the crew. One man drowned and three went insane before they were able to break out from the ice and return to South America.

Determined to avoid the fate of the *Belgica*'s crew, Shackleton viewed teamwork as critical to the survival of the *Endurance*'s crew and effective conflict management as one of his most critical leadership tasks. As in other aspects of his leadership, Shackleton was first and foremost a role model. He knew that it was critical for him—as the leader of the expedition—to set an example in dealing with the inevitable tensions and strains caused by the close quarters and by the physical and emotional stress suffered by the crewmembers.

Shackleton was not a man without emotions—in fact, he was known to have a quick temper. He worked, however, to maintain his composure, to step back and assess difficult situations, and to help his men find a resolution. This was especially true in times of ambiguity or stress when he "appeared to drop his moods . . . and stretch out a soothing hand."[7]

Shackleton also encouraged his men to keep him informed of any disagreements so that he could keep abreast of mounting tensions or damaging alliances. During the first months of the expedition, for example, the eccentric Orde-Lees had a number of encounters with the other men on the ship. He was one of the few who had spent time in the military, and he continued to adhere to many of the protocols of service life.

This was often a source of conflict. On one occasion, in his role as storekeeper, he asked a sailor for a receipt for some Heinz chutney. The practice of asking for receipts was common in the Royal Navy, but it offended his mate, who complained to Shackleton. According to Orde-Lees's diary, Shackleton "said that it was contrary to the spirit of . . . the Merchant Service . . . he was very nice about it . . . but I could see he was displeased."[8]

Shackleton used instances such as these to communicate what he found acceptable and unacceptable behavior. He was also able to be proactive and defuse problems that could distract the men or sap their much-needed energy. Furthermore, resolving a problem early on prevented it from becoming a larger issue.

In spite of all this attention to conflict, there were times when tensions ran high. The most serious conflict took place during the first July, when *Endurance* was beset in the ice. John Vincent—an able seaman and by all accounts a bully—began exchanging words with several other crewmembers. In Hurley's words, Vincent began to call the men "evil names" and he "struck them."[9] When Shackleton got wind of the altercation, he made it clear that this behavior would not be tolerated under his command. Vincent was demoted and that was the last recorded incident of physical violence.

Perhaps this incident, early on in the journey, reinforced in Shackleton a view that the men needed to be able to release on a daily, if not hourly, basis the stress and negative feelings they felt. Small arguments took place throughout the day. The men would argue about which way the wind was coming from, or how far they had floated in the previous week. A person who stepped on another as he left a crowded tent was subjected to fierce reproach. A man who failed to close the tent flap when going out in the middle of the night to relieve himself heard about it from everyone. If snow were knocked into shoes or chores were not done correctly, people would be reminded of their transgression in no uncertain terms.

This norm of releasing anger in small doses did not depend solely on Shackleton's skillful leadership. It continued under Frank Wild, who was left in charge of the party on Elephant Island. In fact, Wild had a superb ability in knowing just how to orchestrate the conflict dynamics of the men under his charge:

> For men growing heartily sick of the same faces around them, bizarre, lurking conflict was a part of daily life. . . . Everybody at some time wrangled with neighbors in the hut about encroachment on their floor space. Wild would allow them all to let off steam and then, just when they appeared on the verge of blows, would defuse the situation with sweet arbitration.[10]

The daily life of the *Endurance* crew, then, was an endless stream of small arguments and minor disagreements. They were sometimes good-humored and sometimes not. But there were few hostile or serious interactions. This culture of letting off steam defused conflict, and it prevented incidents from gaining momentum and becoming serious. Said another way, a series of small tremors prevented a major earthquake.

Lessons for Leaders

Conflict is a pervasive element in any organization, particularly in those that press their performance limits. The challenge is not how to eliminate conflicts but, rather, how to manage them in productive ways that strengthen bonds among team members.

Ironically, the emphasis on teamwork in today's corporate culture can serve to drive conflicts underground. In this subterranean state, unresolved issues become latent sources of tension. How often, for example, have you attended a "polite" meeting that ended with smiling faces—only to hear subsequent hallway and restroom discussions about the "real" issues? Or seen deep differences of opinion devolve into a lukewarm compromise that no one truly supports?

There are several reasons why conflict, anger, and negative feelings need to be dealt with directly and in small doses. First, conflict not expressed means that problems are not being confronted. Second, conflict not expressed directly surfaces in other, nonproductive ways. Unnecessary arguments erupt over peripheral issues, and team members sabotage others in subtle and not-so-subtle ways. Finally, as in survival situations, conflict not expressed and resolved can escalate out of control, with disastrous business consequences.

In spite of the importance of managing conflict, being proactive about dealing with disagreements can be difficult for many leaders. In an honest but misguided desire to promote harmony, otherwise skillful executives avoid the tough issues or fail to create a climate in which conflict is freely expressed.

Perhaps the first step in promoting healthy conflict is to understand—and really to internalize—that conflict and caring are not mutually exclusive. The extraordinary example of Shackleton's crewmembers sharing their milk in the middle of a heated argument makes this point vividly.

The second step in dealing with conflict is to create an effective process that encourages team members to surface their differences and to identify those lurking problems that need to be addressed. An approach that I have found quite effective for this purpose comes from an unusual source.

Some years ago, when I first began to work with senior leadership teams, I encountered a great deal of difficulty and frustration in getting executive teams to confront sensitive issues, and that affected their performance. At the time, I was teaching a course at Yale in which I used a "family systems model" as a lens for looking at the dynamics of organizations.

With this approach, I analyzed organizations as if they were families to see what insights this perspective might generate. I understood that organizations were not really families, but I thought this metaphor might provide a fresh perspective on organizational dynamics. I also thought it might help explain the persistence of organizational problems that defied rational analysis. After all, no one expects families to be rational!

One aspect of the family systems theory that proved to be particularly valuable was the notion of the "family secret." Family secrets are emotionally charged, taboo topics. In family life, they often center on drug or alcohol dependencies, marital difficulties, and personal idiosyncrasies of various kinds. Most family members are aware of the "secrets," but these forbidden subjects are never openly discussed. When conversation moves in the direction of a secret, the anxiety level rises palpably.

The executive teams I was dealing with seemed to resist sensitive issues in much the same way that families avoid confronting secrets. So I decided to try an experiment and approach these taboo team topics as if they were family secrets. The next question was how to surface the issues.

Family systems therapists use a number of images to represent secrets, but none of them seemed quite appropriate for use in an organizational setting. After some thought, I chose a metaphor I thought would work: the *Moose on the Table*.[11] It seemed to me that the image of a large, hairy, ungainly moose—sitting in the middle of a table and blocking communication—vividly symbolized the issues being avoided by the group. And, while imposing, the moose was a goofy enough critter that it would add an element of humor to otherwise tense situations.

With some trepidation, I began to use the Moose on the Table in my consulting work. Although the metaphor initially raised some eyebrows, I was amazed at the ability of the Moose to surface issues that had long been ignored. In one leading technology organization, for example, the CEO and his team were struggling with their inability to create and manage new businesses successfully. They knew this was a fundamental problem, but they were unsure of why it persisted.

As part of a study organized to unravel the mystery, I presented the family systems model and conducted a "Moose Round-Up." The results were astonishing. The "Moose List" in the team's final report included the following issues:

▶ We approach every new product as if it must be a home run, achieving the same level of success as our earliest successes.

▶ We are, in fact, becoming a technology-averse company.

▶ The revenue plan drives our resource allocation and decision-making process.

▶ We have developed a tolerance for mediocrity.

▶ We are looking for a "magic product" to save the company.

▶ We have no real competitive marketing competence.

▶ The operating plan cycle is not flexible enough to allow timely response to business initiatives.

The report (see Figure 7-1), along with a stuffed moose, was presented to the CEO, who accepted it with a smile. The conclusions were not ones he was delighted to hear, but he knew that—once identified—the issues were ones that could be systematically attacked.

Over the years, my colleagues and I have brought the Moose on the Table to scores of organizations throughout the world. There are times in which substitute animals are needed: For example, the Water Buffalo on the Table made an appearance in Asia. Whatever the form, however, the image has always succeeded in getting conflict out in the open, where it belongs.

Why is the Moose metaphor so effective? I believe that this ungainly animal does several things very well. First, it legitimizes and rewards people for being open, and it provides a shared vocabulary for doing so. "In the spirit of the Moose, I'd like to say . . ." becomes a common phrase. Second, the comic image takes the edge off issues that can create tension and divisiveness. Third, identifying an issue as a Moose provides psychological distance. It reframes the issue from an internal conflict to an external problem to be solved. Once the conflict becomes a shared problem, team members can work together to find solutions.

Figure 7-1. The Moose on the Table.

Why New Business Initiatives Fail

Engage Dissidents

The men of the *Endurance* spent countless hours, day after day, talking or sleeping in their crowded tents to avoid the elements and pass the time. Shackleton recognized that these close quarters could be breeding grounds for discontent, and his keen awareness of the difference in people's personalities and needs was vital in minimizing destructive conflict among the crew.

Shackleton studied everyone and appeared to know when he, or others, might have gone too far. Macklin, the surgeon, described Shackleton as someone able to ask you "little things about yourself, how you were getting on . . . and all that sort of thing. . . . Sometimes when you felt he'd been perhaps a bit ruthless, pushing you round a bit hard, he seemed to have the knack of undoing any bad effect . . . with these little intimate talks."[12] Shackleton clearly recognized that hurt feelings needed immediate attention to prevent anger or resentment from building.

During the crew-selection process and early in the expedition, Shackleton identified individuals whose attitudes or behavior could either adversely affect morale or be seen as a challenge to his leadership. Instead of limiting his contact with these men, he brought them closer into his fold.

The photographer, Frank Hurley, for example, always needed to feel that others saw him as one of the leaders of the group. If he felt slighted of the attention he thought he deserved, he would become aggressive and difficult. Hurley's need to be recognized earned him a place in Shackleton's tent, and the Boss consulted him on key decisions. This supported, in Hurley's mind, his own prominence among the ranks, and thus helped ensure his support.

Shackleton saw value in selecting certain other tentmates as well. He bunked with the physicist, Reginald James, out of concern that his "withdrawn academic manner" would cause him to be teased by the other men. Shackleton did not want to expose one person to excessive ridicule for fear it could escalate into a full-blown altercation.

When Shackleton had to choose his crew for the open boat journey from Elephant Island to South Georgia Island, he was again mindful of allowing potential troublemakers unlimited access to the emotionally and physically worn-out crew. Shackleton felt that McNeish's skills as a carpenter could prove invaluable on a wooden boat, but he also wanted McNeish to accompany him for another reason: Shackleton was concerned that, left behind, McNeish could stir up discontent.

He also selected Vincent to make the trip. Because of Vincent's reputation as a bully, Shackleton thought better of leaving the seaman behind to create trouble for Frank Wild. Finally, Shackleton chose Crean, who was less of a team player and was also likely to create problems for the marooned castaways.

In retrospect, Shackleton's foresight and his willingness to deal directly with dissidents is rather astounding. When he needed to select a team for the most difficult challenge he had yet to face—the crossing to South Georgia—more than half of his crew consisted of potential troublemakers. Shackleton's willingness to maintain close relations with these questionable characters, however, undoubtedly mitigated the conflicts that occurred on Elephant Island, and it helped Wild with his formidable task of maintaining morale among those left behind.

Lessons for Leaders

In difficult leadership situations, we are often tempted to ignore or isolate individuals whose personalities rub us the wrong way or who have a knack for stirring up trouble. Although this is an understandable reaction, it is the wrong one. It only creates space for further problems, and rejecting dissidents is ultimately detrimental to the organization. A more productive response—however counterintuitive it may seem—requires doing just the opposite:

- ➤ Identify those individuals or groups that might be undermining your leadership.
- ➤ Be proactive and keep troublemakers close by.
- ➤ Find ways to minimize the negative impact of their behaviors.
- ➤ Make sure these people are engaged, in some way, in the decision-making process.
- ➤ Treat everyone, including dissidents, with respect, even when they are antagonistic.
- ➤ Be willing to set limits, and make it clear that this works both ways. Inappropriate, rude, or bullying behavior cannot be tolerated.
- ➤ Avoid the temptation to denigrate malcontents and keep your personal opinions about people to yourself—and your closest advisers.

Leaders who are proactive in dealing with individuals who have the potential to be dissidents can avoid antagonistic relations further down the road.

In one company, two men were equally capable for the job of CEO. One got the job and one became the COO. In order to prevent unnecessary conflict, the CEO decided to share the limelight by insisting all public appearances be attended by both of them, including all photographs and company meetings. This reinforced the message that they were a team, and the inherent acknowledgment of the COO's work in making the new venture a success was a huge motivating factor for the COO. As a result of these efforts, what could have been a disaster turned into a complementary relationship. Together, they led the company in creating a new culture, a solid friendship, and an exciting new venture.

Avoid Needless Power Struggles

In December 1915, more than a year after the *Endurance* crew had set sail from South Georgia, there was still no prospect of rescue and no end of the journey in sight. Shackleton could feel the morale of his men slipping. He had heard grumbling that, since the ship had been destroyed and they could not carry out their mission, the men would not be paid. Some began to believe that they were enduring these torturous conditions for nothing, and they worried for the safety of their family members at home who were depending on the income.

Shackleton believed that he had to act. He could not let his men continue to feel sorry for themselves and wallow in anger or frustration. He thus decided that they would make a second march across the ice toward land. On December 22, the party celebrated Christmas early, eating as much as they wanted to fortify themselves for the journey ahead, and then they started out at 4:30 the next morning.

As before, two teams of fifteen men each pulled the boats and sledges weighing over 1,000 pounds. As in the previous march, they would sink to their knees in the soft, wet snow. Their progress was excruciatingly slow. They were averaging just two miles a day. Four days into their journey, McNeish, who was close to collapsing from the combined effects of exhaustion, starvation, and exposure to the elements, simply decided that he would no longer go on.

Worsley ordered McNeish to pick up his section of the rope and continue. McNeish refused, arguing the march was useless. Worsley, himself on the verge of exhaustion, called for Shackleton, who stood facing the angry and frustrated carpenter. McNeish argued that the march over the ice was not in their best interests because they would never be able to cover the distance they needed to reach their destination.

Shackleton stood quietly by while McNeish lashed out. The carpenter declared he did not have to obey any orders, because the ship's articles were not enforceable. He argued that he was no longer obligated to follow orders, since the articles he had signed were to serve "on board," and they were no longer aboard the *Endurance*.

With all of his men watching the first real challenge to the Boss's authority, Shackleton turned his back on McNeish and walked away. He knew that he could not reason with the carpenter, and did not want to waste energy on a pointless argument. Shackleton simply left the carpenter standing in the snow—giving him time to come to his senses.[13] After weighing his options, McNeish took his position at the rear of the sled when the expedition set out again. The one-man mutiny had been put down without further conflict.

Lessons for Leaders

It is vital to decide which battles are worth fighting and which are not. The battles worth fighting should be engaged with all available resources; those not central to your mission should be let go.

When a situation cannot be resolved immediately, you may, like Shackleton, choose to leave your "McNeish" standing in the snow until you can assess the situation realistically. It is better to wait until you are prepared than to respond in haste and further escalate the problem.

It is particularly important to avoid creating situations in which people feel trapped, causing them to escalate conflicts because they see no way out. The Roman general Scipio advised giving opponents a "golden bridge," an avenue of retreat, arguing that an enemy with no way out will fight with unprecedented ferocity.

Scipio's maxim applies to nonmilitary situations as well. A golden bridge resolved a business conflict among three colleagues—Tom, Elizabeth, and Patrick—who were at loggerheads over a dissolving partnership. Their hopes of maintaining a profitable business with strong friendship had not been realized and—after months of trying to revive the firm—it became clear that there was no chance of solving their differences.

Patrick, in particular, felt aggrieved and rejected. He responded by making financial claims that Tom and Elizabeth found unreasonable. The haggling continued, lawyers were called, and the careers of all three were stalled. Finally, Elizabeth came up with an idea.

All three had made an initial investment in the company, and the amount remaining in the partnership bank account included this investment, plus a small additional sum. Elizabeth proposed that the partners each withdraw their initial investment and that Patrick receive the remainder. Although the leftover money amounted to only a few hundred dollars, Patrick accepted the offer. The proposal provided a golden bridge, a way to end the stalemate. A needless power struggle was avoided and the three partners moved on with their lives.

Expedition Log

1. What are the norms about conflict in your organization? What is the level of openness? Do team members share their opinions openly and deal with problems directly, or do they raise conflict in oblique, indirect, or passive-aggressive ways?

2. What changes can you make that will allow anger to be dealt with productively and in small doses?

3. How many Mooses are there in your organization? Are there taboo topics that affect performance but are never discussed? Consider a Moose Round-Up, or some other proactive way of initiating a discussion about these off-limits topics.

4. What is your characteristic style of dealing with troublemakers,

skeptics, and malcontents? Do you engage them or push them away? Is there a dissident you could "pull into your tent" and engage productively?

5. Are you, or others, engaged in any nonproductive power struggles? Is there anyone who is your "McNeish in the snow"? If so, how can you move your expedition forward without compromising your authority and position of leadership?

8

Lighten Up!

Strategy 8:
Find something to celebrate and something to laugh about.

The disappearance of the sun is apt to be a depressing event in the polar regions, where the long months of darkness involve mental as well as physical strain. But the *Endurance*'s company refused to abandon their customary cheerfulness, and a concert in the evening made the Ritz a scene of noisy merriment in strange contrast with the cold, silent world that lay outside.[1]

—Ernest Shackleton

This strategy incorporates what is probably the most counterintuitive behavior of all the ten strategies for leading at *The Edge*. In stressful circumstances, when times are grim, celebration is usually the farthest thing from anyone's mind. Under survival conditions, laughter is an unnatural act, and in tough business situations, humor can seem frivolous, inappropriate, or out of touch.

Yet, under extreme pressure, the ability to lighten up, celebrate, and laugh can make all the difference. It can break a spiral of depression and stimulate creativity. It can enable people to step back and get psychological distance on their problems. It can cut through fear and tension. Finally, it can enable a team to refocus, reenergize, and surmount daunting obstacles.

This chapter shows how these behaviors influenced the outcome of the Shackleton saga and the course of other survival situations. It also illustrates how effective leaders have used these qualities to make their businesses successful. Above all, it makes the case that, at *The Edge*, celebration and humor are neither superfluous nor luxuries. They are imperatives.

Find Something to Celebrate

From the very beginning, Shackleton's expedition had a certain celebratory atmosphere that characterized the life of the group. It created an upbeat mood and a way of thinking about life that sustained the men through the grimmest of times.

This atmosphere of celebration contributed to the sense of cheerfulness and optimism, as described in Strategy 3, but it was more than simple cheerfulness. It reflected the complexity of Shackleton's leadership and his ability to be both deliberate and spontaneous in shaping the culture of the team.

Shackleton grasped any excuse—some rather far-fetched—in finding things to celebrate. On May 24, 1915, for example, they marked Empire Day, an occasion originally created as an opportunity to encourage patriotism among British children. To celebrate Empire Day, the crew of the *Endurance* sang songs in the Ritz, seizing the occasion to honor their native land.[2]

Later, while still aboard *Endurance*, Shackleton continued the festivities by calling for a "Dog Derby." In this twilight celebration, dogsled races stimulated merriment, laughter, and heavy betting involving chocolate and cigarettes.[3] The following week, on June 22, they celebrated Midwinter's Day. It was an occasion that gave the physicist, Reginald James, an opportunity to display his "witty and truly unintelligible" acting ability with a tongue-in-cheek "Dissertation on the Calorie" by Herr Prof. Von Schopenbaum.[4]

In those early days, when times were not so bad, celebration came easily. What is most impressive, however, is that the spirit of celebration continued throughout the darkest of days, when cheerful rituals could easily have turned to deep despair.

The day of December 5, 1915, marked one full year since the crew had left civilization. Their ship had been crushed two months earlier, and they had been carving out a harsh existence on the ice floes. According to the original plan, they would have been heading home by now, so this anniversary might have turned into a gloomy reminder of their predicament.

Shackleton, realizing the significance of the day and the potential for disappointment, decided to be proactive. Exemplifying the aphorism "If you can't fix it, feature it," the Boss declared a holiday to celebrate the anniversary of their departure from South Georgia. What could have been a day of depression turned, instead, into a day of celebration.[5]

Later, at Patience Camp, the living conditions continued to deteriorate. Food was in such short supply that discarded seal heads and flippers had to be dug from the ice in a desperate search for any last scrap of blubber. They lived hand to mouth, relying on the few penguins and seals that could be snared. All of the suet had been used, so any meat that was brought in had to be fried in fishy seal blubber.

These were not times that cried out for celebration. Yet Shackleton still found occasions for festivities:

> On Leap Year day, February 29 [1916], we held a special celebration, more to cheer the men up than for anything else. . . . The last of our cocoa was used today. Henceforth water, with an occasional drink of weak milk, is to be our only beverage.[6]

The living conditions of the expedition continued to worsen, but the commitment to celebration did not. By June 1916, the abandoned castaways were living in the desolate squalor of Elephant Island. Blackborow's foot, which had been frostbitten on the open boat journey, got progressively worse. It was clear that an amputation had to be performed to save his life, and Macklin and the other surgeon, James McIlroy, went about their business.

A blazing pile of penguin skins created enough warmth to vaporize the chloroform needed as an anesthetic. McIlroy removed the bandage from Blackborow's foot and systematically severed each of the gangrenous toes at the ball joint. At the end of the fifty-five-minute operation, the stowaway opened his eyes, smiled, and asked for a cigarette, which the surgeon rolled using a page from the *Encyclopaedia Britannica*.[7]

These were not the hopeful, fun-filled early days of the expedition. This was life at its harshest, most severe, and frightening limit. And yet, a week later, a second Midwinter's Day celebration was held. The occasion was marked with a concoction of nut pudding, biscuits, sledging rations, and powdered milk.

Amazingly, the castaways summoned enough energy to put on a program of twenty-six different acts, including poetry and music. Although the members of the audience lay in their sleeping bags, the event was spirited. Not only did Hussey play the banjo, but James also sang a clever song about Frank Wild and their primitive living conditions.

The celebration ended with a toast to Shackleton and the crew of the *James Caird*, followed by the only available libation: "Gut Rot, 1916."[8] The concoction—made with stove alcohol, water, ginger, and sugar— was not Dom Perignon, but it served its purpose. They had celebrated together and broken the endless monotony of waiting for rescue. Shackleton's ability to use celebration and ceremony to boost team morale seemed to come naturally. It is surprising, though, that many leaders fail to understand the importance of ceremonies—or conduct them so ineptly that spirit is diminished rather than enhanced.

The story of the *Karluk* provides numerous illustrations of failures in leadership. The sinking of the ship, for example, served as an occasion for Captain Bartlett to indulge himself in a unique and bizarre ceremony. Although the rest of the crew had abandoned the doomed vessel, Bartlett stayed aboard. He built a roaring fire in the galley stove and proceeded to play all the gramophone records aboard the ship, one by one. As each record was finished playing, he threw the disk into the galley fire . . . save one. He played Chopin's Funeral March, then set it aside for later.

When the end finally came and water reached the deck of the *Karluk*:

Captain Bartlett placed the Funeral March on the Victrola. With
the water running along the starboard side of the deck and
pouring down the hatches, he waited at the rail until it came
down level with the ice. Then he stepped off. . . . The Canadian
Blue Ensign fluttered until it cut through the water. Captain
Bartlett, deeply moved, stood right alongside her until she was
gone.[9]

Watching the *Karluk* sink to the strains of Chopin's Funeral March
undoubtedly served some need of Bartlett's. But imagine the effect of this
lugubrious scene on the twenty-two men, one woman, sixteen dogs, and
a cat that watched the funeral event. It was not a ceremony likely to build
hope, confidence, and morale.

Lessons for Leaders

Effective leaders find ways of building celebration into the culture of their
organizations, and there are as many methods to bring teams together
as there are reasons to celebrate. I've worked with teams that celebrate
business-related achievements such as promotions, employees making
partner, and departments achieving sales goals, or personal events, such as
birthdays and engagements.

Companies recognize employees with celebrations ranging from elab-
orate annual holiday parties to monthly half-hour gatherings around a
birthday cake. For a more personal touch, team members can send colleagues "thank you" notes for specific contributions to projects.

Some businesses have structured recognition systems, such as a drop
box where employees can nominate each other for monthly awards. At
the month's end, the department leader draws three names from the box
and publicly recognizes the staff members' contributions.

One marketing research department uses its annual planning and
midyear meetings as occasions to recognize employees with personalized
awards. For example, "The Dazzling Diva" award was bestowed on an employee who had auditioned for, and won, her first leading operatic role. The
award took the form of a large, sparkling star inscribed with her name for

her dressing room door. "The Life Savers" award, including flowers and rolls of Life Savers candy, was given to an employee who frequently came to the rescue of her coworkers. Other awards took a similar tone.

These awards were inexpensive but heartfelt, and imbued with humor and sincerity. Great care had obviously gone into their selection and preparation. The division leader had personally created the Dazzling Diva star. In the process, she had covered her home with sparkles, which she jokingly said had risked a domestic disturbance. It was clear that the awards, while simple, were thoughtful and personal. They meant something, and that was the point.

A survey of friends and colleagues working at different organizations produced the following list of company celebrations. You may want to consider adding to this list by surveying your colleagues:

> ► We hold quarterly events to energize and excite the team for the upcoming quarter and to celebrate achievements from the previous quarter. We had a Fiesta Friday and an offsite Crab Feast with Maryland Bay Crabs. We try to make them themed dinners to support our diversity initiatives.

> ► We celebrate quarter end (surviving!), audits, and employee anniversary milestones.

> ► We celebrate new project awards, annual growth, employees joining the company, baby showers, work anniversaries, birthdays, promotions, departmental transfers, and community efforts by employees.

> ► We celebrate when interns receive their offers, annual promotion day, and we all drink champagne when someone makes partner.

Find Something to Laugh About, Too

Shackleton and Wild set aside specific times for special celebrations, but humor, banter, and merriment were constants in the life of the expedition. Shackleton, in particular, went to great lengths to make sure that the mood of the group would be as lighthearted as possible under the circumstances.

In a dramatic gesture (described in fuller detail in Chapter 2), Shackleton threw gold sovereigns into the snow to emphasize the absolute necessity of ridding themselves of extra weight during their sledge journey. In a surprising move, however, the Boss went back to the wreckage of *Endurance* and retrieved Hussey's treasured "zither banjo." He presented the twelve-pound instrument to Hussey, who recalled the incident as follows:

> "It's rather heavy," I said dubiously. "Do you think we ought to take it?"
> "Yes, certainly," was the chief's prompt answer. "It's vital mental medicine, and we shall need it."[10]

Shackleton made the right decision, and the banjo contributed in important ways to the continued positive morale of the expedition. Although Hussey had a limited repertoire—six tunes to be exact—many nights were spent listening to the "cheery twang" of the banjo.

Hussey's music was supplemented by another favorite form of entertainment: good-natured banter. Captain Frank Worsley recalled:

> Hussey was a brilliant wit, and his keen repartee was one of the few joys left to us. Often we would combine to provoke him just for the pleasure of hearing his clever retorts, and invariably he would emerge the victor, no matter how many of us tried to best him. On an ice-floe any little diversion is more welcome than people living in civilized conditions perhaps can imagine.[11]

Hussey was not the only one to lighten the atmosphere. First Officer Greenstreet was also noted for his ability to "fool around" for a laugh. And then there were the inevitable impersonations. Impersonations were one of the most encouraged forms of amusement. They had the effect of lightening the mood while alleviating tension and subsurface conflict. Some of the more annoying characteristics of crewmembers were often the focus of these short expositions.

Orde-Lees, for example, had a habit of being a little too anxious to please Shackleton. McIlroy, the surgeon, thus saw an opportunity to mimic an interaction between the two, and Orde-Lees described the imperson-ation in his diary:

> "Yes sir, oh yes certainly sir, sardines sir, yes sir here they are (dashes to pantry and back) and bread sir, oh yes sir, bread sir. . . ." (Another dash to pantry and much groveling effusion. . . .) "And may I black your boots sir," and so on.[12]

Banter and impersonations broke the monotony, but humor also had its place in sustaining the crew through the darkest crises. The loss of *Endurance* was one of the lowest, most demoralizing points in the journey. When the ship finally succumbed to the unbearable pressure of the ice, Shackleton ordered all hands onto the floe. As they were going over the side, Shackleton turned to Orde-Lees and said:

> "We've got it in the neck all right this time, haven't we?"
> "Well, no, I don't think so," [Orde-Lees] ventured. "You would-n't have had anything to write a book about, if it hadn't been for this."
> "By Jove, I'm not so sure you aren't right," [Shackleton] re-marked [at] which we both had a good laugh.[13]

Humor is a consistently effective tool for dealing with adversity, as I rediscovered in a conversation in Washington, D.C. I had the opportunity to present the Shackleton story and the ten *Leading at The Edge* strategies to then-Secretary of the Navy John Dalton. The meeting, held at the Pen-tagon, was attended by a number of the Secretary's staff members, many of whom had their own personal experiences at the *Survival Edge*.

The discussion that followed my presentation was a stimulating one, and it expanded my understanding of the ten strategies. Afterward, a naval officer wearing pilot's wings approached me. He said that he had enjoyed the presentation and asked whether I had heard about the "toga party."

I remembered the toga party in the movie *Animal House*, with John Belushi. These were not the kinds of parties sanctioned by the Naval

Academy, so I had no firsthand experience with such events. The officer's comment did, however, raise a vivid image of comedian John Belushi hosting a fraternity toga party wearing only a sheet and a mischievous smile. So I knew exactly what he was talking about, but just how it related to leadership was completely obscure.

It became clear, however, when he told me the story of *Alfa Foxtrot 586*, a Navy patrol plane that left Adak, Alaska, on October 26, 1978. The plane, a four-engine turboprop, had taken off with its crew of fifteen on a routine ocean-surveillance and antisubmarine mission. What was to be an uneventful flight turned into a crash landing at sea and a fight for survival. Their plight—desperate though it was—sheds light on one strategy for leading at *The Edge.*

After my conversation at the Pentagon, I gathered every piece of information that I could find about the crash. I read U.S. Navy incident reports and found other written material, including the Patrol Squadron Nine web page. I also corresponded with those involved in the rescue operation and survivors of the ordeal. As a result, I was able to make the connection between the toga party and *The Edge.*[14]

As the Navy patrol plane flew over the North Pacific, the weather worsened and winds increased. Of greater concern, however, was the performance of a propeller on the left wing of the aircraft. The engine was running erratically and was stopped, but the 1,200-pound propeller began to increase the speed of its rotation, from 103.5 percent of normal to 110 then 120, and finally 129.5 percent—the maximum that could be recorded. The prop was on the verge of shearing from its mount and causing great damage. Had this happened, the inevitable outcome would have been a nonsurvivable crash and the death of all aboard.

The pilot, Jerry Grigsby, climbed to slow the prop. At 1,100 feet, however, its speed was still much too high. Then, without warning, the engine burst into flames. The runaway prop was out of control.

The flight engineer, Harold "Butch" Miller, was able to extinguish the blaze with firefighting compound, but the action depleted the limited supply of the compound. There were sure to be other outbreaks, and the situation was grim. They were now 800 miles from Adak, an impossible distance to make in their current state, and 337 miles from the

Air Force station on the island of Shemya—still light-years away for the crippled aircraft.

Anticipating an explosion, Grigsby brought the plane down to 1,000 feet. Then the fire alarm went off again. Miller used the last of the fire-fighting compound to douse the blaze. Grigsby continued to descend, to 500 feet, and they limped toward Shemya.

Anticipating the worst, the crew donned life vests and survival suits. The fire alarms went off again, smoke streamed from the crippled engine, and Matt Gibbons, the flight's tactical coordinator, radioed the plane's co-ordinates and added, "This is five eight six. Out."

With those final words, Grigsby landed the aircraft in the frigid twenty-five-foot swells of the North Pacific. As the plane hit, the right wing came off, fuel tanks ruptured, and the engines exploded in balls of steam. The fuselage cracked open and water flooded in, but the plane was down.

In the jarring crash, many crewmembers had been buried in debris and caught in the wreckage. But the radar man was able to launch two life rafts, one large and one small. Grigsby stayed on the aircraft, counting his crew, until he was certain that everyone had made it off. Then he swam for the large raft.

After repeated efforts, Grigsby failed to reach the raft, and he was lost in the swells. The pilot then tried for the second raft and was within twenty-five feet of it when those aboard threw him his last hope—a rope anchored with an emergency radio. It fell short by a few feet, and Grigsby disappeared from sight.

Four men huddled in the large raft, which was designed to carry twelve, while nine men jammed into the smaller raft, designed to carry seven. The small raft, with no tarpaulin cover, was awash with breaking waves from the freezing ocean. In their desperate attempt to bail with the boat's metallic survival blanket, they inadvertently opened an air valve.

The rafts drifted helplessly in the heavy seas while planes from Shemya searched for survivors. In the bitter cold and rain, the men—sea-sick and in a state of shock—began to lose their alertness and coordination. Finally, one airman in the seven-man boat realized that something was desperately wrong. The raft was deflating, and they were slowly sinking. This startling observation jarred the others from their near-comatose state, and they began a frantic search for the leak. Finally, the loose valve was discovered and closed.

As the hours went by, water entered the torn survival suit of Technician Gary Hemmer, and his eyes began to close. Master Chief Garland Shepard slapped Hemmer's helmet until he regained consciousness. James Brooner, a sonobuoy technician who had gone into the water in an effort to save Grigsby, slowly slid into the water sloshing around in the raft. Soon only his head was visible. Three others pulled him up, talked to him, slapped him, and shook him. But they were all slowly dying.

In this grimmest of moments, the pivotal event occurred. Matt Gibbons and Navigator/Communicator John Ball[15] had been engaged in a gallows humor conversation about their plight. As part of a mock qualifying exam, Gibbons asked Ball to describe the aircraft electrical system. "It's under water," Ball responded. Gibbons shot back, "Qualified!"

The wandering conversation led to a fanciful reminiscence about a wild party at Ohio State University, and the image of John Belushi in a sheet emerged. Then, slowly, the chant started: *To-ga . . . To-ga . . . To-ga . . . To-ga.* Somehow, from the foggy depths of despair, the image of the comedian dressed in a sheet at a fraternity party had entered the consciousness of the survivors. As Ball recalls, "When we were at the lowest point of our morale, chanting, 'Toga, Toga, Toga' became a mantra for our raft."

The chant, feeble at first, grew in strength and rallied the survivors, just as Belushi had rallied his despondent fraternity brothers. This strange combination of humor and determination breathed a last element of life into the group, which was finally rescued by the Soviet fishing vessel *MYS Synyavin.*

In all, five died in the crash. One crewmember went down with the aircraft, three others died of exposure, and the pilot, Jerry Grigsby, was lost at sea. He was later awarded the Distinguished Flying Cross for "extraordinary heroism and professionalism above and beyond the call of duty."

The story does not have a Hollywood ending, but survivors of the crash hosted a reunion twenty-six years later. It was dubbed "26th on the 26th" an allusion to the twenty-sixth anniversary of their ditching on the twenty-sixth of October. Alexandr Alexeevich Arbuzov, captain of the Russian rescue vessel, was an honored guest.

Dennis Mette, navigator/communicator on the first rescue aircraft to reach the scene, described the reunion as "a time of remembrance, and a time to thank rescuers from the Air Force, Coast Guard, and Navy, as well as Captain Arbuzov. This was an event where seamen and airmen from two countries put the Cold War aside to rescue those in peril."[16]

In the end, the ten who survived the crash of *Alfa Foxtrot 586* owe their deliverance to perseverance, the support of their comrades, and—ironically—the humorous spirit of the toga party.

Lessons for Leaders

Humor is one of the most effective leadership tools. The ability to use humor skillfully has served American presidents with political views as disparate as John F. Kennedy and Ronald Reagan. The absence of humor also undermined the effectiveness of Richard Nixon, who often appeared grim or mean-spirited.

The multipurpose nature of humor makes it a sort of leadership Swiss Army knife. Kidding that is truly good-natured—not hurtful—can strengthen interpersonal bonds. A joke can break the monotony of routine work, some of which is inherent in any job. Laughter can create a relaxed atmosphere and stimulate creativity. Humor, even dark humor, can cut through tension, fear, and anxiety.

Herb Kelleher, former CEO of Southwest Airlines, is one leader who understands the power of humor in creating organizational success and bottom-line profitability. In *Nuts! Southwest Airlines' Crazy Recipe for Business and Personal Success*, authors Kevin and Jackie Freiberg outline Kelleher's formula.[17]

The playful attitude he encouraged began with casual clothing, or "fun ware," which was designed to engender a lighthearted perspective. Kelleher himself appeared at meetings dressed as Elvis, General Patton, and Corporal Klinger from the *M*A*S*H* television show.

A tabloid-style internal publication titled *Southwest Airlines Plane Tails* shared stories of employees who had developed innovative solutions to problems, along with humorous, tongue-in-cheek articles. One piece, for example, discussed the nuances of eating Southwest Airlines Peanuts.

A sense of playfulness can permeate an organization, affecting the way employees interact with both customers and one another. The "Southwest Way to a Sense of Humor" included these guidelines:

▶ *Think funny.* Look for the flip side of situations, and make outrageous thoughts fun.

▶ *Adopt a playful attitude.* Stay open to silly or nonconformist thoughts and behaviors.

▶ *Be the first to laugh.* Try to be the first to find humor in stressful situations.

▶ *Laugh with, not at.* Promote healthy, constructive humor.

▶ *Laugh at yourself.* Take work seriously, but not yourself.[18]

In reading this list, I was struck by how well these guidelines fit the norms of the Shackleton expedition. Almost a century later, they still work.

Expedition Log

1. Do you celebrate the major successes and achievements of your team?

2. Do you look for opportunities to celebrate the "small wins" as they occur?

3. How would you characterize the culture of your organization: grim and serious, or playful and spontaneous?

4. Do those you manage feel free to be themselves and to find humor in work situations? If not, what can be done to promote a relaxed atmosphere?

5. Do people joke with others in healthy, constructive ways?

6. When things go wrong, do you use humor to defuse tension?

7. Can you laugh at yourself?

9

Risk

Strategy 9:
Be willing to take the Big Risk.

> . . . Shackleton was (paradoxically enough) an exceedingly cautious
> man. It may sound fantastic to call an Antarctic explorer of his cal-
> iber cautious, but I claim that it was true of him. He was brave, the
> bravest man I have seen, but he was never foolhardy. When necessary
> he would undertake the most dangerous things, and do so fearlessly;
> but always he would approach them in a thoughtful manner and
> perform them in the safest way. He was proud of his reputation for
> carefulness, and therefore, the nickname that he had won on his first
> expedition, that of "Cautious Jack," which tickled him immensely.[1]
> —Frank A. Worsley

I once presented my perspective on leading at *The Edge* to a group of
senior executives in the insurance industry. These executives, many of
whom were actuaries, raised a number of thoughtful questions about this
strategy. Their business, one commented, was not one in which taking
"the Big Risk" is viewed favorably.

Risk taking for its own sake, however, is not the subject of this chapter. Needless risk taking is a form of bravado that endangers organizational
stability, or even lives. Clearly, there are times to stay the course, and there

are situations in which risk should be minimized. Unfortunately, there are also times in which taking what appears to be a safe course is actually a dangerous move. This chapter explores both dimensions of risk.

Never Take an Unnecessary Chance

The very nature of Antarctic exploration involves risk. Nevertheless, Shackleton was incredibly disciplined in his ability to avoid taking unnecessary chances, and there are numerous examples of this restraint.

He severely disapproved of any carelessness that might tempt fate. Soon after the loss of *Endurance*, for example, Macklin and Greenstreet decided to combine seal hunting with a joy ride on a small floe. Poling along merrily, they were as happy as college students punting on the river. Then they sighted the Boss and, like "guilty schoolboys," promptly ended their excursion. When the two returned to the camp, Shackleton's "awful look" made it clear that this was their last bit of reckless horseplay.

Shackleton's caution was tested again and again. By March 9, 1916, the Patience Camp had drifted far enough north that the crew began to feel a slight movement caused by the swells of open water. The motion broke through the apathy that had set in among the crew, who were eager to launch the lifeboats at the earliest opportunity. Two days later, the pack opened up and a large stretch of open water appeared. They prepared to launch the boats, but the Boss hesitated. Something inside him signaled caution, and he gave the order to remain on the floe. He had been wise to trust his intuition, as the ice closed soon after.[2]

The pressure to launch the boats continued to build. It peaked again on March 23, 1916, when the party sighted land—the northernmost point of Antarctica. The expedition had been drifting for five months of claustrophobic monotony, and the thought that they might escape the floe sent shock waves of excitement through the camp. Here was a chance to make a sledge journey that would put them on dry land.

Shackleton and Worsley climbed to the top of a hummock to assess the situation. They scanned the horizon with binoculars, and Worsley posed the question foremost in everyone's mind: Would they attempt to make it across the ice? Worsley describes what happened next:

> [The Boss] did not reply at once, and I could see by his ex-
> pression that he disliked having to say the word that would dis-
> appoint all of us. At length he said shortly: "No . . . I can't risk
> the danger of crossing ice that will be opening and closing rap-
> idly under the influence of the tides and currents between us
> and the land. The boats might get crushed. We might get sepa-
> rated. Many things could happen. But if we keep on as we are
> for another hundred miles or so, we are bound to drift to open
> water, and then we will make for the nearest whaling station."[3]

Shackleton could not foresee the dangers that lay ahead. But he was
sure that, having safely brought the expedition 2,000 miles since they
were first trapped in the ice, he was not going to make an impetuous
move that would risk the expedition.

When a Risk Is Justified, Do Not Hesitate

The landing on Elephant Island had given the crew a brief respite, but it
was only a temporary sanctuary. Anyone searching for the crew of the
Endurance would expect them to be somewhere in the south of the Weddell Sea, far from the expedition's current position, so there was effectively no hope of rescue from Elephant Island.

In addition to this grim fact, there was another, more immediate
problem nagging at Shackleton: their food supply. Clark had managed to
add variety such as limpets to their menu, and Green, the cook, continued to make hot meals, but the hard reality was that the food supply
would not last forever. Worsley recalled:

> . . . [T]he day dawned when Shackleton had to face the fact
> that he would not be able to feed his men through the winter.
> I remember that day. He asked me to walk with him to our
> usual lookout promontory, and there he confided to me his
> ever-growing anxiety. "Skipper," he said, "we shall have to make

that boat journey, however risky it is. I am not going to let the men starve."[4]

This was not a time for wishful thinking about rescue, or for imagining that the food supply would be sufficient to sustain the men. It was a time for carefully calculating the odds, and for having the courage to do what no one had ever done before: risk the 800-mile sail to South Georgia.

It is hardly possible to exaggerate the dangers involved in the boat journey, but Shackleton's logic in choosing this course was impeccable. Sailing in subfreezing temperatures across 800 miles of stormy ocean in an open boat was extremely hazardous, but he reasoned that the venture would add nothing to the risks of the men left on the island. First, there would be six fewer mouths to draw on the limited food supply at Elephant Island. Second, Shackleton planned to take only a small amount of rations—one month's provisions—for the crew of the *James Caird*. He knew that if they had not made South Georgia in one month, they were not going to make it at all.

The Boss balanced the odds and concluded:

> The risk was justified solely by our urgent need of assistance. The ocean south of Cape Horn in the middle of May is known to be the most tempestuous storm-swept area of water in the world. The weather then is unsettled, the skies are dull and overcast, and the gales are almost unceasing. We had to face these conditions in a small and weather-beaten boat, already strained by the work of the months that had passed.[5]

The lifeboat *James Caird*, only twenty-two feet, six inches long, was hardly built for such a voyage. The passage was one of extreme danger and hardship, a constant battle against the seas and the gale-force winds. Those men not on watch sought protection from the bitter cold, but there was no respite. Every part of the small vessel was soaked by the relentless waves.

Space was so cramped that Shackleton had to direct the movement of each man during watch changes to avoid collisions and bruises. Boulders that had been taken for ballast had to be moved constantly to trim the boat, a "weary and painful" task. Their clothes and reindeer-skin sleeping bags were always wet and, as the bags disintegrated, the reindeer hair contaminated their drinking water.

The *James Caird* was often in danger of swamping. The tiny boat took water with each cresting wave, and one man bailed furiously at all times. They were often forced to crawl forward on the decking to chip the ice that was weighting down the boat. Each effort meant a risk of life: If a man had gone over the side, he would have been lost forever.

The ice continued to accumulate and the boat became "more like a log than a boat." To regain buoyancy, they discarded everything not absolutely essential for survival, including spare oars and two of the wet frozen sleeping bags, each of which weighed some forty pounds.

By the sixth day of the journey, each man suffered from frostbite and showed blisters on his hands. They ate, treated their wounds, and prayed for better weather. Good weather meant more than relief from the cold. To navigate accurately, they needed to see the sun. The sky had been so cloudy that they had no way to fix their location.

On the seventh day, the sun eventually came out, and Worsley—hanging on the mainmast with his sextant—was finally able to get a shot at the sun and determine their position. The news was good: They had covered more than 380 miles and were almost halfway to South Georgia. Still, the emergence of the sun showed clearly how tiny the *James Caird* was in the vast ocean. Shackleton recalled:

> So low in the water were we that each succeeding swell cut off our view of the sky-line. We were a tiny speck in the vast vista of the sea. . . . For a moment the consciousness of the forces arrayed against us would be almost overwhelming. Then hope and confidence would rise again as our boat rose to a wave and tossed aside the crest in a sparkling shower. . . .[6]

On the tenth night, Worsley was so cramped from his turn at the helm that he could not straighten his body. He had to be dragged below and massaged until he could crawl into his sleeping bag.

The next day, Shackleton was at the tiller when he saw what he thought was a line of clear sky. As he called out the good news to the others, Shackleton realized he had not seen an opening in the sky. What he had seen was the foam on the crest of a wave—a wave larger than any he had seen in his life.

As Shackleton called out, "For God's sake, hold on!" the wave lifted the boat like a cork. The *James Caird*, half filled with water from the giant wave, was still afloat, but just barely. Fighting for their lives, the men bailed with anything that they could find. Slowly the boat regained its stability, but the voyage had almost ended in disaster.

If conditions had previously been severe, now they were horrible. The food and cooking stove were soaked, and drinking water was running low and was contaminated by salt. With dry mouths and swollen tongues, they strained for a sight of land. Finally, on May 8—fourteen days after their departure from Elephant Island—they sighted the dark cliffs of South Georgia.

They were desperate to land and find water, but the forbidding coast offered no safe haven. Waves broke over the rocky coast and splashed thirty and forty feet into the air. They had no choice but to stand off and search for a better landing point.

As dawn broke the next day, they found themselves being driven onto the shore, which was a sheer wall of rock. In the treacherous seas and hurricane-force winds, the *James Caird* was shipping water heavily. It was agonizing to have come this far and face disaster. Then fate turned. The wind shifted and freed them to maneuver. Shackleton recalled:

> . . . [J]ust when things looked their worst, they changed for the best. I have marveled often at the thin line that divides success from failure and the sudden turn that leads from apparently certain disaster to comparative safety.[7]

As the wind stopped, the pin that held the *Caird*'s mast fell out. If the pin had given way earlier, during the hurricane, the mast would have "snapped like a carrot," and they would have been driven onto the rocks to a certain death. Once more, they searched for a landing point, tired to the point of apathy and dehydrated to the point of death from thirst. Their last water—strained through gauze to separate the liquid from reindeer hair—had long been used.

Finally, on May 10, they found a gap in the reef. Fighting shifting winds, they tacked again and again to hit the opening and, on their fifth try, navigated the narrow opening to the safety of the cove beyond. Shackleton sprang ashore with a line and held the *James Caird* against the outgoing waves. After narrowly escaping a twenty-foot fall to the rocks below, the Boss secured the line and the crew came ashore.

As they stood on the beach, they heard a gurgling sound and turned to see a freshwater stream. They fell to their knees and drank the ice-cold water. They had risked the Southern Ocean, and they had triumphed. At last, they were safe.

In retrospect, Shackleton's decision to leave the ephemeral safety of Elephant Island was the right one. He gambled and he won. But knowing that a risk is called for and actually taking it are two different things. My own experience in Vietnam brought that point home clearly, and one particular day forever shaped my perspective on the issue of risk. Although the events of that day are not happy ones, I will relate them now in the belief that there is significant value to the underlying lesson in the story.

Toward the end of my tour in Vietnam, I was the commanding officer of a Marine rifle company—an infantry unit of about 200 men. My company, India Company, had been given the task of providing security for a convoy of forty vehicles traveling north from the Marine airstrip at Chu Lai to the base at Da Nang.

The distance, about fifty miles, was relatively short, but moving any distance along Route 1 was potentially treacherous. Appropriately named "Rough Riders," convoys traveling along the elevated road were much like moving ducks in an amusement-park shooting gallery. They followed a fixed, predictable route, and they were exposed and vulnerable to enemy fire at numerous points. In addition, much of the road's pavement had been destroyed, creating opportunities for the Viet Cong to plant mines and other explosive devices.

The convoy left Chu Lai early in the morning. Each truck was filled with either cargo or Marines from my company. I was in one of the lead trucks, surrounded by my radio operators and a forest of antennas. We sat on layers of sandbags placed as protection against explosions from mines. Their value was more psychological than real.

Included in the convoy were several armored vehicles, including a peculiar Marine contraption called the *Ontos*. The Ontos, from the Greek word for "thing," had a great deal of firepower but often broke down. In addition to this problem, the Ontos was armed with six recoilless rifles that, when fired, create a dangerous back-blast from the explosion. Nothing can be behind an Ontos in action.

We were escorted by a helicopter gunship that would provide immediate air cover. We also had the capability to call in "fast movers"—jet aircraft that could deliver additional air support in case of significant trouble. In theory, we had a lot of firepower that could balance the odds in case of an ambush.

As with so many days in Vietnam, things started to go wrong early. I had been given the wrong frequency for the gunship, which circled the convoy repeatedly trying to raise us on the radio. Unless we could communicate, the helicopter could not be used, so I had no choice but to stop the convoy until the problem was fixed.

Finally, the exasperated pilot landed the chopper so we could talk in person and straighten out the problem. The incident would have been just another annoyingly comical moment, but the delay had cost time. Time meant losing daylight, and getting caught out in the open at night meant losing the ability to use aircraft effectively—a situation I did not want to think about.

As the convoy moved north, there was another delay at the small town of Tam Ky. The Viet Cong had planted a large mine set to detonate when a very heavy load—such as a military truck or tank—went over it. An unfortunate Vietnamese farmer, in a small truck filled with heavy bags of rice, had detonated the mine. The farmer had been killed and his truck blocked the road until it could be removed.

Throughout the day there were delays at each point in the road where pavement had been destroyed. Each of these sections had to be swept by a combat engineer team using mine detectors. The team, led by Naval Academy classmate Bill Gleeson, used the most sophisticated detectors available to methodically examine every square inch of dirt for buried explosives. The engineers also went into the water to check for wires and explosives that might be planted in culverts. It was a tedious task, but it could not be rushed.

After several hours on the road, I received a radio message that a battalion of the North Vietnamese Army (NVA) was operating in the vicinity, so we should be on the alert. Intelligence reports were frequently wrong, but the warning raised my level of vigilance another notch. It meant that an ambush, if it occurred, would be a serious firefight with the NVA, not a limited skirmish with the Viet Cong.

With all these delays, it was getting to be late in the afternoon, and I was becoming more and more concerned about still being on the road when night fell. Still, there was no way of avoiding the time-consuming process of sweeping for mines. At one stretch of road, the driver of a lead truck refused to move forward—even after the road had been swept. Gleeson waved him across from the far side, but the driver pointed at himself and shook his head, "No." Unconvinced that the road was clear, the driver thought he was being used as a human mine detector. Gleeson walked back to the truck, flashed his signature smile, climbed in beside him, and said, "Let's go!"

The convoy rolled forward and the lead trucks, including mine, passed safely. But as I looked back, a truck exploded in an inferno that instantly killed the two Marines aboard. A mine, fashioned from several hundred pounds of high explosives, had been buried so deep that it could not be detected. It apparently had been "command detonated" by a nearby enemy soldier who was trying to hit my truck, marked with antennas, but he hesitated and hit a vehicle following behind. The delay cost lives and time. The burning truck had to be pushed off the road, and medevac helicopters brought in to take out the casualties.

We cleared the wreckage and the convoy moved on. As we passed through another small village, we were hit by sniper fire and lost another Marine. Another life, another delay, and it continued to get dark.

We finally began picking up speed and made it to a small village about twenty miles from Da Nang. The village sat at the entrance to a long bridge across one of the many rivers in the area. A large wooden gate at the entrance to the bridge controlled traffic movement.

The lead vehicles with the minesweeping team crossed the bridge, and my truck approached the gate. When we were about twenty-five yards away, the gate slammed shut. The village erupted with a series of explosions that was unlike anything I had ever experienced in Vietnam. Hundreds of tracers streaked across the road like strands of a fiery spiderweb.

As soon as the ambush was triggered, the Ontos ahead of my truck turned to return fire. This meant that the road ahead was now blocked by the back-blast from its six recoilless rifles and by the closed gate. We were now caught in the withering fire of the NVA battalion, armed with mortars, rockets, automatic weapons, recoilless rifles, and other heavy weapons. The closed gate and the back-blast had stopped the convoy; the trucks were fixed targets. Marines piled out of the trucks to take cover and return fire.

The sustained din of explosions and small-arms fire was so great that it was impossible to hear someone shouting only a few feet away. I tried to raise the rear of the column on the radio but could hear nothing but the thumping of the .50-caliber machine gun mounted on my truck. As I crouched by my radioman trying to decide what to do next, I came to the sudden, chilling realization that we were in the killing zone.

Every ambush is carefully designed with an area of entrapment appropriately called the "killing zone"—and we were in it. The NVA had driven the civilians out of their homes, and the entire village was now a free-fire zone designed for death. If we stayed where we were, we would all die.

I should have realized this sooner. The immediate action in an ambush situation is to move forward, no matter what. But the blocking of the road by the closed gate and the back-blast of the Ontos had taken me by surprise. In addition, I am sure there was a part of me that wanted to engage, not run, but this was not a time to fight.

I got the Marines back onto the trucks and we broke through the gate. As we approached the bridge, the NVA troops began firing at my truck with a recoilless rifle. If they had hit my lead vehicle, every other truck would have been stopped on the bridge and the situation would have been hopeless.

Then the firing from the recoilless rifle stopped abruptly. I later learned that Gleeson, whose engineer team had made it safely across the river, had risked his life to come back and silence the weapon with a grenade launcher. We moved onto the bridge and were now fully exposed to enemy fire.

Tracers were everywhere, and it seemed impossible that the convoy could make it across the full length of the bridge. There was no choice, however, but to keep moving. As the lead trucks rolled onto the bridge, the rear of the convoy was heavily engaged. The NVA troops were attacking with fixed bayonets prepared for close combat. The last truck in the convoy was on fire, and its wounded driver was rescued only through the courageous efforts of one of my men. He ran back to the truck, threw the driver over his shoulder, and—firing an M-60 machine gun from his hip—carried the driver to safety.

When the convoy reached the far side of the river, we regrouped. Every vehicle was riddled with bullet holes, and two had been destroyed. As I look back, it still seems unbelievable that the company survived the ambush. We reached Da Nang late that night.

I have since thought a great deal about that day. There was great risk for everyone in driving across the open bridge and being directly exposed to the full force of the ambush. The greater risk, though, was standing in place, taking what cover could be found and eventually—inevitably— running out of ammunition and being overrun. In the killing zone, there is only one course of action: *Move, move, move.*

Lessons for Leaders

Henry David Thoreau once said, "A man sits as many risks as he runs." There are times when doing nothing, or making a "safe choice," actually entails greater risks than a bold gamble. Shackleton could have avoided sailing 800 miles across the Scotia Sea, and it is possible that, by some miracle, the expedition would have been rescued. It is far more likely, however, that they all would have suffered slow starvation on Elephant Island.

The situation Shackleton faced was analogous to being caught in the killing zone of an ambush. In both cases, the crucial leadership decision is whether to stay in a deteriorating situation or risk greater immediate danger to reach a position of ultimate safety. Under these circumstances the decision that appears to be the safe choice is often the one that carries with it the greatest risk.

These life-and-death situations, while extreme, are metaphorically similar to those faced by leaders in a number of adverse business situations. In their book *The Profit Zone*, for example, Adrian Slywotzky and David Morrison point out that information technology, global competition, and business design have combined with other forces to create changes in the old economic order. As a result of these changes, market share and volume growth no longer guarantee business success. Yet many managers cling to the illusion of the security they provide. In doing so, they stay pinned down in the "no-profit zone":

> No-profit zones are the black holes of the business universe. In a physical black hole, light waves go in, but never come back out. In an economic black hole, investment dollars go in, but the profit dollars never come back out.[8]

A business that stays caught in the no-profit zone will, like a military unit in the killing zone, meet with disaster. Getting out of the zone requires, first, recognizing the danger and, second, taking the risk of doing things differently—of reinventing the business.

There are some situations in which the economic danger is difficult to ignore. Under these conditions—a losing situation with little hope of a turnaround—it makes sense to take major risks because there is little real alternative. In other instances, risk aversion does not result in disaster, but neither does it create change. Risk takers make things happen.

Randy MacDonald, senior vice president of human resources for IBM, has a reputation for taking big risks that make a real difference. In describing MacDonald, Ted Hoff, human resources vice president of global sales and sales incentives, put it this way: "Randy embodies the ability to take calculated risks!"[9]

MacDonald took such a risk in response to CEO Sam Palmisano's call to make IBM a *Globally Integrated Enterprise*. The challenge facing MacDonald and IBM Human Resources was to develop a system to measure and track the capabilities of each member of its global workforce. Having this information would enable IBM to shift employees to growing markets and be more responsive in deploying talent.[10] To achieve this goal, however, MacDonald would have to fundamentally change the company's approach to human resources management.

MacDonald and his team devised a pioneering program called the *Workplace Management Initiative*.[11] They created a new HR structure, replacing the old siloed arrangement. Instead of grouping by function—for example, benefits, compensation, or diversity—MacDonald formed cross-functional teams of specialists. Each team was then assigned to a specific business unit where functions worked together to ensure that their efforts were aligned with business unit objectives.[12]

With the new HR structure in place, MacDonald set out on the next challenge: inventorying the skills and experience of IBM's 330,000 employees.[13] MacDonald and his team created an assessment taxonomy to catalog expertise and career ambitions.[14] After each employee completed an instrument that encompassed 4,000 skill areas,[15] HR teams reviewed the results of the assessments. With this knowledge, they were able to identify critical skill gaps and ensure that employees' skills were well matched with their assignments. These actions enabled other HR functions, such as workforce development and recruiting, to be carried out more effectively.[16]

Did the *Workplace Management Initiative* bring Palmisano's global vision to life? Although there were some setbacks, the overall conclusion was that the transformation helped IBM's bottom line during difficult economic times. One concrete payoff was optimized labor costs, as IBM was able to redeploy employees to vacant positions requiring a particular skill set. The program also helped IBM recruit the right individuals, an enormous benefit. More difficult to measure, but perhaps most important, the *Workplace Management Initiative* contributed to improved service for IBM clients. Having the right people at the right place and at the right time can make all the difference.

The concept of the *Workforce Management Initiative* was powerfully simple, but execution was massively complex. Not only did it require a $100 million investment, but no organization in the world—not even the U.S. military—had ever attempted such an in-depth assessment of capabilities. The program involved an investment in databases and software applications, and it also demanded something even harder. Each IBM business had to change the way it managed a massive and growing global workforce.

Reflecting on the experience, Ted Hoff underscores the importance of MacDonald's leadership:

> There were language issues, workforce laws, cultural issues, and government-mandated practices. We were on the "bleeding edge," and our success involved teamwork, perseverance, and innovation. We all gave it our best, but the vision and determination all came from Randy.[17]

As the IBM story clearly demonstrates, leaders at *The Edge* need to be comfortable with the discomfort of risk. Unnecessary risks should be avoided, but there are times for bold moves. Understand the risks you face and evaluate them carefully. Then balance risk and return, and have the courage to step up to those calculated risks that are worth taking.

Expedition Log

1. Think about a risk you might take to improve the effectiveness or profitability of your organization. Using the Risk Assessment Matrix (see Figure 9-1), list the best- and worst-case outcomes you anticipate. What does this analysis tell you about whether or not to take the risk?

2. Is your assessment of the risks involved consistent with the views of others on your team?

3. If you are anticipating taking a significant risk, have you developed a plan for communicating this risk to others? Have you made a compelling, logical case that will facilitate understanding and commitment?

4. Is there a risk you might take to improve your own effectiveness as a leader? Use the Risk Assessment Matrix again, writing out the best- and worst-case outcomes, to analyze this opportunity.

Figure 9-1. Risk Assessment Matrix.

	Best Case	Worst Case
Do It! Take the Risk		
Don't Do It! Don't Take the Risk		

10

Tenacious Creativity

Strategy 10:
Never give up—there's always another move.

> Without a sea anchor, the boat bobbed and squirmed and shipped
> plenty of green water. The compass glass was broken, but repaired
> with sticking plaster from the medicine chest.[1]
> —Frank A. Worsley

F inding creative solutions to daunting problems is a difficult task under
the best of circumstances. It is even more challenging at *The Edge*.
Fear, physical exhaustion, and psychological weariness are integral parts of
the journey faced by those at the limits of survival—or by organizations
striving to achieve the highest possible levels of performance. Yet it is
precisely in these stressful situations that the ability to solve problems becomes most critical and that the need for innovation is the greatest. This
chapter explores tactics for approaching this formidable challenge.

Encourage Relentless Creativity at *The Edge*

The survival accounts in this book have emphasized teamwork under adversity. Self-leadership, however, is an important element in leading others, and there are numerous accounts of individuals who have demonstrated exceptional resourcefulness. One of the most colorful stories I have encountered involved a Texan who was bitten by a poisonous coral snake. He saved himself by biting off the snake's head, slitting its body lengthwise, and using the skin for a tourniquet until help arrived.

Less bizarre than the coral snake story, the adventure of Steven Callahan is an individual journey that exemplifies tenacious creativity in the face of enormous challenge. Callahan was sailing his small sloop, the *Napoleon Solo*, from the Canary Islands bound for the Caribbean when the boat sank during a heavy gale. Apparently rammed by a whale, the *Solo* went under in a matter of minutes. Callahan escaped in a small inflatable raft, the *Rubber Ducky III*, and embarked on a remarkable 1,800-mile journey that lasted seventy-six days.[2]

Each day of the ordeal that followed was a continuing fight for survival. The solar stills intended to produce freshwater malfunctioned. Sharks attacked the small, five-and-a-half-foot raft, rubbing their backs against the floor and biting at the ballast pockets underneath. Ship after ship—nine in all—passed by without seeing the sailor in distress.

Short of water and slowly starving to death, Callahan finally managed to spear a triggerfish, and its nourishment brought him back to life. His equipment continued to deteriorate, however, and waves crashed into the small craft. Every day was a delicate balancing act:

> I must work harder and longer each day to weave a world in which I can live. Survival is the play and I want the leading role. The script sounds simple enough: hang on, ration food and water, fish, and tend the still. But each little nuance of my role takes on profound significance. If I keep watch too closely, I will tire and be no good for fishing, tending the still, or other essential tasks. Yet at every moment that I don't have my eyes on the horizon is a moment when a ship may pass me. If I use both stills now, I may be able to quench my thirst and be in better shape for keeping watch and doing jobs, but if they both wear out I will die of thirst. . . . It is a constant struggle to keep control, self-discipline, to maintain a course of action that will best

ensure survival, because I can't be sure what the course is . . . all
I can tell myself is, "You're doing the best you can."[3]

On day twenty-three, Callahan lost the power strap to his speargun
while attempting to capture a dorado, a powerful fish that reaches sixty
pounds. This one, skewered in the tail, thrashed through the water dragging the raft until it finally broke free.

The speargun was Callahan's only means of gathering food and was
thus essential to his survival. Lashing the arrow to the shaft with cod line,
he created a jerry-rigged weapon now powered only by his arms. This
new limitation demanded what seemed like endless, motionless waiting—
like "an ancient bronze statue of a bowless archer"—until his prey reappeared.

Lacking sugars, starches, and vitamins, Callahan's body withered. Salt-
water sores began as small boils and soon burst, leaving dozens of open
sores. Remarkably, he forced himself to perform yoga exercises in the
early morning, at dusk, and at night. The routine was slow and painful: It
took an hour and a half to do what could normally be accomplished in
a half hour. Through sheer force of will, however, he did what he could
to maintain his strength.

After forty days at sea, Callahan noted ironically that he had reached
the maximum amount of time that his raft was guaranteed by the man-
ufacturer. Nevertheless, he had cause for celebration. Callahan estimated
that he had, by that time, drifted more than halfway toward the Caribbean.
He had also managed to seal the leaking distillation stills and—by acting
as a "human bellows"—to keep them inflated. He had also improved his
rainwater collection system. Callahan used the awl of his knife—a Cub
Scout model he had found when he was twelve—to bore holes in a Tup-
perware box he mounted on top of the raft.

His situation was momentarily stabilized, but disaster struck again on
day forty-three. A speared dorado ran the sharp tip of the spear into the
lower tube of the raft, creating a gaping hole four inches long. Huge air
bubbles rushed through the hole until the tube was completely deflated.
The *Rubber Ducky*, now kept afloat only by her top tube, floated a mere
three inches above the water.

Callahan's life now depended on repairing the lower tube. If he failed, he would not be able to spear fish, and even if he caught them, he could not dry them for food. Sleep would be impossible, and his legs would hang down as the lowest point on the craft. Harassing sharks would now attack his legs rather than the ballast tubes.

The plugs from the raft repair kit were useless—they were much too small. Thinking quickly, Callahan looked at the gaping hole in the raft as if it were an open mouth. Into the mouth he stuffed a "tongue" made of part of a foam cushion salvaged from the *Solo*. Holding the torn edges of the raft, he wrapped light line around the foam until he had created a seal.

This first effort was only a momentary success. Fifteen minutes after it was inflated, the tube was flat again. Callahan tried for five hours to fill the gaps in the seal, but it was still leaking badly. He calculated that 3,000 pumps a day would be required to keep the raft afloat. That amounted to about two hours of strenuous exercise—far more than he could manage.

For eight days, Callahan tried to patch the leak. It had to be repaired if he were to survive. As calmly as possible, he thought the problem through:

> You've got to come up with something. . . . Go back. Identify
> the problem . . . lashings working off. I have to keep them on.
> What equipment have I got? Space blanket, flare gun, useless
> lighter, plastic bag. . . . What else have I got? First aid kit, band-
> ages, scissors, twine, and line. And the stuff I've already used—
> spoon, fork, radar refl . . . The fork! Of course, why you stupid
> bloody idiot! "It's the fork!"[4]

Energized by the hope that the fork would provide the answer, Callahan lay awake all night planning the repair. When morning came, he carefully broke the tines off the fork and inserted the fork handle through the foam tongue. Then he rewrapped the plug with lines of various sizes to create a makeshift tourniquet that sealed the leak.

In his weakened condition, Callahan was forced to rest between each stage of the operation. It was midafternoon before the repair was completed and he could begin pumping. What would normally have been a five-minute job took a half hour. After the exhausting work of pumping, the tube finally inflated, but not for long: In an hour and a half, the air was gone.

Depressed but determined, Callahan tried once more. Tightening the tourniquet and adding a second, he again painfully inflated the bottom tube. This time it worked:

> *Ducky* gorges on air, picks herself up out of the water, and drifts forward again like a lily pad cut free from its roots. . . . Twelve glorious hours pass before *Ducky* needs another feeding. . . . My body hungers, thirsts, and is in constant pain. But I feel great! I have finally succeeded![5]

The raft continued to drift—slowly, but inexorably—westward toward the Caribbean. Each day presented new problems and renewed demands for improvisation. Callahan devised a water-collection cape from part of his space blanket. He scraped the sticky gum from the back of repair tape to create a goop that would plug a hole in the solar still. He lashed three pencils together to make a "low-budget" sextant that allowed him to determine his latitude.

Sharks continued to harass the boat, and replenishing his food supply was a daily challenge. His spear, damaged by the thrashing of the dorados, needed constant repair. During one ferocious battle, a fish unscrewed the point and swam away.

Callahan repaired the tip with a thin knife from a Boy Scout utensil kit made of flat stainless steel. But the tip bent too easily, so he contrived a new spear tip by lashing the butter knife together with another small knife he had salvaged from the *Solo*. Both were weak, but together they provided enough strength to spear a fish when thrust at just the right angle.

The restricted diet and exposure continued to take their toll on him, but Callahan's creativity enabled him to adjust to his surroundings:

> By now the habitat in which I live, Duckyville, has become a neighborly suburb. The fish and I are so familiar I can chat with them individually . . . I recognize a dorado's nudge, a trigger's

peck, or a shark's scrape the way you recognize different neighbors' knocks on the back door. Often I know which individual fish is whacking the raft with its tail or butting it with its head. . . .[6]

On day seventy-five of the journey, Callahan sighted a soft glow of light, first to the south, then to the north. Then a beam of light swept the horizon—a lighthouse! Dancing up and down in the small confines of the raft, he hugged an invisible companion, shouting, "Land! Land ho!"

On the following day, a small white boat carrying three astounded fishermen sighted the *Rubber Ducky III*. After being hauled on board the rescue craft, Callahan calmly opened his water tins and drank five pints of hoarded water. He was soon safe ashore on the island of Marie Galante, near Guadeloupe. Through determination, creativity, and force of will, he became the only person in history to have survived more than a month at sea in an inflatable raft.

Draw on the Creativity of the Team

Although Shackleton's journey was of longer duration than Callahan's, the crew of *Endurance* had an advantage: Its members were able to draw from each other. This support and creativity enabled them to persist when, individually, each might have given up. The story of the Imperial Trans-Antarctic expedition is replete with examples of tenacity, and it is impossible to look back over the journey and not be impressed by the remarkable resilience and dogged perseverance of the crew.

At each critical point in the journey, the crew could have given up—when *Endurance* was crushed; when the two sledge marches failed; when they found themselves marooned on Elephant Island; when they faced the glaciers of South Georgia; and when repeated attempts to rescue the castaways had failed. Each time, however, the party persisted and its members eventually found their way to safety.

The expedition's ability to reach safety was due to more than simple persistence. The success of Shackleton's crew also depended on the ability to stand in the face of death and think creatively about potential solutions. Interestingly, many of these out-of-the-box ideas came from the photographer, Frank Hurley, and the carpenter, McNeish, both of whom Shackleton had labeled as potential troublemakers.

As Shackleton contemplated taking the fragile *James Caird* through the roaring waves and gale-force winds of the Drake Passage, he called on McNeish to make the boat more seaworthy. McNeish fashioned a makeshift decking of canvas, lids of cases for equipment and supplies, and four sled runners that had been saved for overland travel.

The canvas was frozen stiff and had to be thawed out over the blubber stove before it could be sewn, nailed, and screwed into position. The nails were salvaged from packing cases, another improvisation. They were a bit short, but they did the job. Although the result was not pretty, the *James Caird* could never have survived the voyage without it.

Another invaluable tool was the bilge pump that Hurley had made from the Flinders bar used to adjust the ship's compass. This iron cylinder, moving in a brass tube, was exactly what was needed to create a pumping action, but no one—other than Hurley—saw the connection.[7]

It was not surprising that Hurley was the one to come up with the idea. He was an experienced metalworker, but he also had a record of ingenuity. He had earlier, for example, constructed a superb camp stove out of the ash chute from the wreckage of *Endurance*. Since most of his tools had been lost, he had chipped the quarter-inch steel with a blunt chisel.[8]

As the *James Caird* made its way through heavy seas, the compass glass was broken. Because the instrument was critical for navigation, the loss of this essential navigational tool was potentially devastating. The problem was solved, however, with sticking plaster from the medicine chest.

The crew responded with creativity in the face of adversity throughout the remainder of the journey. After the *Caird* had arrived safely at South Georgia, Shackleton and his crew were still some 150 miles by sea from the safety of the whaling station at Stromness. Because of the condition of the boat, and the weakened state of several of the men, there was little alternative but to attempt an overland crossing of the island.

Shackleton believed that they could shorten the journey by sailing farther up bay, but the *Caird* had lost its rudder in the surf. So they contrived another rudder with an oar that had survived the passage. As they launched the *James Caird* once more, the lost rudder miraculously appeared floating in the water—a sign they all took as a good omen.

When the men reached their point of departure for the overland journey, they had to contend with the fact that they were wholly unprepared for a climbing expedition. Once again, McNeish's inventiveness came in handy. The carpenter removed screws from the *Caird* and put eight in each boot, point down. The makeshift crampons were especially important for Shackleton. With characteristic generosity, he had given away his heavy Burberry boots and was now wearing a light leather pair in poor condition. Shackleton's rule, as cited by Worsley, was "that deprivation should be felt by himself before anyone else."[9]

Shackleton, Worsley, and Crean began the assault of South Georgia on Friday, May 19, 1916, at 3:00 A.M. To minimize the pain of separation from the others, the crossing party left quickly and moved out with a minimum of equipment: two compasses, fifty feet of rope, and a carpenter's adze that would have to substitute for an ice axe. The only map they had was incomplete and showed no details of the mountains.

Traveling by moonlight, they sloshed through knee-deep snow, skirting precipices that fell hundreds of feet into blackness. The terrain was confusing in the darkness, and they often had to backtrack. Retracing their steps was exhausting and demoralizing.

At one point, they encountered a deep pit in the ice, as though made by a huge meteorite. In the fog, each feared the other had fallen into the gaping hole. Thereafter, they roped themselves together to ward off such a tragedy.

Meals were eaten while perched precariously in the snow, each man taking turns using his body to shield the Primus stove and prevent it from blowing out. When the rations were warm, they took turns scooping out a spoonful of the life-giving food. The good-natured banter that had become so much a part of the life of the expedition continued: Shackleton accused Crean of having a bigger spoon, and Crean accused Worsley of having a bigger mouth.

As the journey continued, the weary team explored one pass after another, never knowing quite what was on the other side until they reached the summit. Each time, they found themselves blocked by impassable chasms and were forced to retreat over hard-won terrain. These return trips, made in bitter cold, were horribly discouraging. After they unsuccessfully attempted to negotiate three passes, only one more remained. As they struggled to this fourth and last pass, heavy fog rolled in from the sea. It obscured everything around them and was so heavy that the climbers had difficulty seeing each other.

Their position was truly desperate. As they sat perched at the top of the fourth pass, some 4,500 feet high on the glacier, fog had cut off their retreat, and darkness cloaked the way forward. It was a steep descent, but how steep? If they waited for moonlight, they would freeze to death. Even with light, the tedious process of cutting steps with the adze would still take too long. It had taken them a half hour to descend a hundred yards, and they had thousands of feet to go.

They needed a creative solution, a way out. Sitting on a large step he had cut out on the mountain, Shackleton thought for a moment and then said:

> I've got an idea. We must go on, no matter what is below. To try to do it this way is hopeless. We can't cut steps down thousands of feet. . . . It's a devil of a risk, but we've got to take it. We'll slide.[10]

The prospect of sliding down the steep slope into uncertainty was indeed daunting. Anything that lay in their path—a rock, a crevasse, anything at all—would have meant the end. Yet this was the only hope for them, and for their shipmates waiting on Elephant Island. Worsley recalled thinking that "if we were killed, at least we had done everything in our power to bring help to our shipmates." Then he recounted what happened next:

> We each coiled our share of the rope until it made a pad on which we could sit to make our glissade from the mountaintop. We hurried as much as possible, being anxious to get through the ordeal. Shackleton sat on the large step he had carved, and I sat behind him, straddled my legs round him and clasped him

round the neck. Crean did the same with me, so that we were locked together as one man. Then Shackleton kicked off.

We seemed to shoot into space. For a moment my hair fairly stood on end. Then quite suddenly I felt a glow, and knew that I was grinning! I was actually enjoying it. It was most exhilarating. We were shooting down the side of an almost precipitous mountain at nearly a mile a minute. I yelled with excitement, and found that Shackleton and Crean were yelling too. . . . To hell with the rocks![11]

Whether Shackleton and Crean shared Worsley's excitement, or whether they were yelling out of sheer terror, is not entirely clear. When they reached the bottom of the steep slope, they all shook hands and the Boss remarked, "It's not good to do that kind of thing too often."

Nevertheless, they had successfully tobogganed some 1,500 feet down the mountain without crashing into a rock or creating an avalanche. The slide, which had taken about three minutes, provided a creative alternative to freezing to death on the mountain. And it embodied the spirit of Strategy 9 (Be willing to take the Big Risk) and Strategy 10 (Never give up—there's always another move).

This was not, however, the last time they would need to be creative on the journey across South Georgia. As they neared the whaling station, the trio once more found itself in a precarious position on a nearly vertical ice precipice. Again, they attempted to cut steps with the adze, and again the process was too slow. The threat of a blizzard loomed large, and had they been exposed to gale-force winds on the open mountain, they would have been carried into the void.

In this untenable position, able neither to walk nor crawl, Shackleton made a discovery: The slippery ice was, in fact, covering a layer of snow that had been deposited by the winds. As Shackleton negotiated the descent, the possibility occurred to him that the heel of his boot could be used to smash through the ice crust, thereby forming a small step. He tried it, and it worked! The others followed suit, and the three weary climbers descended the mountain, literally walking on their backs!

With the factories and ships of the whaling station in sight, the exhausted travelers shouted and waved, but they were much too far away to be heard. As they stumbled onward, one last obstacle emerged: A glacial waterfall blocked their path. With nothing to secure the rope, Worsley held the line fast while Shackleton and Crean slid down the waterfall. Wedging the frayed rope into the rocks and holding his breath, Worsley followed. The rope was left dangling in the waterfall.

At 3:00 P.M. on May 20, 1916, the three exhausted explorers reached the whaling station at Stromness. Halting only to eat, and with no map to guide them, they had crossed the uncharted glaciers of South Georgia in thirty-six hours.

The men walked up to the station manager, Thoralf Srlle, who stared at the disheveled trio with disbelief. Srlle, who knew Shackleton as a friend, found him unrecognizable. "Don't you know me?" Shackleton asked. "I know your voice," the station manager replied. "My name is Shackleton," the Boss responded.[12]

It is said that Srlle turned away with tears in his eyes. And at that, the three grimy, bearded "ruffians" were welcomed inside to food, hot baths, and clean clothes. Their heroic journey across South Georgia had saved their shipmates. It remains a tribute to unremitting effort—and to tenacious creativity at *The Edge*.

Lessons for Leaders

Chapter 3 stressed the importance of maintaining an optimistic attitude when leading organizations in challenging situations. But having an optimistic outlook does not mean creating rosy, unrealistic expectations of smooth sailing. Optimism at *The Edge* means believing that somehow, someway, the team will succeed—in the long run. In the short run, however, problems are inevitable.

It is somewhat paradoxical that, in everyday life, we are seldom surprised when things go wrong. Keys are lost, cars do not start, people forget appointments, and computers crash. But when organizations are at *The Edge*, these expectations can change. I have seen leaders become furious at the small problems and "normal accidents" that inevitably occur when people and machines are stretched to the limits.

Rather than expecting things to go right, successful leaders under these conditions should be prepared for things to go wrong. In fact, when at *The Edge*, a realistic expectation is that things will go wrong with greater frequency and magnitude than ever before. Once this reality is accepted, daunting problems become a normal part of the journey. Then the leadership challenge becomes one of mobilizing the collective creativity of the team to find a solution.

Steven Callahan's journey in *Rubber Ducky III* took him 1,800 miles in the course of seventy-six days. Shackleton's open boat journey in the *James Caird* lasted sixteen days, and he sailed over 800 miles. Chesley B. "Sully" Sullenberger's journey was different. It lasted a total of six minutes, and he landed in the same city from which he departed. But all three stories share the same fundamental theme.

When Sullenberger, Captain of US Airways Flight 1549, took off from LaGuardia, he had no thought of becoming a national hero. Two minutes later, he had embarked on a journey to save the lives of his crew and 150 passengers when a "double bird strike" disabled both engines. It was, as Sully recalled, like the worst thunderstorm he'd ever heard growing up in Texas.[13]

A flock of Canada geese engulfed the plane. Some crashed into the windscreen; others were sucked into the impeller blades of the jet engines. Sully felt the impact, heard the thump, and finally smelled the odor of the birds crippling the engines.

The Airbus 320 lost all thrust at low altitude, low speed, and over one of the most densely populated cities in the world. The aircraft stopped climbing and began to stall. It was a shocking, horrifying situation. Everyone aboard could die in a matter of seconds.

Sully recovered from the shock of the strike and began the protocol for transferring control of the aircraft. He spoke to First Officer Jeff Skiles sitting beside him and said, simply, "My aircraft." "Your aircraft," came the response. Sully was now flying the airplane.

Sully's career had spanned forty-two years. He had flown Air Force fighters and gliders. He was an experienced pilot. But Sullenberger knew that this flight, and the landing, was going to be like nothing he had ever seen before. He was now flying a seventy-ton jet engine glider.

Thirty seconds after the engine failure, the aircraft—call sign "Cactus 1549"—was at 3,000 feet and Sully was furiously running through the options as he alerted air traffic control of their situation: "This is Cactus 1539, hit birds, we lost thrust in both engines. We're turning back towards LaGuardia."[14]

On the ground at LaGuardia, Air Traffic Controller Patrick Harten was hyperfocused. He had dealt with a dozen or so emergencies over his ten-year career but this was his first aircraft with zero thrust.[15] He knew the odds, but he spoke calmly: "OK, yeah, you need to return to La-Guardia. Turn left, heading of two-two-zero."

Sully responded with equal composure, "Two-two-zero." But his mind was racing. Making it back to LaGuardia would mean banking the aircraft to turn, then more banking to line up with the runway. Each maneuver would increase the risk of a stall or spin. It might be theoretically possible, but there is a reason that pilots call an attempt to turn back after engine failure "the impossible turn." In trying to reach the LaGuardia runway, he could kill everyone on the airplane. People on the ground could die as well.

Harten thought quickly. Maybe LaGuardia runway 1-3 would work. "Cactus 1529, if we can get it to you, do you want to try to land runway 1-3?" Sully responded, "We're unable. We may end up in the Hudson."

Thirty-five seconds had elapsed since the report of the bird strike. Sully was now both flying the plane and working the radio, while Skiles tried to restart the engine. The aircraft was losing altitude rapidly. Sully needed another option, and Harten continued the search for an answer: "Alright, Cactus 1549, it's going to be left traffic to runway 3-1."

"Unable."

"OK, what do you need to land?" Harten got no response. "Cactus 1549, runway 4 is available if you want to make left traffic to runway 4?" The tone of his question was relaxed and conversational, almost as if he were asking Sully which table he wanted at a restaurant. But Harten was anything but relaxed.

Sully discarded the option of LaGuardia but saw another possibility: "I'm not sure we can make any runway. What's over to our right? Anything in New Jersey? Maybe Teterboro?"

"OK, yeah off to your right side is Teterboro Airport. Do you want to try to go to Teterboro?"

"Yes."

Harten had worked with Teterboro before. He quickly coordinated with their controllers, clearing runway 1 for an emergency landing. Runway 1 was the best option: It meant that Cactus 1549 would be landing into the wind, adding lift to the crippled aircraft. Harten radioed Sully: "Turn right two-eight-zero. You can land runway 1 at Teterboro."

"We can't do it."

"OK, which runway would you like at Teterboro?"

"We're going to be in the Hudson."

It had been one minute and fifty-two seconds since the report of the bird strike. Sully had now concluded that the only viable option was a smooth, level place large enough to land an airliner. And that place was going to be the Hudson River.

"I'm sorry, say again Cactus?" Silence. "Cactus, uh, Cactus 1549, radar contact is lost. You also got Newark Airport off your 2 o'clock and about seven miles." No response. Another pilot answered for Sully: "I don't know, I think he said he was going in the Hudson."

Harten tried one more time: "Cactus 1529, you still on?" Sully's radio was on, but he was no longer trying to land on a runway. He was focused on avoiding the fate of an Ethiopian airliner that landed in the Indian Ocean in 1996. The aircraft had broken into pieces, killing most of the passengers on board.

Avoiding a similar tragedy would not be easy. Sully needed to touch down with the wings exactly level, and with the nose slightly up. The descent rate had to be survivable—just above the minimum flying speed but not below it. And all of these things needed to happen simultaneously.

Sully scanned the water, glimpsing boats at the south end of the river. He had been trained to ditch in the water near boats, facilitating rescue, and that's where the airplane was headed. Training and luck were converging, but Sully had to force himself to be calm. He had to concentrate.

Ninety seconds before they hit the water, Sully spoke three words over the intercom: "Brace for impact." Ninety seconds. Long enough to let the flight attendants prepare, but short enough to minimize the agony of terrified passengers.

Seconds after Sully's announcement, the flight attendants began their commands in unison. Over and over again, he could hear them shouting: "Heads down. Stay down. Heads down. Stay down. Heads down. . . ." Almost a prayer chant, their words comforted Sully. He knew that if he could land the aircraft, the flight attendants could get the passengers out.

They hit the water. It was a hard but smooth landing, and Cactus 1549 slid along the surface of the river. The nose came down, and they started to slow. The aircraft turned slightly to the left and then it stopped. Sully and Skiles looked at each other: "Well, that wasn't as bad as I thought."

It was a heroic, almost comedic moment reminiscent of Shackleton's remark after his slide down the glacier. Had Shackleton been on the airplane, his comment would have been appropriate: "It's not good to do that kind of thing too often."

It had been six minutes from takeoff to landing, and the plane had ditched without breaking up. But there was no time to savor the moment: The pilots and crew now shifted their focus to the challenge of getting everyone out of the aircraft alive.

The evacuation was—in view of the circumstances—relatively orderly at the front, where two flight attendants opened the cabin doors and deployed the slides. At the rear, things were different. The impact had been far more violent and the exits were below the river. As icy water filled the cabin, a terrified passenger opened the rear door and more water rushed into the aircraft.

Flight Attendant Doreen Welsh, who had gone from accepting death to seeing life, focused on getting people out, shouting at passengers to climb over the seats. At the end, Sully walked the aisle twice looking for passengers to make sure everyone was safely out before abandoning the aircraft.

Rescue boats were on the scene almost immediately. It took Firefighter Tom Sullivan, Captain Richard Johnson, and Helmsman John Rizzo five minutes to cover forty blocks in their fast response boat,

Marine 1 Alpha. Sullivan threw life preservers to passengers huddled on the partly submerged wing of the aircraft. He helped women and children first, then others without life jackets. Beverly Waters, the first person Sullivan rescued, recalled being pulled up "like it was nothing for him."[16]

The crew of *Marine 1 Alpha* rescued twenty passengers, leaving them at a triage center at the Circle Line terminal. In keeping with the spirit of New York and its firefighters, Sullivan looked at the survivors and wise-cracked, "Welcome to New York."[17]

All 150 passengers and five crew members were rescued in what has come to be known as the "Miracle on the Hudson." It was, in many ways, a miracle. And people did pray. Asked later if he had prayed, Captain Sullenberger said that he had not. He had concentrated on flying the aircraft, confident that people in the back were taking care of that job.

The Miracle on the Hudson may have been guided by divine intervention, but ultimate success demanded exceptional leadership and teamwork. The pilots, flight attendants, air traffic controllers, and rescue workers embodied the spirit of Strategy 10: Never give up—there's always another move. In Sully's words:

> During every minute of the flight, I was confident I could solve the next problem. My first officer, Jeff Skiles, and I did what airline pilots do: we followed our training, and our philosophy of life. We valued every life on that airplane and knew it was our responsibility to try to save each one, in spite of the sudden and complete failure of our aircraft. We never gave up.
>
> Having a plan enabled us to keep our hope alive. Perhaps in a similar fashion, people who are in their own personal crises—a pink slip, a foreclosure—can be reminded that no matter how dire the circumstance, or how little time you have to deal with it, further action is always possible. There's always a way out of even the tightest spot. You can survive.[18]

The tenacious creativity exemplified by Shackleton and Sully requires recognizing what works and what doesn't. When a strategy fails, acknowledge it and find another one. When the obvious moves are exhausted, keep looking for new ones. Do not dismiss any idea, no matter how far-fetched, without thoroughly considering it. Think the unthinkable, and encourage others to do so as well. The unshakable belief that there is always another move will give you the energy to search for solutions, and creativity will give you the ability to find them.

Expedition Log

1. How would you characterize your core beliefs about problems and obstacles? Do they always come as unpleasant surprises, or do you expect them to occur?

2. What are your typical reactions when things go wrong? What is your tolerance level for potentially frustrating events?

3. Do you have a systematic process for identifying problems and finding solutions? Do you involve all members of the team—including your "troublemakers"—in a search for creative solutions?

4. What are the breakthroughs that would need to occur for you and your organization to reach *The Edge*? Have you demonstrated tenacious creativity in making them happen? What other moves would enable your expedition to reach its full potential?

PART TWO

Continuing Your Expedition

11

Learning to Lead at
The Edge

It's never too late to be what you might have been.

—George Eliot

The ten strategies outlined in Part One of this book provide a roadmap for leaders who want to take their organizations to *The Edge*—to help them achieve their greatest potential. This chapter focuses on the personal dimension of the journey—the behaviors, attitudes, and ways of thinking about life that help individuals to realize their full potential as leaders. Specifically, it outlines a number of qualities and actions that—in my experience—contribute to living, learning, and thriving at *The Edge*.

Cultivate Poised Incompetence

When my son, Jonathan, turned sixteen, he got his own car, a Toyota Celica that was in good condition for a vehicle with about 90,000 miles on the odometer. Trying to be a good father, I spent a lot of time going over the importance of car maintenance, trying to remember everything *my* father told me to do.

Each parent stresses certain lessons or tasks as if they are the most important in the world. For my mother, it was choosing exactly the right word and pronouncing words exactly the way they were supposed to be pronounced. For my father, one of the central tasks in life was checking the engine oil and keeping an eye on the dipstick.

I was not as religious about watching the oil as my dad, but in an effort to be a good parent, I did my best to pass on the tradition to Jonathan. As a result, my son put all his teenage energy into getting the Celica into shape: washing; waxing; scraping off rust; dabbing on touch-up paint; and, most important of all, watching the oil.

Jonathan watched the dipstick like a hawk, waiting for his big moment to add oil. When the time finally came, I was inside playing my guitar. Jonathan came in, brimming with excitement, and asked for a funnel. I went out to the garage, got him one, and then went back to playing.

A little while later, he came in and said, "Dad, this one's too big. I need a smaller funnel." So I went out to the garage a second time and got another funnel, saying, "This should do it. It's the smallest I have." It never occurred to me to ask why he needed such a small funnel.

After a while, I went outside to see how he was doing. He had an extremely frustrated expression on his face. "What's the problem?" I asked.

He pointed at the engine. I looked down and saw an extraordinary creation. It was a marvel of mechanical engineering. Jonathan had taken a roll of duct tape and attached a piece of glass tubing from his chemistry set to my small funnel. With this contraption, he was pouring oil . . . can you guess where? He wasn't pouring it into the normal hole on top of the engine, but into the hole for the dipstick, which is about the size of a pencil. He said, "Dad, this is taking forever!" And it probably would have.

When I showed him the two-inch hole over the manifold that most people use to add oil, it came as quite a revelation. The story did have a happy ending. We finished the job in about three minutes, and we still laugh about Jonathan and the dipstick.

What's the point of this story? Leaving aside my limitations as an auto mechanics coach, I can think of two. One is that—in the spirit of Strategy 10 ("Never give up")—with enough creativity and determination, you can accomplish the mission even if your strategy is not perfect.

Jonathan was getting oil into the engine, even if it was taking him a while to do it.

A second point is that developing any skill is a journey that starts at the beginning with a certain level of ignorance and incompetence. When we look at people who are exceptional at their craft, we often think they were born with that knowledge. One of the interesting aspects about getting older is that you find that some of your friends actually make it to positions of real responsibility—and you knew them when.

Two of my Naval Academy classmates fit this description. John Dalton became the Secretary of the Navy, and Chuck Krulak became the Commandant of the Marine Corps. Both were talented individuals who showed early promise. But when I saw them at the Pentagon, thirty years after graduation, with everyone saluting, I did a double-take. I knew them both from plebe year at Annapolis, when we were first learning how to spit-shine our shoes, and before they had distinguished themselves as exceptional leaders.

In doing research on Shackleton's life, I discovered, to my amazement, that before his first trip to the South Pole he had never pitched a tent, he had never slept in a sleeping bag, he had never slept in a tent overnight, and he had never lit a Primus stove. He had never done any of these basic tasks and yet, eventually, he developed the skills to lead an expedition that would triumph over overwhelming obstacles in the most hostile environment on earth.

I do not recommend going to Antarctica without knowing how to set up a tent. I do know, however, that we all have to start somewhere. The first key to learning to lead at *The Edge* is this: Cultivate poised incompetence. You have to be willing to be incompetent in order to learn. Just because you don't know what you are doing doesn't mean you have to be embarrassed or upset or convinced something's wrong with you.

There are countless stories of people who moved from incompetence to great proficiency: The Red Baron crashed on his first solo landing; Michael Jordan was cut from his high school basketball team; and in the beginning of his administration, Abraham Lincoln was seen as an equivocating, mediocre president.

To achieve the ultimate level of skill in any profession—particularly the profession of leadership—means accepting a level of incompetence. It also means continually raising the bar and learning the next task while maintaining a sense of poise, grace, and good humor.

Learn to Love the Plateau

I once had an opportunity to spend some time with a writer and martial arts expert named George Leonard, and I was impressed by many of his ideas. Leonard, who has studied the topic of mastery, argues that a basic ingredient in the process involves a willingness to live in that most dreaded of all places—the plateau, the level place in the learning process.[1]

Our culture places tremendous emphasis on instant gratification, quick fixes, and sound bites. We are busy people, and we do not have time for things that take time. In fact, there is no higher compliment than being called a "quick study." I actually saw an infomercial for a videotape called *Become a Zen Master in Thirty Minutes.* Presumably, for $29.95 and a half hour of your time, you can compete with the Dalai Lama for enlightenment!

In this culture of ever-increasing clock speed, if events do not move quickly, we are easily convinced that something is seriously wrong. What's taking this plant so long to grow? Let's pull it up and see what the problem is.

The truth is that some things do not happen overnight. Yes, there can be spurts of learning, but they often occur after extended periods of practice in that flat place, the plateau. Whether you are learning a martial art or learning to be a leader, you need to develop the patience to stay in that frustrating place when there are no immediate signs of progress.

Now, there are many ways of being on the plateau. You can kick back and coast. You can tune out and pretend it does not exist. Or you can embrace the plateau with the same focus, energy, and passion that you would if you were getting the instant reinforcement and affirmation that we all love.

I believe that the journey of learning to lead means accepting the reality that leadership skills are developed through long periods of striving with only moderate signs of progress. This means that learning to love the plateau is an essential part of learning to lead at *The Edge*.

Come to Terms with Fear

Although most people don't like to talk about it, fear seems to be an integral part of life. Every leader that I have been close to—close enough that they would really level with me—has described times that fear has loomed large in his or her life. Dealing with uncertainty, managing ambiguity, and not always knowing what to do come with the territory of being a leader.

In fact, nature has programmed us to be afraid of perceived threats, and this physiological mechanism has an important function: It helps us avoid danger. Biologists have identified a part of the brain called the amygdala whose function is just that—producing the reaction of being afraid.

Thanks to many years of biogenetic programming, we are quite skilled at being afraid. The problem is that to make a difference in the world, you often have to enter into territory where things can go wrong. Where there is risk, you can fail. You can be embarrassed. Sometimes there are more severe consequences: People can lose jobs, and sometimes, people can even die. There are many circumstances or events that trigger fear.

If fear is that much a part of life at *The Edge*—if it is that important a part of being human—we ought to know something about it. We ought to make a friend of it, as Joe Hyams suggests in his book *Zen in the Martial Arts*.[2] Making a friend of fear means understanding what is most personally intimidating to us and embracing it rather than pulling back.

The things that provoke fear are different for each of us. Some people are afraid to stand up in front of a group of people to deliver a speech. Others are afraid to take a personal financial risk or deal with the unknown. As Virginia Satir, the well-known family therapist, once remarked, "Most people prefer the certainty of misery to the misery of uncertainty."

Making a friend of fear means, first of all, understanding what it is that scares you. Second, it means understanding your personal reaction to fear. For example, when you are fearful:

▶ How does your body respond?

▶ What do you say to yourself?

▶ How do you feel?

You might be like Roberto Goizueta, the former CEO of Coca-Cola, who was asked whether he slept well at night, given all the competition in his industry. "Yes, I sleep like a baby," he replied. "I wake up every two hours and cry."[3]

Finally, making a friend of fear means developing a way to detoxify the fear so that you can maximize your own effectiveness. For example:

▶ You can write about it.

▶ You can talk to other people about it.

▶ You can think about ways in which you have successfully dealt with fear in the past.

▶ You can ask friends for suggestions.

▶ You can do something else so terrifying that you forget about what you were afraid of in the first place.

A final observation on fear: Sometimes fear is an obstacle that prevents us from accomplishing something. We say to ourselves, "I can't do that, I'm afraid." However, I learned in Vietnam just how much people are capable of achieving while being really scared.

Experiencing fear, therefore, does not mean that you cannot accomplish something. It doesn't even mean that something is wrong. In many circumstances you are supposed to be afraid. It just means that while you are doing it, you are going to be afraid—perhaps even terrified. The more you accept and engage your fears, the less they will stand in the way.

Find an Environment That Supports Learning

If you want to develop the ability to lead at *The Edge*, then find an organization that promotes good leadership. Robert Scott learned to be a
leader at Dartmouth, where he received the best education the Royal
Navy could provide. He later honed his skills by observing naval leaders
firsthand, drawing his own conclusions about what it meant to be a leader.

As I have noted earlier, however, the Royal Navy of the time was a
flawed institution, still basking in the glow of Horatio Nelson's past victories. Only such a navy would be content with muzzle-loading weapons
while others had adopted the cutting-edge technology of breech-loaded
guns. A complacent organization will produce complacent leaders.

The Royal Navy of the 1880s is ancient history, but what strikes
closer to home are modern examples of complacency and inadequate
leadership. David Nadler, in his provocative book *Champions of Change*, recounts the eighteen months during 1992 and 1993 in which the CEOs
of more than a dozen companies were forced to leave their jobs. Some of
the most respected CEOs in the country were forced out of their jobs at
IBM, General Motors, American Express, Eastman Kodak, Eli Lilly, AlliedSignal, Westinghouse, Digital Equipment Company, and Compaq.
Nadler argues persuasively that the common denominator was that each
was an industry leader with a sustained record of success. Each CEO was
a victim of the "success syndrome."[4]

The characteristics of the success syndrome are eerily reminiscent of
the old Royal Navy:

- *Codification.* Informal policies once successful become rigid policies.

- *Internal Focus.* Threats from outside forces, such as competitors,
  are ignored.

- *Arrogance and Complacency.* Competitive problems are viewed as
  "only temporary."

- *Complexity.* Internal politics and the preservation of power become primary objectives.

➤ *Conservatism.* The culture becomes risk-averse.

➤ *Disabled Learning.* New insights are not incorporated into the organizational memory.

As history demonstrates, the presence of these factors can have dire consequences for the organization. These characteristics also have direct implications for leadership. "Junior officers" model their successful seniors; and they behave in ways that are reinforced by the dominant culture of the organization.

The essential point is this: If you want to realize your full potential as a leader, look at the culture of the organization where you work. If it fits the characteristics of the success syndrome, find another. In the right environment, you are much more likely to become an Ernest Shackleton—not a Robert Scott.

Practice the Art of Thriving

Chapter 4 dealt with the vital importance of maintaining one's stamina as a leader at *The Edge.* There is, however, a more expansive way of thinking about taking care of yourself. I refer to this broader perspective as "the art of thriving."

The art of thriving focuses on sustaining career achievement and personal well-being throughout the life cycle. I believe that people who do this successfully are able to integrate the five components of the life structure shown in Figure 11-1.

Each individual has a unique set of needs. The ability to develop a sense of mastery in each of these five areas—work, relationships, physical health, renewal, and sense of purpose—while also establishing a balance among them is essential to personal vitality and thriving.

Work

It is interesting to look at work from the perspective of those who experience it with a sense of passion and excitement. In talking about

Figure 11-1. The "art of thriving" life structure.

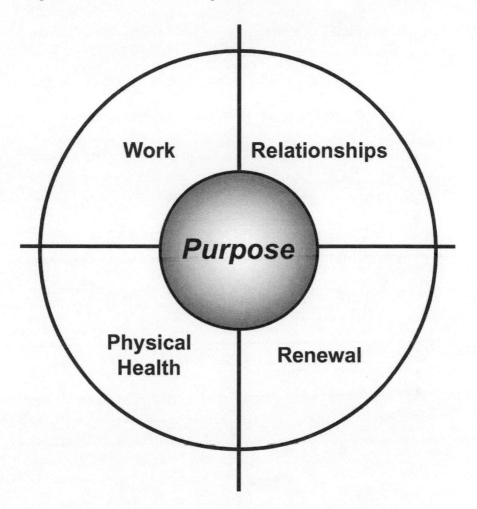

performing his music, Isaac Stern remarked that playing the violin is not just a "job" but a way of life. "It's a way of speaking, a way of expressing something . . . this ecstatic moment when you are at one with the phenomenon of man's creativity. That's very special. That's what is meant by being a musician."[5]

You don't have to be a violinist to experience work as creative expression. On the contrary, I think it can happen in any profession, from computer technology to investment banking. The critical task is to make sure that your unique strengths are brought to bear on a task that provides satisfaction and meaning. In testing the extent to which work contributes to a sense of vitality in your life, here are some questions you might want to ask yourself:

► Are you using your unique strengths and distinctive abilities in your work?

► Are you enjoying what you are doing? Are you having any fun?

► Are you intrinsically interested in the work you are doing? Do you find the substance of the work engaging?

► Is your work a creative expression of who you are?

If the answers to these questions are generally yes, then you—like Isaac Stern—are fortunate. If the answers are generally no, however, it is time to rethink this part of your life. The problem might lie with the work itself, or it may be a systems problem, originating somewhere else in the life structure.

Relationships

The importance of supportive social relationships in managing stress and promoting individual well-being has been demonstrated repeatedly. Having others to whom you can turn provides a "psychic balm" that heals many wounds. For high achievers, however, establishing such relationships can be a problem. Life in the fast track leaves little time for developing the kind of mutual relationships that give the greatest support.

This is especially true during times of transition—such as when you are moving, joining a new organization, or starting a new job. During these periods of change, previous social support systems are often uprooted. To make matters worse, the challenges of a new environment and the attendant anxieties about "measuring up" may make it seem as if there is no time for socializing.

Taking the time to develop relationships is more important than ever in times of transition, but you will need to give the relationships in your life special attention. Some questions you might want to ask yourself periodically are:

▶ Where are your sources of support and nurturance?

▶ Who are the people in your life who care about you as a person, rather than simply as a representation of a job title?

▶ Do you have a sense of belonging in some group or community other than work?

▶ Are you making time to nurture the relationships that are important in your life?

Physical Health

The Spartans had an expression: "You cannot have a healthy mind without a healthy body." Physical health contributes to good decision making, and many successful leaders I have studied point to sheer energy as an important contributor to their achievement. Unfortunately, the importance of having a sound physical foundation is overlooked when things get hot. Basic needs such as sleep, food, and regular exercise are worth tracking. Some questions to ask:

▶ Are you getting enough sleep, and are you resting well when you fall asleep?

▶ Are you eating a balanced diet? Are you using caffeine as a substitute for sleep or exercise?

▶ Are you getting enough exercise? Regular exercise is a proven stamina builder. It doesn't mean you need to participate in a triathlon. Just walking briskly three times a week makes a major contribution, and walking can be done without equipment while you are on the road. The critical point, especially while traveling, is to plan your exercise in advance and to think of it as an important part of your job.

▶ Are you setting aside time—at least fifteen minutes a day—for concentrated relaxation and decompression?

Renewal

Some people attend to all the factors previously mentioned and still experience a sense of burnout and ennui. This problem often originates from a failure to create space for what I call "renewal"—the uniquely personal activities that bring a sense of revitalization into your life. Here are some questions about renewal to examine:

- ▶ Is there space in your life for you to engage in regenerative activities?
- ▶ Are there times when you can forget the needs of others and lose yourself in nonwork activities that are absorbing and renewing?

Sense of Purpose

The fifth element in the art of thriving involves the ability to find a deeper sense of meaning in life. This sense of purpose is ultimately grounded in an underlying set of values about what is important, right, or worthwhile. For some people, this purpose has a spiritual basis. For others, it is connected to beliefs about the importance of scientific progress, technological advances, or creating knowledge. For still others, a sense of purpose is rooted in the need to contribute to humanity or to give to others. Once again, I return to Isaac Stern as an example. He said: "I've been playing concerts since I was fifteen. The world has been very nice to me, and I've taken a lot of things. I have to give something back."[6]

Whatever the source, an ability to find meaning and purpose is an extremely important determinant of "stress hardiness" and longevity. Keeping track of the way you are feeling about these deeper issues is important. Lacking this underlying sense of direction, it is extremely difficult to maintain peak performance and personal effectiveness. Spend some time reflecting on the following questions:

- ▶ How do you feel about the direction your life is taking?
- ▶ What are the deeper values that guide your work?

> ▶ Are the other parts of your life—work, relationships, physical
> health, and renewal—consistent with this sense of purpose?

Balance

The final skill in the art of thriving is the ability to find balance among
all five elements. Of course, no one can create and maintain perfect balance in life. Personal and professional growth involves change, experi-
mentation, risk, and mistakes. The art of thriving is not based on an
artificial attempt to establish rigid equanimity. On the contrary, its essence
lies in the ability to know when life is out of balance and when you need
to restore balance.

Developing this ability is a lifelong process. Morihei Ueshiba, the famous martial arts teacher, was once asked by a student, "Master, how is it
that you are never off balance when you are attacked?" His reply serves
as a metaphor: "I am often off center—but I recover so quickly you never
notice."

Mastering the art of thriving, then, means having the courage to explore the unknown, the willingness to risk losing your balance, and the
tenacity to find that balance again. It is a demanding journey, but the rewards are great.

Relax . . . It Takes Time to Play Like Yourself

A final observation on leading at *The Edge* comes from my ongoing quest
to play the tenor saxophone. On this journey I have spent a great deal
of time on the plateau—perhaps even at "base camp"—but have yet to
be discouraged. One reason for my perseverance is the encouragement
of my teacher, Steve, a superb player who brings out the best in everyone.

I always tape my lessons so that I can hear what Steve does, and also
so that I can listen to myself and learn what I need to do to perform better. I usually have to grit my teeth when I listen to my own playing, but
one day I went to a section of the tape where I had been improvising
over a song called "Blue Bossa." I was amazed. I was incredible. I was fluid.

I was creative. I was almost flawless. Then the tape continued and I heard my own voice asking a question. Wow, I was so great I could talk and play the tenor saxophone at the same time.

Then it hit me: I had actually been listening to Steve. It was deflating, to be sure, but I recovered. At my next lesson, I said, "Steve, I'm very discouraged. Am I ever going to be able to improvise like that?" He took out his pencil and wrote out one word on my music: T-I-M-E.

Learning takes time. Once you understand that, you realize that the process of becoming a leader, or a musician, has to unfold. Yes, you need to practice. Yes, you need to work hard. Yes, there are tricks and techniques. But the uniqueness of your personal style has its own timetable. As the great trumpet player Miles Davis once said, "I can always tell when someone is trying to copy me or another musician. Sometimes you have to play for a long time before you can play like yourself."

12

Epilogue:
What Makes an
Exceptional Leader?

For scientific discovery give me Scott; for speed and efficiency of travel give me Amundsen; but when disaster strikes and all hope is gone, get down on your knees and pray for Shackleton.[1]
                                                          —Sir Edmund Hillary

Set in the most hostile environment on Earth, the sagas of Antarctic explorers clearly illustrate how leadership style, personality, strategy, and openness to innovation interact to determine success or failure. These stories demonstrate how the best leaders are able to extend their reach by bringing out the best in others. And they illustrate how perceptions of leadership are altered by the changing lenses of culture and popular sentiment.

After writing *Leading at The Edge* over a decade ago, I continued to study the explorers who had courageously ventured into the frozen south. I traveled to Antarctica to see for myself the places where Shackleton had landed on his famed expedition. And I learned more about the historic race to the South Pole, one of the most exciting and controversial chapters in the history of leadership under adversity.

The Race

There is no question about who "won" the race: The victor was Norwegian explorer Roald Amundsen. With their exceptional skiing and dog-handling ability, the Norwegians moved across the terrain with relative ease. They traveled only six hours a day, reserving the remainder for sleep and rest. Thanks to their carefully planned diet and well-marked depots, food was never an issue.

Amundsen and his men arrived at the South Pole on December 14, 1911. Recognizing that all five had risked their lives on this adventure as a team, Amundsen insisted that they plant the Norwegian flag together.

While Amundsen basked in the warmth of his victory, Scott and his party still struggled southward, unaware that they had already lost the race. Scott had begun his journey almost seventy miles farther from the Pole than Amundsen had, and his decision to use ponies as well as dogs had created a further delay. As a result, they established their last food depot, "One Ton Camp," approximately twenty-five miles short of their goal. This shortfall, along with poor weather and a number of errors and miscalculations, was to prove fatal for Scott and his polar party.

On January 3, 1912, Scott made a late decision. Although plans for the polar assault had been based on a team of four, Scott inexplicably announced that he would take one extra man on the final leg of the journey. The sleds were equipped with supplies for only four men and the tents were designed to accommodate four, so this change complicated their movement. They had also brought only four sets of skis, so the entire polar party was restricted to a walking pace.

Scott and his men arrived at the South Pole on January 17, 1912— thirty-five days after Amundsen. Finding the Norwegian tent, Scott wrote: "Great God! This is an awful place, and terrible enough for us to have labored to it without the reward of priority.... Now for the run home and a desperate struggle. I wonder if we can do it."[2]

They could not. One member died a month later after sinking into a coma. The next month, a second man—Titus Oates—stepped out into a blizzard never to return. Suffering from severe frostbite, Oates apparently sacrificed his life rather than continue to delay his comrades.

On March 19, a blizzard again enveloped the surviving three members of the polar party. Imprisoned just over eleven miles from One Ton Depot, they had enough food for only two days. Scott's last entry on March 29 reads: "We shall stick it out to the end . . . and the end cannot be far. . . . For God's sake look after our people."[3]

Eight months later, expedition survivors came upon the tent of the polar party. When Scott and his two companions were eventually found, their sledge had included thirty pounds of geological specimens. The weight of these specimens, confirming Scott's dedication to science, was not the principal cause of his tragic death. But the stones, although of scientific importance, symbolize the inherent contradiction of trying to finish a race while carrying rocks.

Leadership Lessons from the Race to the Pole

Fascination with the race continues to the present day. For most of the twentieth century, Scott was considered a heroic figure. Toward the end of the century, historians began to question his leadership. Instead of a hero, Scott was cast as a bungler whose errors in judgment had cost him not only the conquest of the Pole but also the lives of his men. Amundsen, the winner of the race, has been criticized for his single-minded determination and perceived duplicity in "stealing the prize." And Shackleton, who had turned back on his 1909 attempt at the Pole, was attacked as being unpatriotic: His failure to sacrifice his life, and the lives of his men, enabled a foreigner to win the race. Yet he went on to distinguish himself as an extraordinary leader, bringing every man home alive after 634 days of unbelievable hardship.

Of the three, is there a single, best leader? And what, then, are the fundamental leadership lessons we can draw from their adventures of the Frozen Edge?

Effective Leadership Requires a Clear Strategic Focus

Amundsen's original ambition was to stand first at the North Pole. When Cook and Peary claimed that prize, however, Amundsen immediately shifted his attention to winning the race to the South Pole. This new goal became the sole focus of his expedition. With single-minded determination, Amundsen set his plans and priorities. This uncompromising clarity contributed to his success in reaching the Pole and to his ability to bring his men safely home.

Scott, in contrast, lacked such focus. To support his scientific goals, he assembled the most capable scientists and the best-equipped expedition ever to explore Antarctica. Yet, he had also stated that one of the major objects of the expedition was to reach the South Pole, securing the honor of that achievement for the British Empire. Striving for both goals, Scott failed to win the race, and his grueling march to an arbitrary geographic point was inconsistent with the pursuit of scientific research.

Successful Leaders Are Open to New Ideas

A second lesson from the race concerns the leader's critical role in fostering innovation. The process of innovation depends on an openness to new ideas, coupled with the ability to learn from experience. On this dimension of leadership, there were striking differences between Amundsen and both Scott and Shackleton.

The Norwegians owed much of their success to the use of superior technology for polar travel—skis, dogs, clothing, and diet. Skiing was an integral part of their culture, while the British knew relatively little of the art. But Amundsen continued to refine his skills throughout his life. He learned from his earliest experiences on the *Belgica*, he imported ideas from the Eskimos, and he systematically developed an integrated set of competencies for polar life and travel. Consequently, his trip to the Pole was remarkably routine, and he was able to avoid the extreme weather that Scott had to endure.

Scott and Shackleton, in contrast, were surprisingly resistant to the use of these proven methods. It is easy to understand their failure to use the best technology on their first journey toward the Pole in 1902—although Scott's admission that none of their equipment had been tested is still surprising. In later expeditions, however, their persistent reliance on unproven or inferior methods is difficult to understand.

Scott believed that he had learned from earlier mistakes, but the evidence suggests otherwise. On later expeditions, both Shackleton and Scott experimented unsuccessfully with motor sledges and ponies, but neither made effective use of dogs and skis. Ultimately, both relied on the slow, exhausting technique of man hauling.

Though Scott possessed the promise and energy of youth, he often failed to display an openness to new ideas and the ability to learn from mistakes. In his final "Message to the Public," Scott attributes the cause of the tragedy simply to "misfortune." Scott's lengthy journey did subject his party to the misfortune of particularly cold weather—conditions that Amundsen escaped through a rapid assault on the Pole. But Amundsen's success was no accident. The triumph was made possible through careful planning, preparation, and experience with polar travel. In his words:

> I may say that this is the greatest factor—the way in which the expedition is equipped—the way in which every difficulty is foreseen, and precautions taken for meeting or avoiding it. Victory awaits him who has everything in order—luck, people call it. Defeat is certain for him who has neglected to take the necessary precautions in time; this is called bad luck.[4]

Leaders Need to Draw on the Collective Wisdom of the Team

As a leader, Scott believed it was his unique responsibility to analyze situations and draw conclusions. His decisions were closely held and sometimes revealed at the last minute—witness his decision to take a fifth man to the Pole. One consequence of Scott's decision-making style was that he often failed to use the opinions of others to find the best possible course of action. In addition, because they were not involved in the process, members of his expedition had only a limited understanding of the rationale behind his decisions.

In sharp contrast to Scott, both Amundsen and Shackleton made a point of soliciting the ideas of their team members. As a result, their actions were better informed, and the process itself—because it gave people a sense of control—resulted in greater ownership and commitment.

The Best Leaders Forge Strong Team Bonds

The contest to be first at the Pole shows that teams under the best leaders form cohesive bonds that enable everyone to work together in the face of daunting adversity. On this point, Scott again stands apart from Shackleton and Amundsen. Scott did inspire loyalty among some key members of his team, and his doomed polar party stayed together until the very end. But Scott's detachment, his emphasis on hierarchy, and his unilateral decision-making style created barriers to team cohesion.

Neither Shackleton nor Amundsen led perfectly harmonious expeditions, but both leaders demonstrated the critical skills needed to maintain a unified team. Although their personalities were different, the leadership practices of the ebullient Shackleton and the understated Amundsen were remarkably similar. They were both acutely sensitive to the emotions of their men and consciously intervened when morale dropped. They were skilled at managing conflict and winning over potential troublemakers. They placed greater emphasis on individual ability than on rank or social status. And they participated in the most menial camp chores, never isolating themselves from other members of the expedition. These behaviors, both practical and symbolic, reinforced the message of unity.

Scott may not have demonstrated the same level of emotional intelligence as Amundsen and Shackleton, but these famous explorers did share some important characteristics. All were able to endure extraordinary hardship through exceptional perseverance, determination, and courage. Those qualities are crucial for any leader—no matter what race must be run.

A Perspective on Success and Failure

For leaders at *The Edge* confronting today's challenges, another question arises: Was Shackleton a success or a failure as a leader? True, he led his crew to safety in what was arguably the greatest adventure in the history of polar exploration. The fact remains, however, that the Imperial Trans-Antarctic Expedition did not achieve its goal: It did not cross Antarctica.

Shackleton's critics have argued that, given the severe ice conditions, he never should have left South Georgia in the first place; that he should have had more or different equipment; and that he failed to plan for every possible contingency, as well as listing other flaws. On the other side of the ledger, there are those who lionize Shackleton as the essence of everything that a leader should be.

I believe that any attempt to categorize Shackleton as a success or a failure misses the point. There is no debate about whether the expedition met its original goal. It did not. The question of whether Shackleton was successful as a leader does not have a simple or definitive answer. Any conclusion depends on the criteria by which Shackleton's leadership is judged.

There is little doubt that as an individual Shackleton demonstrated an extraordinary level of determination and tenacity. But he did more than that. He also created a team with such strong bonds that, on the verge of starvation, they were willing to share their last rations. It was a team that worked together against enormous odds to overcome staggering obstacles. Although Shackleton failed to cross Antarctica, he delivered on the promise contained in the original advertisement for the expedition: Those who sailed on *Endurance* did, indeed, receive "honor and recognition."

Depending on the yardstick used to measure success, Shackleton can be seen as a success or a failure, or a little of both. I believe that the more important question raised by Shackleton's adventure, and by the other accounts in this book, is a much more personal one: How do you measure your own success as a leader? What are the standards by which you assess your own performance?

One obvious benchmark of success is whether you accomplish what you set out to do—whether you achieve your stated goals. Even this straightforward measure, though, is more complex than it first appears. Whether you reach your objective depends not only on your own effort and ability but also on external forces—the metaphorical equivalents of sea and ice conditions.

There are other variables in the equation that directly affect the probability that you will accomplish what you set out to do. What is the degree of difficulty of your goal? How far are you willing to reach? How high do you want to set the bar? You can greatly improve your odds of succeeding by setting low targets and easy goals. That strategy, while ensuring "success," is not at the core of leading at *The Edge*.

The spirit of reaching for *The Edge* is one of exploration—of breaking new ground and pressing the limits. This process of exploration carries with it the inherent risk that your original mission will fail, or that it might have to be changed as a result of new discoveries.

Of course, nobody likes failure, or even unpredictability—especially in today's business environment. I have tried to imagine the questions that would be directed toward Christopher Columbus if he were a CEO meeting with Wall Street analysts:

> Mr. Columbus, you promised to sail to Japan, to establish a trading station with Asia, to build a relationship with the Emperor of China, and to bring back spices and gold. You accomplished none of this. Instead, you landed in the wrong place, and you brought back only corn, cotton, hammocks, and, well . . . some cigars. You may have discovered a New World, but you failed to deliver on your commitments. How do you explain your lackluster performance?

Unfortunately, the decision to explore new terrain—whether geographical, intellectual, or economic—carries with it inherent risk and uncertainty. There is simply no assurance that things will work out exactly as planned. Furthermore, there is no formula for determining the right level of difficulty at which goals should be set. What is certain, however, is that individuals who want to do extraordinary things—to reach for *The Edge*—must be willing to set lofty goals. And they must also be willing to risk the possibility that others will see the outcome of their efforts as a failure.

There are, then, many standards for judging success. Some of them include:

- ▶ Achieving your stated goals
- ▶ Achieving new goals, if the original goals must be changed
- ▶ Accepting bold challenges
- ▶ Avoiding failure
- ▶ Finding honor and recognition
- ▶ Achieving economic success
- ▶ Demonstrating loyalty to comrades

Each person must decide which of these (or other) standards are important and how each should be weighted. This weighting is, ultimately, a question of values. These values, in turn, determine how a leader will behave.

Vilhjalmur Stefansson, the leader of the *Karluk* expedition, displayed his values in an early dispatch from the Arctic that declared:

> ... [T]he attainment of the purposes of the expedition is more important than the bringing back safe of the ship in which it sails. This means that while every reasonable precaution will be taken to safeguard the lives of the party, it is realized by both the backers of the expedition and the members of it, that even the lives of the party are secondary to the accomplishment of the work![5]

The values embedded in this message left Stefansson free to abandon the expedition. They also later enabled him to minimize the deaths of eleven men, arguing that "the loss of a dozen lives for scientific progress" was small when compared with the millions who perished in World

War I. He neglected to add the roles that arrogance, dereliction of duty, and incompetent leadership had played in the tragedy. From Stefansson's perspective, however, the expedition was a great success. It furthered our understanding of "the friendly Arctic," and it enhanced his personal career ambitions.

Shackleton, in stark contrast, was as completely committed to bringing his crew safely home as Stefansson was nonchalant about the fate of *Karluk* and its crew. The night after the destruction of *Endurance*, Shackleton lay awake in his tent completely focused on his responsibility:

> The task was now to secure the safety of the party, and to that end I must bend my energies and mental power and apply every bit of knowledge that experience of the Antarctic had given me. The task was likely to be long and strenuous, and an ordered mind and a clear programme were essential if we were to come through without loss of life.[6]

It was this sense of responsibility that led him, time and again, to think of others before he thought of himself; to give his mittens and boots to those in greater need; and to volunteer for the first, and longest, watches.

On the boat journey to South Georgia, it was Shackleton's concern for the well-being of those left behind that moved him to confide in Frank Worsley, "Skipper, if anything happens to me while those fellows are waiting for me, I shall feel like a murderer."[7] This same sense of responsibility enabled him to work tirelessly to find a ship and rescue his comrades on Elephant Island.

This level of genuine concern was what inspired the unswerving loyalty that Shackleton generated to the end of his life. It was what moved Worsley to later say:

> ... [W]hen looking at Shackleton's grave and the cairn which we, his comrades, erected to his memory on the wind-swept hill of South Georgia ... it seemed to me that among all his achievements and triumphs ... his one failure was the most glorious. By self-sacrifice and throwing his own life into the balance he saved every one of his men. ...[8]

However others may view his accomplishments, there is little doubt about how those closest to Shackleton felt about him as a leader—and as a comrade.

I believe that Shackleton and others who have faced the limits of human endurance have left an invaluable legacy. This legacy incorporates the leadership strategies outlined in this book, but it extends beyond that. The lessons drawn from the experiences of others can help individuals to clarify their personal values and to make decisions about the kind of people they want to be as leaders. By defining ourselves, we will be better able to reach *The Edge*—wherever and whenever we choose to pursue it.

PART THREE

Tools for Leading at *The Edge*

Expedition Toolkit

Τhis section of the book contains several tools designed to help you continue the process of developing your leadership skills. The *Critical Leadership Skills Survey* is an instrument to help you assess the extent to which you typically practice the ten strategies outlined in *Leading at The Edge*. The survey is intended to stimulate thinking about your leadership style; it is not meant to be a final, categorical assessment of your leadership ability.

The questionnaire will, however, allow you to step back and reflect, and it can be an effective feedback instrument as well. I have found that having others complete the *Critical Leadership Skills Survey* to assess my leadership style is an enlightening, productive experience.

The second tool—*Your Leadership Expedition: A Personal Development Plan*—provides a way of bringing together, in a comprehensive plan for professional development, your insights from the *Critical Leadership Skills Survey* and your responses to the questions posed in the Expedition Log at the end of Chapters 1 through 10.

Identifying Hidden Conflicts: Conducting a Moose Round-Up is the third tool, which is designed to help leaders identify issues that hamper productivity and team unity. The guide provides examples of situations in which the tool is most effective, along with detailed instructions for conducting a "Round-Up."

A fourth tool, *Resolving Conflicts: Lessons from the Martial Arts*, enables leaders to work through sticky issues once the sources of friction have been identified. This collaborative method uses principles from the martial art of aikido to give leaders a new perspective on conflict resolution.

Finally, *Further Readings from* The Edge includes a list of books dealing with experiences at the *Survival Edge*. It includes books recounting the Shackleton saga as well as books about other survival stories.

One of my goals is to continue to expand the list with other stories that illustrate effective and ineffective leadership and teamwork at *The Edge*. I am interested in accounts that illustrate the use of the ten strategies in both business and survival situations. If you have a story to contribute, I would be pleased to hear from you. I can be contacted through my email address, Dennis.Perkins@SyncreticsGroup.com, or at:

The Syncretics Group, Inc.
869 Boston Post Road, Suite 201
Madison, CT 06443
Phone: 203-779-5329
www.SyncreticsGroup.com

Critical Leadership
Skills Survey

Instructions

In answering these 30 questions, think about your behavior in a particular role or situation. For example, your frame of reference might be:

➤ The way you demonstrate leadership as the formal head of a group or organization

➤ Your peer leadership as a member of a work team

➤ The way you lead and inspire yourself when dealing with personal or professional adversity

Please answer the questions about yourself using the following scoring categories:

1 = Never or almost never true

2 = Seldom true

3 = Sometimes true

4 = Often true

5 = Almost always true

If you have difficulty answering a question, choose the category that comes closest to describing the way you are.

Critical Leadership Skills Survey

	Never or Almost Never True	Seldom True	Sometimes True	Often True	Almost Always True
1. You have a clear image of the organization's future direction.	1	2	3	4	5
2. You use symbols and images to communicate what needs to be done.	1	2	3	4	5
3. You imbue others with a sense of optimism and self-confidence.	1	2	3	4	5
4. You maintain stamina with sleep, exercise, and good diet.	1	2	3	4	5
5. You frequently communicate the importance of team unity.	1	2	3	4	5
6. You demonstrate a willingness to take on "low status" jobs.	1	2	3	4	5
7. You diffuse tension by dealing with conflict in small doses.	1	2	3	4	5
8. You find events to celebrate—even in difficult circumstances.	1	2	3	4	5
9. You demonstrate a willingness to take appropriate risks.	1	2	3	4	5
10. You persevere in the face of adversity.	1	2	3	4	5

	Never or Almost Never True	Seldom True	Sometimes True	Often True	Almost Always True
11. You clearly communicate the organization's future direction to others.	1	2	3	4	5
12. You use personal example to emphasize the importance of key actions.	1	2	3	4	5
13. You are realistic in assessing your situation (including both threats and opportunities).	1	2	3	4	5
14. You let go of guilt about mistakes.	1	2	3	4	5
15. You illustrate ways in which each person's skills contribute to the group.	1	2	3	4	5
16. You minimize symbols and special privileges that create status differences among team members.	1	2	3	4	5
17. You avoid needless power struggles by ensuring that people focus on problems rather than personalities.	1	2	3	4	5
18. You use humor as a device for defusing tension.	1	2	3	4	5
19. You encourage experimentation with new ideas.	1	2	3	4	5
20. You communicate a message of hope for the future.	1	2	3	4	5

	Never or Almost Never True	Seldom True	Sometimes True	Often True	Almost Always True
21. You direct others' energy toward realistic short-term goals.	1	2	3	4	5
22. You use metaphor and stories to communicate ideas.	1	2	3	4	5
23. You consider the merit of contradictory or "negative" views.	1	2	3	4	5
24. You build renewal and relaxation into your daily life.	1	2	3	4	5
25. You bring together the entire team for meetings and special events.	1	2	3	4	5
26. You demonstrate genuine respect and concern for others.	1	2	3	4	5
27. You maintain contact with "troublemakers" and dissidents.	1	2	3	4	5
28. You provide opportunities for regular social activity.	1	2	3	4	5
29. You emphasize learning from mistakes.	1	2	3	4	5
30. You encourage people to step back and mobilize their creativity when faced with difficult problems.	1	2	3	4	5

Scoring Instructions

STEP #1. Record your score for each question below. Each strategy is measured by three questions. Then total the scores for the three questions for each strategy.

Strategy 1:
Vision and Quick Victories

Questions	Score
1	_____
11	_____
21	_____
TOTAL	_____

Strategy 2:
Symbolism and Personal Examples

Questions	Score
2	_____
12	_____
22	_____
TOTAL	_____

Strategy 3:
Optimism and Reality

Questions	Score
3	_____
13	_____
23	_____
TOTAL	_____

Strategy 4:
Stamina

Questions	Score
4	_____
14	_____
24	_____
TOTAL	_____

Strategy 5:
The Team Message

Questions	Score
5	_____
15	_____
25	_____
TOTAL	_____

Strategy 6:
Core Team Values

Questions	Score
6	_____
16	_____
26	_____
TOTAL	_____

Strategy 7:
Conflict

Questions	Score
7	_____
17	_____
27	_____
TOTAL	_____

Strategy 8:
Lighten Up!

Questions	Score
8	_____
18	_____
28	_____
TOTAL	_____

Strategy 9:
Risk

Questions	Score
9	_____
19	_____
29	_____
TOTAL	_____

Strategy 10:
Tenacious Creativity

Questions	Score
10	_____
20	_____
30	_____
TOTAL	_____

Critical Leadership Skills Profile

STEP #2. Next, plot your profile below, using the "Totals" from Step 1, to create a graph.

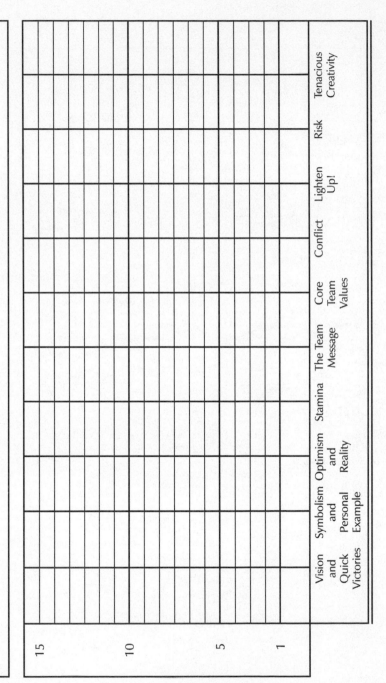

Critical Leadership Skills Analysis Guide

1. Were there any surprises in your profile—low points or high points—that you didn't understand?

2. If so, examine the individual questions that made up each of the ten dimensions (corresponding to the ten strategies) you have plotted. Does that help explain your profile?

3. Of the ten strategies, which are your strongest or most developed?

4. Which of the strategies need to be strengthened or further developed?

Your Leadership Expedition: A Personal Development Plan

When embarking on an expedition, it is always useful to have a map. I have found that the following conceptual map is helpful in the leadership development process. It depicts a systematic process consisting of five stages:

1. **Assessment.** Who are you now?

2. **Vision.** Who do you want to be?

3. **Overcoming barriers.** What are the obstacles that stand in your way, and how can they be overcome?

4. **Action.** What are the specific steps needed to move toward your vision?

5. **Sustaining.** How will you deal with setbacks and maintain momentum?

The stages are only guideposts, of course, and the development process does not always flow in one direction. In clarifying your vision, for example, you will probably gain insight into the person you are right now. The questions and exercises that follow will help clarify each of these stages, and they will refine your understanding of the leadership journey you have undertaken.

Assessment

1. What are your strengths as a leader—the skills, knowledge, and personal qualities that contribute to your ability to lead at *The Edge*?

2. What are your development needs—the areas that, if developed, would increase your effectiveness as a leader?

3. What are the activities that you find energizing—activities that stimulate you and that you find intrinsically enjoyable?

4. What are your core values about leadership—the deep beliefs that provide guidance and meaning?

Vision

1. Imagine that it is some time in the future. You have realized your full potential as a leader and are able to lead others to the limits of their performance.

2. Write a detailed, vivid description of who you are and what you will be doing. What is a typical day like for you? What will you be thinking and feeling? Try to capture that image in as much detail as possible.

3. Write a one-sentence, high-concept statement that captures the essence of your vision.

4. Is there a concrete image that symbolizes your vision?

Overcoming Barriers

1. What are the barriers that stand between you and your vision? These obstacles may be external or internal—the *limiting beliefs* that prevent you from fully using your abilities. List them here, casting each barrier in the form of an "I"

statement (e.g., "I can't be a charismatic leader because I'm too introverted").

2. Select the barriers that represent the most problematic obstacles—those over which you have some degree of control.

3. Now generate as many ideas as possible for dealing with these obstacles. It is often helpful to get help from friends and colleagues who may see solutions that elude you. Some other strategies for generating ideas are:

  ▶ *Opportunity framing.* What hidden opportunities might be found in the problem?

  ▶ *Using a metaphor.* What concrete images can be used to represent the problem (e.g., a brick wall, a mountain, or an ice pack)? In thinking about how you would deal with these symbolic barriers, you might find a solution.

  ▶ *Chunking down.* Try to break the obstacles down into smaller pieces. Can you now get a toehold or a "lead in the ice"?

Action

1. Now that you have developed a vision and a set of strategies for overcoming obstacles, you can create a set of goals for moving toward your vision. To be most effective, these goals should be:

  ▶ *Specific.* For example, your goal may be to "take the conflict resolution seminar offered by X university," rather than more generally to "improve my conflict resolution skills."

  ▶ *Positive.* Goals should be stated in terms of "doing" rather than "avoiding" or "not doing."

> ► *Challenging yet attainable.* Stretch yourself, but don't set unreasonable expectations.

2. It is often helpful to create both a set of long-term (i.e., three to five years) goals and a set of short-term (i.e., six months to one year) goals.

Sustaining

List below the things that will enable you to sustain your leadership development process. Some questions to consider are:

1. What are your external sources of reinforcement? How will you get help and support from others?

2. What is your backup plan for dealing with adversity and setbacks?

3. When and how will you take time to reflect on your progress?

4. How will you reward yourself and celebrate success for interim accomplishments?

5. What are the tangible symbols that will help you stay focused on your vision?

Your Leadership Expedition Map

Using a large sheet of paper, construct a map or flowchart that shows the route of your planned expedition. The point of departure is *your assessment* of where you are right now. The destination is *your vision*. Trace the route that you will follow, showing key milestones with expected completion dates, along with major obstacles and how you will get past them. Feel free to be creative and to use vivid images with strong personal associations.

Identifying Hidden Conflicts: Conducting a Moose Round-Up

One of the key issues leaders face is how to uncover conflicts that may slow down the expedition. Until the sources of friction are identified, problems will persist and potentially get worse. The challenge is how best to create a safe venue where issues can be discussed and ultimately resolved. If leaders truly wish to understand and work through problems, the following exercise can help.

As described in Chapter 7, a *Moose* is a latent conflict that everyone knows about but no one discusses. Examples include performance problems, ineffective organizational structures, and leadership actions that send a mixed message. The *Moose Round-Up* is intended to identify these problems so they can be dealt with openly.

At first impression, the Moose metaphor might seem too contrived, but we have found that the metaphor—sometimes employed with a stuffed moose and even a moose call—is remarkably effective.

Before starting a Round-Up, it's important to ask three questions. First, is this the right time to engage in the process? Although many con-

flicts need to be dealt with, if the expedition is in the middle of an avalanche it might make sense to wait until the sliding stops. Second, are you
really open to honest feedback? The exercise will be effective only if the
leader and the team are willing to talk candidly about problems and to
work together to find solutions. Third, is this an issue that needs to be resolved in a group setting, or is it best dealt with one-on-one? A caveat
here is that some leaders attempt to resolve group issues with a series of
one-off conversations. If it's a group problem, then it needs to be solved
in a conversation with the entire team.

Assuming the answers to these questions are affirmative, the next step
is to designate a *Moose Wrangler*. The Wrangler—ideally someone who
does not report directly to the leader—should be someone who understands the organization and who can be trusted to talk about issues in
confidence. The Wrangler will be responsible for collecting the issues for
discussion—for "rounding up the Mooses."

Once the Wrangler has been identified, the leader brings the team together to explain the concept of the Moose, the process for rounding
them up, and the outcome: what the team can expect from the exercise.

If there are any questions or concerns, people should be encouraged
to raise them. It is important for the leader to establish an atmosphere of
trust and demonstrate a genuine willingness to address concerns.

Next, the Wrangler asks the team to identify any "Mooses on the
loose" in the organization. The worksheet provided asks team members
to rank each Moose on a scale from 1 to 10, with 1 on the response scale
equivalent to "mildly annoying" and 10 signaling "extremely problematic." Worksheets are completed anonymously, then returned to the Wrangler for compilation. Confidentiality is critical, especially since some
people may be concerned that their handwriting could compromise
anonymity.

Once all the worksheets are collected, the Wrangler compiles the
findings. Each Moose is given a score by averaging the ratings from the
individual employees. For example, if one issue appears on four different
worksheets, the ratings are added together and divided by four. The Wrangler and leader review the results, which list Mooses in order of size.

The leader–Wrangler meeting should occur shortly before a full team

Moose Round-Up Worksheet

A *Moose* is a latent conflict that everybody knows about but nobody discusses. In the space below, list any difficult issues or conflicts that get in the way of organizational effectiveness. Rank each Moose on a scale of 1 to 10, with 1 being "mildly annoying" and 10 being "extremely problematic."

Moose	Rank (1–10)

meeting. The leader needs to understand the issues that will surface, but not so much in advance as to ruminate excessively. At the full team session, the Wrangler presents the results of the Moose Round-Up and provides an opportunity for discussion and clarification.

Once the Mooses are identified, the leader and the team can start the process of working through the issues together. Although solutions often take time, once conflicts are out in the open they are no longer Mooses—only undiscussable secrets qualify!

Resolving Conflicts: Lessons from the Martial Arts

There are many ways to think about conflict resolution. The challenge for a leader is finding the right set of lenses for looking at a particular situation. One metaphor suggests that "argument is war," and it implies that there will be a winner and a loser. This perspective works well in combat, but it is poorly suited for most organizational conflicts. People who need to work together shouldn't think of each other as enemies.

Organizational conflicts are best resolved when opposing parties work together to find creative solutions that meet each other's needs. Unfortunately, this constructive partnership is sometimes hard to establish and maintain. For many people—even seasoned executives—conflict can create visceral reactions that block effective problem solving.

It seems hard to believe, but I have seen leaders exhibit excessive anger, including threats of physical violence; withdrawal and disappearing acts; and inflexibility, also described as the "threat-rigidity" response. Overcoming these negative reactions to conflict isn't easy, but it is possible. To effectively resolve conflicts, leaders must:

▶ Be aware of the situations that trigger these responses.

▶ Have effective strategies for constructively resolving differences.

▶ Mentally rehearse these strategies.

▶ Be able to see conflict situations as opportunities to use and improve their skills.

Improving conflict resolution skills can be a daunting task, and sometimes it is necessary to "break set" and get out of the usual patterns we use to think about familiar situations. Personally, I have found a helpful approach to conflict resolution in the principles of the Japanese martial art of aikido.

Although the origins of aikido are ancient, the current method was developed at the beginning of the twentieth century by renowned martial artist Morihei Ueshiba. Translated, the word *aikido* suggests a method for creating harmony with the spirit or energy of others. One of aikido's unique characteristics is the ethical imperative to defend oneself without harming others.[1] Practically, those who study aikido learn to blend with the force of an attack and redirect it, rather than oppose it head-on. It's a particularly helpful way to think about conflict in organizations that call for a win/win outcome.

Specifically, the metaphor of aikido works well in situations where finding a mutually agreeable solution is important; there is value to maintaining a positive relationship with another person, and it is worth investing the time. When these conditions exist, the aikido concepts listed here can help you achieve a positive outcome.

Aikido Principles for Conflict Resolution

1. **Develop expanded awareness.**

   ▶ *Know yourself.* Understand your own reactions to conflict—that is, what you say to yourself, what you feel, and how you behave. Be aware of your emotional triggers and when those triggers may lead you to act aggressively or inappropriately.

- ➤ *Know the other person.* Think about how the other person has responded to conflicts in the past, how that person is likely to respond to different approaches, and the potential for emotional triggers. Are there specific things likely to create a negative reaction, and can those traps be avoided?

- ➤ *Know the situation.* Is this a problem that requires a confrontation, or is it a needless power struggle similar to the McNeish mutiny described in Chapter 7? If it can be avoided without creating a Moose, it might be easier to simply step aside. This option is rarely contemplated in emotional situations, but it is a move that is often employed in aikido.

2. **Cultivate balance: Stay centered and grounded.**

- ➤ *Maintain your space.* Though you are watching out for your opponent, you're not a doormat. Don't allow yourself to be run over.

- ➤ *Stay physically relaxed.* When we deal with difficult issues, it is natural to tense up. Monitor the state of your muscles; if you find your shoulders next to your ears, relax!

- ➤ *Breathe.* Deep, diaphragmatic breathing is sometimes given a near mystical quality in yoga and the martial arts. But breathing deeply and slowly—several deep breaths with slow exhaling—can have remarkably positive effects.

- ➤ *Use self-talk.* Think of a short phrase or phrases that will help you stay balanced when dealing with emotional issues (for example, "Stay Cool," "Don't Take the Bait," or "Count to Ten").

- ➤ *Use humor.* The role of humor in defusing tense situations is highlighted in Chapter 8 (Find something to celebrate and something to laugh about), and it can make an important contribution to conflict resolution. The critical thing to keep in mind is that humor should be used to make a statement that is genuinely funny, not as a sarcastic weapon to be used against your opponent.

➤ *Find the right place.* Choose a relaxing or calming environment, not a public setting where your conversations can be overheard. To minimize power imbalances, consider a neutral venue where there are no territorial concerns.

➤ *Pick the right time.* Just as it is important to conduct a Moose Round-Up at an appropriate time, it is best to confront difficult problems when other stressors are minimized.

➤ *Use tangible reminders.* Before going into an emotional conflict, think about the way you want to be and how you want to present yourself. For example, you could imagine yourself to be a bamboo plant, rooted in the ground but flexible. Or you could picture someone you know (or know of) who handles conflict well and keep the image of that person in mind.

3. **Blending: Merge your energy and ideas with that of the other person.**

➤ *Fully engage the conflict in a nonconfrontational way.* When you meet to discuss an issue, be fully present and take a position. Give the other person something solid to deal with.

➤ *Genuinely try to see the situation from the other person's point of view.* Make sure that you understand the other person's statements before reacting. Summarizing what you have heard before responding is a very useful technique.

➤ *Find something about the situation you can agree on.* Identifying a point of convergence, however small, creates movement.

4. **Leading: Channel the energy of the conflict toward positive resolution.**

➤ *Visualize how you want the situation to end.* Skip Barber, founder of a well-known race car driving school, is often quoted as saying, "You go where you look, so you'd better look where you want to go." Aikido instructors think the same way, encouraging students to extend their *ki* (their inner energy) through visualization. Having a clear picture of a successful resolution is an important steering device in heated conflicts.

▶ *When attacked, maintain your position without responding in kind.* Avoid inflammatory statements that escalate the conflict. Acknowledge and move on.

▶ *Focus on the present and the future rather than on the past.* Debating who did what, and when, will only create a distraction from the task of reaching agreement.

▶ *Provide opportunities for the attacker to change position without embarrassment.* Give the individual a "golden bridge," and avoid trying to prove that he or she is wrong.

▶ *Search for alternatives that meet everyone's objectives.* Find the third option, or a "syncretic solution" that integrates several approaches.

▶ *Deal with impasses by moving to another dimension of value.* Create flexibility by finding something you can give on—something that is important to the other person but not too costly to you.

▶ *Restate agreement on mutual goals.* Continue to blend while directing the other person's energy and attention toward the things that bring you together.

Closing Note

Mastering the art of conflict resolution as a leader, much like learning aikido, takes practice and repetition. Often, the best response to a challenge is not the one that is the easiest or the most natural. In fact, the most effective moves might—at least at first—be counterintuitive. And there will be setbacks. When things go wrong, I like to recall the words often attributed to Mark Twain: "Good judgment is the result of experience. Experience is the result of bad judgment." Get some experience!

Further Readings from *The Edge*

Books on Ernest Shackleton

Alexander, Caroline. *The* Endurance: *Shackleton's Legendary Antarctic Expedition*. New York: Alfred A. Knopf, 1999.

Armstrong, Jennifer. *Shipwreck at the Bottom of the World: The Extraordinary True Story of Shackleton and the* Endurance. New York: Crown, 1998.

Fisher, Margery, and James Fisher. *Shackleton and the Antarctic*. Boston: Houghton Mifflin, 1958.

Huntford, Roland. *Shackleton*. New York: Carroll & Graf, 1999.

Lansing, Alfred. Endurance: *Shackleton's Incredible Voyage*. New York: Carroll & Graf, 1998.

McCurdy, Michael. *Trapped by the Ice! Shackleton's Amazing Antarctic Adventure*. New York: Walker, 1997.

Ralling, Christopher. *Shackleton, Greatest of All British Polar Explorers*. London: British Broadcasting Corporation, 1985.

Shackleton, Ernest. *South: A Memoir of the* Endurance *Voyage*. New York: Carroll & Graf, 1999.

Shackleton, Sir Ernest. *South: The Story of Shackleton's Last Expedition, 1914–1917*, ed. Peter King. North Pomfret: Trafalgar Square, 1992.

Worsley, F. A. Endurance: *An Epic of Polar Adventure*. New York: W. W. Norton, 1999.

Worsley, F. A. *Shackleton's Boat Journey*. New York: W. W. Norton, 1977.

Other Survival Accounts

Adams, David, with Caroline Adams. *Chasing Liquid Mountains: Adventures of a Solo Yachtsman*. Sydney: Macmillan, 1997.

Ambrose, Stephen E. *Undaunted Courage: Meriwether Lewis, Thomas Jefferson, and the Opening of the American West*. New York: Simon & Schuster, 1996.

Amundsen, Roald. *The South Pole: An Account of the Norwegian Antarctic Expedition in the "Fram," 1910–12* (1913; reproduced with introduction by Roland Huntford, New York: Cooper Square Press, 2001).

Bailey, Maurice, and Maralyn Bailey. *117 Days Adrift*. Dobbs Ferry, NY: Sheridan House, 1992.

Bickel, Lennard. *Mawson's Will*. New York: Avon, 1978.

Boukreev, Anatoli, and G. Weston DeWalt. *The Climb: Tragic Ambitions on Everest*. New York: St. Martin's Press, 1997.

Bradley, James, with Ron Powers. *Flags of Our Fathers*. New York: Bantam Books, 2000.

Byrd, Admiral Richard E. *Alone: The Classic Polar Adventure*. New York: Kodansha International, 1995.

Callahan, Steven. *Adrift: Seventy-Six Days Lost at Sea*. New York: Ballantine, 1987.

Caputo, Philip. *A Rumor of War*. London: Arrow Books Ltd., 1981.

Cherry-Garrard, Apsley. *The Worst Journey in the World*. New York: Carroll & Graf, 1997.

Dugard, Martin. *Knockdown: The Harrowing True Account of a Yacht Race Turned Deadly*. New York: Pocket Books, 1999.

Franklin, Jonathan. *33 Men: Inside the Miraculous Survival and Dramatic Rescue of the Chilean Miners*. New York: Penguin Books, 2011.

Fredston, Jill. *Snowstruck: In the Grip of Avalanches*. Orlando, FL: Harcourt Books, 2005.

Gonzales, Laurence. *Deep Survival: Who Lives, Who Dies, and Why, True Stories of Miraculous Endurance and Sudden Death*. New York: W.W. Norton & Company, 2003.

Hayhurst, Jim Sr. *The Right Mountain: Lessons from Everest on the Real Meaning of Success*. Toronto: John Wiley & Sons, 1996.

Henderson, Bruce. *Fatal North: Adventure and Survival Aboard USS* Polaris, *the First U.S. Expedition to the North Pole*. New York: New American Library, 2001.

Herzog, Maurice. *Annapurna*. North Salem, NY: The Adventure Library, 1995.

Heyerdahl, Thor. *Kon-Tiki*. New York: Washington Square Press, 1973.

Howarth, David. *The Sledge Patrol: A WWII Epic of Escape, Survival, and Victory*. New York: The Lyons Press, 2001.

Huntford, Roland. *The Last Place on Earth*. New York: Atheneum, 1985.

Junger, Sebastian. *The Perfect Storm: A True Story of Men Against the Sea*. New York: W. W. Norton, 1997.

Kamler, Kenneth. *Surviving the Extremes: A Doctor's Journey to the Limits of Human Endurance*. New York: St. Martin's Press, 2004.

Keith, Agnes. *Three Came Home: A Mother's Ordeal in a Japanese Prison Camp*. London: Eland, 2002.

Kiley, Deborah Scaling, and Meg Noonan. *Albatross: The True Story of a Woman's Survival at Sea*. New York: Houghton Mifflin, 1994.

Kirschke, James. *Not Going Home Alone: A Marine's Story*. New York: Ballantine Books, 2001.

Klaben, Helen, with Beth Day. *Hey, I'm Alive!* New York: McGraw-Hill, 1964.

Knecht, G. Bruce. *The Proving Ground*. New York: Grand Central Publishing, 2002.

Kocour, Ruth Anne, with Michael Hodgson. *Facing the Extreme: One Woman's Story of True Courage, Death-Defying Survival, and Her Quest for the Summit.* New York: St. Martin's Press, 1998.

Kolditz, Thomas. *In Extremis Leadership: Leading As If Your Life Depended on It.* San Francisco: Jossey-Bass, 2007.

Krakauer, Jon. *Into Thin Air: A Personal Account of the Mt. Everest Disaster.* New York: Villard, 1997.

Kranz, Gene. *Failure Is Not an Option: Mission Control from Mercury to Apollo 13 and Beyond.* New York: Simon & Schuster, 2000.

Kuhne, Cecil, ed. *Near Death on the High Seas: True Stories of Disaster and Survival.* New York: Vintage Books, 2008.

Leighton, Kim. *A Hard Chance: The Sydney Hobart Disaster.* Minocqua, WI: Willow Creek Press, 1999.

Leslie, Edward E. *Desperate Journeys, Abandoned Souls: True Stories of Castaways and Other Survivors.* Boston: Houghton Mifflin, 1988.

Lewis, Cam, with Michael Levitt. *Around the World in 79 Days.* Lincolnville, ME: Team Adventure Press, 2001.

Maclean, Norman. *Young Men and Fire: A True Story of the Mann Gulch Fire.* Chicago: The University of Chicago Press, 1992.

McKinlay, William Laird. Karluk: *The Great Untold Story of Arctic Exploration.* New York: St. Martin's Press, 1977.

Millard, Candice. *The River of Doubt: Theodore Roosevelt's Darkest Journey.* New York: Doubleday, 2005.

Mitchell, Richard G., Jr. *Mountain Experience: The Psychology and Sociology of Adventure.* Chicago: The University of Chicago Press, 1985.

Moore, Lt. Gen. Harold (Ret.) and Joseph Galloway. *We Were Soldiers Once . . . and Young.* New York: Harper Torch, 2002.

Mundle, Rob. *Fatal Storm: The Inside Story of the Tragic Sydney-Hobart Race.* Sydney: International Marine/McGraw-Hill, 1999.

Nalepka, James, and Steven Callahan. *Capsized: The True Story of Four Men Adrift for 119 Days*. New York: HarperCollins, 1992.

O'Neill, Helen. *Life Without Limits: The Remarkable Story of David Pescud and His Fight for Survival in a Sea of Words*. Sydney: Bantam Books, 2003.

Philbrick, Nathaniel. *In the Heart of the Sea: The Tragedy of the Whaleship Essex*. New York: The Penguin Group, 2000.

Potterfield, Peter. *In the Zone: Epic Survival Stories from the Mountaineering World*. Seattle, WA: The Mountaineers, 1996.

Read, Piers Paul. *Alive: The Story of the Andes Survivors*. New York: Avon Books, 1975.

Robertson, Dougal. *Survive the Savage Sea*. New York: Sheridan House, 1994.

Rousmaniere, John. *After the Storm: True Stories of Disaster and Recovery at Sea*. New York: International Marine/McGraw Hill, 2004.

Rousmaniere, John. *Fastnet, Force 10: The Deadliest Storm in the History of Modern Sailing*. New York: W. W. Norton & Company, 2000.

Sides, Hampton. *Ghost Soldiers: The Epic Account of World War II's Greatest Rescue Mission*. New York: Anchor Books, 2001.

Simon, Alvah. *North to the Night: A Spiritual Odyssey in the Arctic*. New York: Broadway Books, 1998.

Simpson, Joe. *Touching the Void: The Harrowing First-Person Account of One Man's Miraculous Survival*. New York: Harper Row, 1990.

Steger, Will, and Jon Bowermaster. *Crossing Antarctica*. New York: Alfred A. Knopf, 1992.

Stewart, George R. *Ordeal by Hunger: The Story of the Donner Party*. New York: Houghton Mifflin, 1988.

Trumbull, Robert. *The Raft: The Courageous Story of Three Naval Airmen Against the Sea*. Annapolis, MD: Naval Institute Press, 1992.

Useem, Michael. *Leadership Moment: Nine True Stories of Triumph and Disaster and Their Lessons for Us All.* New York: Three Rivers Press, 1998.

Walters, Humphrey, Peter Mackie, Rosie Mackie, and Andrea Bacon. *Global Challenge: Leadership Lessons from "The World's Toughest Yacht Race."* Sussex, England: The Book Guild, 1997.

Whitmont, Debbie. *An Extreme Event: The Compelling, True Story of the Tragic 1998 Sydney-Hobart Race.* Sydney: Random House Australia, 1999.

Willis, Clint, ed. *Rough Water: Stories of Survival from the Sea.* New York: Adrenaline, 1999.

Notes

The Shackleton Saga

1. Roland Huntford, *Shackleton* (New York: Carroll & Graf, 1999), p. 365.

2. Ernest Shackleton, *South: A Memoir of the* Endurance *Voyage* (New York: Carroll & Graf, 1999), p. 2.

3. Stephen J. Pyne, *The Ice: A Journey to Antarctica* (New York: Ballantine, 1988), pp. 4–5.

4. Distances related to the Shackleton expedition are measured in nautical miles (a nautical mile equals 1.15 statute miles).

5. Alfred Lansing, Endurance: *Shackleton's Incredible Voyage* (New York: Carroll & Graf, 1998), p. 23.

6. Shackleton, p. 4.

7. Ibid., p. 11.

8. Ibid., p. 34.

9. F. A. Worsley, Endurance: *An Epic of Polar Adventure* (New York: W. W. Norton & Co., 1999), p. 20.

10. Lansing, p. 60.

11. Ibid., p. 95.

12. Ibid., p. 116.

13. Ibid., p. 280.

Chapter 1: Vision and Quick Victories

1. Ernest Shackleton, *South: A Memoir of the* Endurance *Voyage* (New York: Carroll & Graf, 1999), p. 82.

2. Roland Huntford, *Shackleton* (New York: Carroll & Graf, 1999), p. 456.

3. Ibid., p. 455.

4. Ibid., p. 456.

5. Adam Brandenburger and Barry Nalebuff, "Inside Intel," *Harvard Business Review* (November/December 1996), p. 168.

6. Don Clark, "Intel Chief Chips Away at Plan Beyond PCs," *Wall Street Journal* (September 8, 2010), and Don Clark, "Intel, Seeking Edge on Rivals, Rethinks Its Building Blocks," *Wall Street Journal* (May 4, 2011).

7. Huntford, p. 224.

8. Norman R. Augustine, "Managing the Crisis You Tried to Prevent," *Harvard Business Review* (November/December 1995), p. 147, and Eileen Murray and Saundra Shohen, "Lessons from the Tylenol Tragedy on Surviving a Corporate Crisis," *Medical Marketing & Media* 27, no. 2 (February 1992), p. 14.

9. Greg Brenneman, "Right Away and All at Once: How We Saved Continental," *Harvard Business Review* (September/October 1998), p. 162.

10. Ibid.

11. "Continental Airlines Receives J. D. Power and Associates Award for Highest-Ranked Traditional Network Airline," www.chron.com/news/article/PRN-Continental-Airlines-Receives-J-D-Power-1561332.php.

12. William Laird McKinlay, Karluk: *The Great Untold Story of Arctic Exploration* (New York: St. Martin's Press, 1977), p. 30.

13. Margery and James Fisher, *Shackleton and the Antarctic* (Boston: Houghton Mifflin, 1958), p. 352.

14. Huntford, p. 390.

15. Ibid., p. 386.

16. Ibid.

17. Fisher, p. 339.

18. Ibid., p. 342.

19. Ibid., p. 356.

20. Huntford, p. 465.

21. J. P. Donlon, "The CEO's CEO," *Chief Executive* (July/August 1998), pp. 28–37.

22. Ibid.

23. Shackleton, p. 162.

Chapter 2: Symbolism and Personal Example

1. Alfred Lansing, Endurance: *Shackleton's Incredible Voyage* (New York: Carroll & Graf, 1998), p. 64.

2. F. A. Worsley, Endurance: *An Epic of Polar Adventure* (New York: Jonathan Cape and Harrison Smith, 1931), p. 18.

3. Ibid., p. 19.

4. Ibid.

5. Ernest Shackleton, *South: A Memoir of the* Endurance *Voyage* (New York: Carroll & Graf, 1999), p. 77.

6. Arthur Laffer, "The Age of Prosperity Is Over," *Wall Street Journal* (October 27, 2008).

7. "Survival of AIG: A Story of Long Odds," *Pittsburgh Tribune* (February 13, 2011). http://www.pittsburghlive.com/x/pittsburghtrib/business/s_722637.html.

8. Speech by Mary Jane Fortin, August 25, 2009.

9. Ibid.

10. Shackleton, p. 83.

11. Worsley, p. 23.

12. Gordon Bethune, *Worst to First* (New York: John Wiley & Sons, 1998), p. 36.

13. Sir Ernest Shackleton, *South* (New York: The Macmillan Company, 1920), p. 135.

14. Quoted from Orde-Lees Diary, Roland Huntford, *Shackleton* (New York: Carroll & Graf, 1999), p. 511.

15. Philip Caputo, *A Rumor of War* (London: Arrow Books, 1981), pp. 91–92.

16. Robert F. Dennehy, "The Executive as Storyteller," *Management Review* 88, no. 3 (March 1999), pp. 40–43.

Chapter 3: Optimism and Reality

1. F. A. Worsley, Endurance: *An Epic of Polar Adventure* (New York: W. W. Norton & Co., 1999), p. 53.

2. Roland Huntford, *Shackleton* (New York: Carroll & Graf, 1999), p. 217.

3. Ibid., p. 92.

4. Martin E. P. Seligman, *Learned Optimism: How to Change Your Mind and Your Life* (New York: Pocket Books, 1998), pp. 207–234.

5. Worsley, p. 6.

6. Ibid., p. 4.

7. Sir Ernest Shackleton, *South* (New York: The Macmillan Company, 1920), p. 121.

8. Huntford, p. 465.

9. Margery and James Fisher, *Shackleton and the Antarctic* (Boston: Houghton Mifflin, 1958), p. 359.

10. Worsley, p. 4.

11. Ibid., pp. 4–5.

12. Alfred Lansing, Endurance: *Shackleton's Incredible Voyage* (New York: Carroll & Graf, 1998), p. 207.

13. Fisher, p. 372.

14. Lansing, p. 235.

15. Hal Lancaster, "Herb Kelleher Has One Main Strategy: Treat Employees Well," *Wall Street Journal* (August 31, 1999), p. B1.

16. Piers Paul Read, *Alive* (New York: Avon Books, 1975), pp. 81–82.

17. The Chinese character is typically not interpreted in this way, with one symbol representing "danger" and the other "opportunity," but both individual elements are embedded in the compound character. I appreciate the assistance of John Montanaro and Diana Ho in helping me with the interpretation of this figure.

18. Burke Davis, *Marine! The Life of Chesty Puller* (New York: Bantam, 1964), p. 267.

19. Allan R. Millett, *Semper Fidelis: The History of the United States Marine Corps* (New York: Free Press, 1991), p. 492.

20. Martin Russ, *Breakout: The Chosin Reservoir Campaign, Korea 1950* (New York: Penguin, 1999), p. 62.

21. Ibid., p. 81.

22. Davis, pp. 280–281. There are variations of this famous quote from this colorful Marine officer.

23. Russ, p. 391.

24. Davis, p. 295.

25. Lansing, p. 105.

26. Patricia Sellers, "CEOs in Denial," *Fortune* 139, no. 12 (June 21, 1999), p. 80.

27. Martha Lagace, "Ruthlessly Realistic: How CEOs Must Overcome Denial," *Harvard Business School Working Knowledge* (March 29, 2010) (http://hbswk.hbs.edu) and Richard S. Tedlow, *Denial: Why Business Leaders Fail to Look Facts in the Face—and What to Do About It* (New York: Penguin, 2010).

28. Albert Rothenberg, M.D., "Janusian Thinking and Nobel Prize Laureates," *American Journal of Psychiatry* 139 no. 1 (January 1982), pp. 122–124.

29. Robert Byrne, ed., *The 637 Best Things Anybody Ever Said* (New York: Fawcett Crest, 1982).

30. Nina Munk, "How Levi's Trashed a Great American Brand," *Fortune* 139, no. 7 (April 12, 1999), p. 82.

31. Ibid.

32. Rachel Dodes, "Levi's Shoots for the High-End Hipster," *Wall Street Journal* (April 14, 2010).

Chapter 4: Stamina

1. F. A. Worsley, *Shackleton's Boat Journey* (New York: W. W. Norton, 1977), pp. 58–59.

2. Roland Huntford, *Shackleton* (New York: Carroll & Graf, 1999), pp. 110–113, 115.

3. Ibid., p. 145.

4. Sir Ernest Shackleton, *South* (New York: The Macmillan Company, 1920), p. 99.

5. Ibid., p. 91.

6. Worsley, pp. 169–170.

7. Huntford, p. 687.

8. Ibid., p. 690.

9. "Keeping Employees Healthy: Trim Staff, Fat Profits?" *Economist* (July 30, 2011).

10. Ibid.

11. Michelle Andrews, "Employers Roll Out Aggressive Wellness Programs," *U.S. News & World Report* (October 25, 2007) http://health.usnews.com/health-news/health-plans/articles/2007/10/25/americas-best-health-plans?PageNr=3.

12. Michael E. Porter and Jennifer F. Baron, "Pitney Bowes: Employer Health Strategy," *Harvard Business Review* (February 24, 2009).

13. Anatoli Boukreev and G. Weston DeWalt, *The Climb: Tragic Ambitions on Everest* (New York: St. Martin's Press, 1997).

14. Jon Krakauer, *Into Thin Air: A Personal Account of the Mt. Everest Disaster* (New York: Villard, 1997), p. 202.

15. Shari Caudron, "Corporate Creativity Comes of Age," *Training & Development* (May 1998), p. 50.

16. Worsley, p. 188.

17. Shackleton, p. 75.

18. F. A. Worsley, Endurance: *An Epic of Polar Adventure* (New York: W. W. Norton & Co., 1999), p. 171.

19. Huntford, p. 613.

20. Joe Simpson, *Touching the Void* (New York: Harper & Row, 1990), pp. 103–104.

21. Ibid., p. 113.

22. Daniel Diermeier, *Reputation Rules: Strategies for Building Your Company's Number One Asset* (New York: McGraw-Hill, 2011), pp. 54–59.

23. Ibid.

Chapter 5: The Team Message

1. F. A. Worsley, Endurance: *An Epic of Polar Adventure* (New York: W. W. Norton & Co., 1999), p. 46.

2. Alfred Lansing, Endurance: *Shackleton's Incredible Voyage* (New York: Carroll & Graf, 1998), p. 17.

3. Margery and James Fisher, *Shackleton and the Antarctic* (Boston: Houghton Mifflin, 1958), pp. 343–344.

4. Jon Krakauer, *Into Thin Air: A Personal Account of the Mt. Everest Disaster* (New York: Villard, 1997), p. 163.

5. Ibid., p. 241.

6. Personal interview with Joan Imhof, Branford, CT, May 7, 1999.

7. The use of the "Tap Code" was taken from the video *Return with Honor* (Santa Monica: American Film Foundation, 1998).

8. Deloitte IABC Excel Award Nomination: Barry Salzberg, p. 5.

9. Barry Salzberg, "Trusting a CEO in the Twitter Age," *BusinessWeek* (August 7, 2009).

10. Ibid.

11. The American Business Awards website, 2010 Honorees (http://www.stevieawards.com/pubs/awards/403_2630_20412.cfm).

12. Salzberg.

13. Roland Huntford, *Shackleton* (New York: Carroll & Graf, 1999), p. 461.

14. Huntford, p. 467.

15. Fisher, p. 343.

16. F. A. Worsley, *Shackleton's Boat Journey* (New York: W. W. Norton, 1977), p. 134.

17. Huntford, p. 424.

18. Worsley, Endurance, p. 53.

Chapter 6: Core Team Values

1. F. A. Worsley, *Shackleton's Boat Journey* (New York: W. W. Norton, 1977), pp. 20–21.

2. Roland Huntford, *The Last Place on Earth* (New York: Atheneum, 1985), p. 523.

3. Several months after this chapter was written, Margaret Holtman came upon a piece in the *New York Times* Book Review ("The Race to the Bottom," October 31, 1999, p. 43) in which Caroline Alexander makes a similar observation. My perspective on Scott was formed and written prior to the publication of the *New York Times* article.

4. Huntford, pp. 562–563.

5. V. E. Fuchs, "Scott and Amundsen," *Geographical Journal* (July 1980) 146, no. 2, pp. 272–274.

6. Huntford, p. 151.

7. Ibid., p. 157.

8. Ibid., p. 151.

9. Ibid., p. 144.

10. Roland Huntford, *Shackleton* (New York: Carroll & Graf, 1999), p. 13.

11. Ibid., p. 57.

12. Ibid., p. 425.

13. Sir Ernest Shackleton, *South* (New York: The Macmillan Company, 1920), p. 92.

14. F. A. Worsley, Endurance: *An Epic in Polar Adventure* (New York: W. W. Norton & Company, 1999), p. 93.

15. Edward Lawler, *From the Ground Up: Six Principles for Building the New Logic Corporation* (San Francisco: Jossey-Bass, 1996), p. 85.

16. Personal interview with Scott Sklar, Novato, CA, June 14, 1999.

17. Huntford, *Shackleton*, p. 456.

18. Worsley, Endurance, p. 106.

19. Alfred Lansing, Endurance: *Shackleton's Incredible Voyage* (New York: Carroll & Graf, 1998), p. 127.

Chapter 7: Conflict

1. Roland Huntford, *Shackleton* (New York: Carroll & Graf, 1999), p. 435.

2. Harold Horwood in *Sea Tales: The Deadly Arctic Expedition* (New York: New Video Group, 1997).

3. William Laird McKinlay, Karluk: *The Great Untold Story of Arctic Exploration* (New York: St. Martin's Press, 1977), p. 99.

4. George R. Stewart, *Ordeal by Hunger: The Story of the Donner Party* (New York: Houghton Mifflin, 1988), p. 63.

5. Ibid., p. 66.

6. Huntford, p. 26.

7. Ibid., p. 499.

8. Ibid., p. 424.

9. Ibid., p. 423.

10. Ibid., pp. 537–538.

11. Dennis N. T. Perkins, *Ghosts in the Executive Suite: Every Business Is a Family Business* (Branford, CT: The Syncretics Group, 1986), p. 11.

12. Huntford, p. 435.

13. Alfred Lansing, Endurance: *Shackleton's Incredible Voyage* (New York: Carroll & Graf, 1998), p. 95.

Chapter 8: Lighten Up!

1. Ernest Shackleton, *South: A Memoir of the* Endurance *Voyage* (New York: Carroll & Graf, 1999), pp. 46–47.

2. Roland Huntford, *Shackleton* (New York: Carroll & Graf, 1999), p. 419.

3. Ibid., p. 428.

4. Ibid., p. 437.

5. Ibid., p. 468.

6. Shackleton, p. 111.

7. Alfred Lansing, Endurance: *Shackleton's Incredible Voyage* (New York: Carroll & Graf, 1998), p. 206.

8. Ibid., pp. 208–209.

9. William Laird McKinlay, Karluk: *The Great Untold Story of Arctic Exploration* (New York: St. Martin's Press, 1977), pp. 67–68.

10. Huntford, p. 472.

11. F. A. Worsley, Endurance: *An Epic of Polar Adventure* (New York: W. W. Norton & Co., 1999), pp. 53–54.

12. Huntford, p. 426.

13. Ibid., p. 448.

14. This story is based on personal correspondence with Dennis Mette on October 21, 2004, and October 4–5, 2011, and personal correspondence with John Ball on October 5, 2011. It was also reconstructed from material taken from the Manual of the Judge Advocate General final investigative report concerning the aircraft mishap involving Bureau Number 159892, which occurred on October 26, 1978; and the VP-9 Memorial Page (www.vpnavy.com/vp9586.html), which includes material from a *Reader's Digest* article, "We Are Ditching, Ditching, Ditching!" by Earl and Miriam Selby, September 1979, pp. 112–118.

15. John Ball was an extra ("plus-in") Navigator/Communicator on the flight, backing up Lieutenant (junior grade) Bruce Forshay. Andrew C. A. Jampoler, *Adak: The Rescue of Alfa Foxtrot 586* (Annapolis, MD: Naval Institute Press, 2003), pp. 14-21.

16. Personal communication with Dennis Mette on October 4, 2004.

17. Kevin and Jackie Freiberg, *Nuts! Southwest Airlines' Crazy Recipe for Business and Personal Success* (New York: Broadway Books, 1998).

18. Ibid.

Chapter 9: Risk

1. F. A. Worsley, Endurance: *An Epic of Polar Adventure* (New York: W. W. Norton & Co., 1999), p. 114.

2. Roland Huntford, *Shackleton* (New York: Carroll & Graf, 1999), p. 497.

3. Worsley, p. 65.

4. Ibid., p. 89.

5. Ernest Shackleton, *South: A Memoir of the* Endurance *Voyage* (New York: Carroll & Graf, 1999), p. 159.

6. Ibid., p. 175.

7. Sir Ernest Shackleton, *South* (New York: The Macmillan Company, 1920), p. 180.

8. Adrian J. Slywotzky and David J. Morrison, *The Profit Zone: How Strategic Business Design Will Lead You to Tomorrow's Profits,* 2nd ed. (New York: Three Rivers Press, 2002), p. 6.

9. Phone interview with Ted Hoff, August 16, 2011.

10. Ibid.

11. Robert Grossman, "IBM's HR Takes a Risk," *HR Magazine* (April 1, 2007).

12. Ibid.

13. Ibid.

14. Phone interview with Ted Hoff, August 16, 2011.

15. Ibid.

16. Ibid.

17. Ibid.

Chapter 10: Tenacious Creativity

1. Roland Huntford, *Shackleton* (New York: Carroll & Graf, 1999), p. 561.

2. Distances for Steven Callahan's journey are measured in nautical miles.

3. Steven Callahan, *Adrift: Seventy-Six Days Lost at Sea* (New York: Ballantine Books, 1987), pp. 138–139.

4. Ibid., pp. 222–223.

5. Ibid., p. 224.

6. Ibid., pp. 210–211.

7. Huntford, p. 462.

8. Ibid., p. 460.

9. F. A. Worsley, Endurance: *An Epic of Polar Adventure* (New York: W. W. Norton & Co., 1999), p. 151.

10. Ibid., p. 155.

11. Ibid., p. 156.

12. Ernest Shackleton, *South: A Memoir of the* Endurance *Voyage* (New York: Carroll & Graf, 1999), p. 208.

13. Chesley B. Sullenberger, III, *Highest Duty: My Search for What Really Matters* (New York: HarperCollins, 2009).

14. Dialogue for this case is taken from the official FAA transcript from the incident with punctuation and capitalization added for ease of reading: http://www.faa.gov/data_research/accident_incident/1549/media/Full%20Transcript%20L116.pdf. There were instances during the transmission when Sullenberger and the air traffic controller referred to the flight by the wrong call number.

15. Alex Caldwell, "Controller Patrick Harten Talks About Flight 1549," *ATC News* (http://www.atc-network.com/News/29122/Controller-Patrick-Harten-talks-about-flight-1549).

16. Liz Robbins, "Hudson River Rescue Still Defines Upgrade of Fire Dept.'s Marine Unit," *New York Times* (January 14, 2011).

17. Ibid.

18. Chesley B. Sullenberger, III, "All I Wanted Was to Talk to My Family, and Get Some Dry Socks," *Newsweek* (February 12, 2009).

Chapter 11: Learning to Lead at *The Edge*

1. George Leonard, *Mastery: The Keys to Success and Long-Term Fulfillment* (New York: Plume, 1992), pp. 39–49.

2. Joe Hyams, *Zen in the Martial Arts* (New York: Bantam, 1982), p. 103.

3. "A Conversation with Roberto Goizueta and Jack Welch," *Fortune* 132, no. 1 (December 11, 1995), p. 96.

4. David A. Nadler, *Champions of Change* (San Francisco: Jossey-Bass, 1997), pp. 67–71.

5. "Violin a Way of Life," *Seattle Times* (March 4, 1990).

6. Ibid.

Chapter 12: Epilogue

1. Sir Ernest Shackleton, *South: The Story of Shackleton's Last Expedition, 1914–17,* ed. Peter King (North Pomfret: Trafalgar Square, 1992), p. 3.

2. C. Neider (ed.), *Antarctica* (New York: Cooper Square, 2000), p. 288.

3. Ibid., p. 267.

4. Roald Amundsen, *The South Pole: An Account of the Norwegian Antarctic Expedition in the "Fram" 1910–12* (1913; reproduced with introduction by Roland Huntford, New York: Cooper Square Press, 2001), p. 370.

5. William Laird McKinlay, Karluk: *The Great Untold Story of Arctic Exploration* (New York: St. Martin's Press, 1977), p. 6.

6. Ernest Shackleton, *South: A Memoir of the* Endurance *Voyage* (New York: Carroll & Graf, 1999), p. 77.

7. F. A. Worsley, Endurance: *An Epic of Polar Adventure* (New York: W. W. Norton & Co., 1999), p. 107.

8. F. A. Worsley, *Shackleton's Boat Journey* (New York: W. W. Norton, 1977), p. 220.

Resolving Conflicts: Lessons from the Martial Arts

1. A. Westbrook and O. Ratti. *Aikido and the Dynamic Sphere: An Illustrated Introduction* (Rutland, VT: Charles E. Tuttle, 1970), p. 17.

Index

Acknowledgments for Previously Published Materials

Grateful acknowledgment is made to the following sources for permission to reprint from previously published material. The publisher has made diligent efforts to trace the ownership of all copyrighted material in this volume and believes that all necessary permissions have been secured. If any errors or omissions have inadvertently been made, proper corrections will gladly be made in future editions.

Excerpts from *ADRIFT* by Steven Callahan. Copyright © 1986 by Steven Callahan. Reprinted by permission of Houghton Mifflin Harcourt Publishing Company. All rights reserved.

Excerpts from *ENDURANCE* by Alfred Lansing copyright © 1959 by Alfred Lansing. Reprinted by permission of Curtis Brown, Ltd.

Excerpts totalling 258 words from pages 103–104, 113 from *TOUCHING THE VOID* by Joe Simpson. Copyright © 1988 by Joe Simpson. Reprinted by permission of HarperCollins Publishers. Extracts from *TOUCHING THE VOID* by Joe Simpson published by Vintage Books reprinted by permission of The Random House Group Ltd.

Extract from *SHACKLETON'S BOAT JOURNEY* by F. A. Worsley copyright © 1977 by W. W. Norton & Company, Inc. Used by permission of W. W. Norton & Company, Inc. Also copyright © 1999 by Frank Worsley. Reproduced by permission of Sheil Land Associates Ltd.

Extract from ENDURANCE: *AN EPIC OF POLAR ADVENTURE* by F. A. Worsley copyright © 1931 by the Estate of F. A. Worsley.

Used by permission of W. W. Norton & Company, Inc. and Sheil Land Associates Ltd.

Excerpts from *RACE TO THE SOUTH POLE* by Dennis N. T. Perkins et al. in *THE ENCYCLOPEDIA OF LEADERSHIP, VOL. 3* (G. R. Goethals, G. J. Sorenson, and J. M Burns, eds.). Copyright © 2004 by Dennis N. T. Perkins et al. Used by permission of Berkshire Publishing Group LLC.

Even the best leaders are only as good as their team . . .

Turn the page to enjoy an excerpt from

Into the Storm

Lessons in Teamwork from the
Treacherous Sydney-to-Hobart Ocean Race

Dennis N.T. Perkins and Jillian B. Murphy

Coming Fall 2012

Get ready for the next adventure at *The Edge*!

Dusk was coming on and I was at the end of my tether and thinking to myself, "If this continues, I can't keep going like this. And
there's no one else that can steer this damn boat, so we're in serious
trouble."

—Ed Psaltis, Skipper, *AFR Midnight Rambler*

Arthur Psaltis watches the boat's digital readout as the wind speed
races from thirty-five knots, to forty, and then forty-five knots. At
sixty knots, the readout suddenly goes blank. Arthur stares at the empty
screen. Then it hits him: The metal fitting that holds the wind meter on
top of the mast has been torn off, rendering the instrument useless.

The next blast of wind flattens the boat, driving its mast into the
water and flooding the cockpit. As the crew has done so many times in
practice, side by side on the rail with their backs to the sea, they calmly
take in the main sail. They know what they have to do. If the sail stays up,
the boat could be rolled 360 degrees and they might never recover.

Conditions are treacherous and getting worse by the minute. The
noise is the most frightening part. It comes as a high-pitched scream, like
an old-fashioned kettle boiling furiously. The wind—reaching speeds of
nearly ninety miles per hour—howls around them, and the waves rise
higher than the fifty-foot mast, dwarfing the thirty-five-foot boat.

The heavy rain and spew from the waves spray the sailors on deck,
pelting their faces like gravel, and the constant noise makes talking nearly
impossible. The crew can communicate only by cupping their hands

around their mouths and shouting into each other's ears. They slap the hull of the boat to warn those below deck of oncoming big waves.

The men below deck are fighting a different battle. They can see nothing of what is happening topside and find themselves in a constant state of anxiety. As Ed expertly steers the boat up the face of the massive waves, the men exhale each time the boat slides down the other side unscathed. It is an extraordinary feat of seamanship.

But not every time. When Ed miscalculates, the boat flies off the wave and hangs in midair until it hits the trough between the waves. The impact is like crashing into a block of cement. Trapped below, the crew waits to see if the boat will explode, the weight of the rigging ramming the mast through the hull like a pile driver. It is a horrible feeling knowing that the boat might fill with water and sink in an instant.

As the boat shoots off the back of one towering wave, Chris Rockell, a tough, rugby-playing New Zealander, is launched from his seated position. He flies through the air, crashing into an exposed bolt that is sticking through the overhead of the cabin. Chris falls backward and his face turns red, covered with blood.

Terrified that his injury will force the team to quit the race, Chris sticks his fingers into the wound to see if he touches "hard or squishy." Relieved to find his skull intact, he insists that the boat continue on and not pull out of the race on his account. Concussed and barred from going on deck, Chris carefully positions his weight on the high side of the boat to act as ballast.

The crew members are literally fighting for their lives, and the worst is yet to come. They are competing in what will become one of the most dangerous and historic offshore ocean races in history.

★ ★ ★ ★ ★ ★

Into the Storm: Lessons in Teamwork from the Treacherous Sydney-to-Hobart Ocean Race recounts the story of the courageous crew members of *AFR Midnight Rambler,* winners of the 1998 Sydney Hobart Yacht Race. Their stunning victory, and the teamwork that made it possible, hold valuable lessons for success in today's demanding environment.

Organizations are always faced with ambiguity and uncertainty, but the current level of turbulence is unprecedented in recent memory. By studying leaders and teams facing extreme challenges, the authors have identified a set of core strategies that are critical to success at *The Edge*.

It's hard to imagine a better place to test these strategies than the iconic Sydney Hobart Yacht Race. This 723-mile, deepwater challenge—often called the "Everest" of offshore ocean racing—is considered one of the toughest in the world. Unpredictable weather and seas make each race demanding, but the 1998 race proved to be the most perilous in the race's sixty-five-year history.

As the fleet of 115 boats sailed down the coast of Australia, they were hit by an unexpected *weather bomb*—a massive storm that created eighty-foot waves and near hundred-mile-an-hour winds. Six sailors perished in the maelstrom, and another fifty-five were saved in what became the largest search-and-rescue operation in Australia's history.

While many boats tried to maneuver around the storm, the crew of *AFR Midnight Rambler* chose to head directly into its path. After battling mountainous waves and hurricane-force winds, they arrived safely in Hobart, three days and sixteen hours later.

The decision to head into the eye of the storm, along with extraordinary tenacity, optimism, courage, and teamwork, enabled this team of "amateurs" to beat professionals sailing much larger and better-financed boats. Ed Psaltis and his crew of six were proclaimed overall winners and awarded the coveted Tattersalls Cup. They were the smallest boat in ten years to win the race.

What were the factors underlying this stunning victory? How has the team sustained its remarkable pattern of winning for more than a decade? This inspiring book answers these questions and provides concrete strategies for building exceptional teams in extraordinary times.